PENGUIN TRAVEL LIBRARY

UNDER THE MOUNTAIN WALL

As a naturalist-explorer, Peter Matthiessen has been a member of expeditions to remote regions of all five continents, including the Amazon jungles, the Canadian Northwest Territories, the Sudan, New Guinea, and Nepal. A former commercial fisherman and charter-boat captain, he participated as a diver in the worldwide search for the great white shark that culminated in his book *Blue Meridian* and in the film *Blue Water, White Death*. Mr. Matthiessen was one of the founders of *The Paris Review*, and his fiction includes *At Play in the Fields of the Lord*, which was nominated for the National Book Award, and *Far Tortuga*. His many works of nonfiction include *Wildlife in America*, *The Snow Leopard*, for which he received the National Book Award in 1978, *In the Spirit of Crazy Horse*, and *Indian Country*.

For an Award of Merit from the National Institute of Arts and Letters given to Mr. Matthiessen in 1963 for this book and *The Cloud Forest*, Robert Penn Warren wrote: "*The Cloud Forest* and *Under the Mountain Wall* depict nature and man with unusual perceptiveness and with dramatic power, in a prose notable for vividness and control."

Also by Peter Matthiessen

■ ■ ■ ■ ■ ■ ■ ■

UNDER THE MOUNTAIN WALL

A chronicle of two seasons in Stone Age New Guinea

PETER MATTHIESSEN

Elisabeth Sifton Books
PENGUIN BOOKS

ELISABETH SIFTON BOOKS • PENGUIN BOOKS
Viking Penguin Inc., 40 West 23rd Street,
New York, New York 10010, U.S.A.
Penguin Books Ltd, Harmondsworth,
Middlesex, England
Penguin Books Australia Ltd, Ringwood,
Victoria, Australia
Penguin Books Canada Limited, 2801 John Street,
Markham, Ontario, Canada L3R 1B4
Penguin Books (N.Z.) Ltd, 182–190 Wairau Road,
Auckland 10, New Zealand

First published in the United States of America by
The Viking Press Inc. 1962
Published in Penguin Books 1987

A portion of the text has appeared in somewhat different form in *Harper's*.

cip data available
ISBN 0 14 00.9548 9

Printed in the United States of America by
R. R. Donnelley & Sons Company, Harrisonburg, Virginia
Set in Caledonia

For Deborah, with love

In warm memory of
MICHAEL ROCKEFELLER
*whose interest and generosity were a major
contribution to the Harvard-Peabody Expedition of 1961.
Though he did not live to see the achievement of the Expedition,
his participation was crucial to its success.*

Contents

Drawings of Kurelu artifacts scattered through the text
are by Otto van Eersel

■ The peaks of the Snow Mountains, on bright mornings, part the dense clouds and soar into the skies of Oceania. Beneath the clouds, like a world submerged, lie the dark rocks which form the great island of New Guinea; climbing abruptly from the Dampier Strait in the East Indies, the range extends eastward fifteen hundred miles until, at land's end in Papua, it sinks once more beneath the ocean.

The Snow Mountains are the summit of western New Guinea. On a high flank in the central highlands lies a sudden valley: here the Baliem River, which had vanished underground some twenty miles upstream, bursts from the mountain wall onto a great green plain. The plain itself, ten miles across, is a mile above the sea. Fifty miles southeast of the valley's head, the river drops into a gorge and passes from the mountains, to subside at last in the vast marshes of sun and mud and sago palms stretching southward to the Arafura Sea.

The Baliem Valley was discovered from the air in 1938, but no white man came to live there until 1954, when a government post was established on abandoned lands of the Wukahupi tribes. Dutch patrols have now explored much of the valley, which supports more than forty thousand people, and the last large blank on the most recent maps is a region of perhaps thirty square miles under the northeast wall.

This remote corner is controlled by those tribes of the Ndani or Dani-speaking peoples known as the Kurelu; the Dani language, with small tribal variations, is spoken throughout the valley and beyond, yet it is but one of many distinct languages in the central highlands. (The origins of these languages, like the origins of the people themselves, are virtually unknown. One may suppose that the mountain Papuans came out from Asia long before the Polynesians— though in the wake of the Australian aborigines—and that they were forced into the mountains by peoples who came after, but the near absence of archaelogical evidence makes any attempt at chronology unintelligent.) The region is bordered in the south by the Aike River and in the west, toward the Baliem, by the lands of the enemy Wittaia. In the north and east it ends abruptly at the mountain wall. The wall rises in a series of steep ridges to an outer rim which varies, around the valley, from ten to twelve thousand feet in elevation; the upper wall is rarely seen. All day, all year, the clouds balance on the rim, as if about to tumble in. They are dark and still and all but permanent, protecting the great valley from infecting winds.

The Kurelu are named for the tribal *kain* or leader: their country, that is, is "Kurelu's Land." The tribe is divided into four main groups: the Loro-Mabell to the northward, the Kosi-Alua from the western grasslands, the Haiman-Halluk, between the Kosi-Alua and the mountains, and the Wilihiman-Walalua, in the south. The Wilihiman-Walalua is the people's contraction of four clan names (Wilil:Haiman-Walilo:Alua) and represents, politically, a union of allied villages. Several such unions, linked by clan or more or less well disposed toward one another, may form a loose confederacy and are led by the most powerful kain—in this case, Kurelu, kain of the Loro-Mabell. Their boundaries are fluid and informal, dependent on the predominance of clan, though the clans are spread throughout the villages. The clan Alua, for example, is well represented not only in the Wilihiman-Walalua but in the Kosi-Alua. The latter groups share a common frontier with the enemy and may be called the southern Kurelu.

Because the southern Kurelu were entirely untouched by civilization, their culture was chosen for study by the Harvard-Peabody Expedition of 1961. The expedition, sponsored in part by the government of the Netherlands, entered the Baliem at the end of March and remained until September, with the cooperation and assistance of the Dutch officials, particularly Dr. Victor de Bruyn of the Office of Native Affairs. Its purpose was to live among the people as unobtrusively as possible and to film and record their wars, rituals, and daily life with a minimum of interference, in order that a true picture of a Stone Age culture—one of the few in which both war and agriculture are important—might be preserved.

This book is a chronicle of two seasons in the Stone Age. The few details and episodes not actually witnessed by the author were supplied and confirmed by other members of the party—Robert Gardner, cameraman and leader of the expedition whose film, *Dead Birds*, concerns the Kurelu; Karl G. Heider, anthropologist; Jan Broekhuyse, anthropologist; Michael Rockefeller, photographer and sound technician. The expedition was joined by photographer Eliot Elisofon for the month of May; by botanist Chris Versteegh for two weeks in June; and by medical student Samuel Putnam in July and August; it was assisted immeasurably by the talents and good company of its Dani interpreter, Abututi, with his wife, Wamoko, and of its cook, Yusip.

All of these have made important contributions to this book, but I am particularly indebted to Jan Broekhuyse, whose year of prior experience with other Baliem tribes proved invaluable in the gathering and assessment of information, and to Karl Heider, who remained with the Kurelu after the departure of the expedition and has since supplied extensive data and corrections. Heider, Broekhuyse, and Gardner have been kind enough to inspect the manuscript for errors and distortions, and within the limits of our present understanding of the culture an honest portrait of the Kurelu has been attempted.

This is the story of the great warrior Weaklekek and of the swineherd Tukum, of U-mue and his family, and of their enemies and friends. The events described were observed to have happened to these tribesmen, called by these names, in the spring and summer of 1961—though occasionally, minor actions of one person have been attributed to another, to avoid a confusing multiplicity of characters. The glossary in the back of the book will serve as a key to the *dramatis personae* as well as to pronunciation.

Reference to the tribe's exposure to the expedition has been omitted, not only because the first reactions of a wild people to the white man, affecting and sad and funny though they are, have been well documented, but because the Kurelu offered a unique chance, perhaps the last, to describe a lost culture in the terrible beauty of its pure estate. The armed patrols and missionaries invaded their land on the heels of the expedition, and by the time this account of them is published, the proud and warlike Kurelu will be no more than another backward people, crouched in the long shadow of the white man.

Photographic Section I:

THE KURELU

2

3

4

5

6

7

9

10

11 ▶

12

13

14

15

16

17

18

19

20

21

23

24

25

26

Under the Mountain Wall

■ One morning in April, in the year when the old history of the Kurelu came to an end, a man named Weaklekek started down the mountain from the hill village of Lokoparek. He did not go by the straight path, which descends through a tangle of pandanus and bamboo onto the open hillsides, but instead went west, through the forest beneath the cliff. The cliff was a sheer face of yellow limestone black-smeared with green algae, and the tree line of its crest wavered in mist. With the sun rising behind it, the mist appeared illumined from within.

The rains of April had been heavy, and the path was a glutinous mire pocked by the hooves of pigs; he walked it swiftly, his bare feet feeling cleverly for the root or rock that would give them purchase, and at the stream he ran across the log. The path climbed steeply to a grove of tropical chestnuts, tall, with small leaves of green-bronze, and there he paused a moment to peer out through the forest shades. Though he could not see it, the sun had mounted from behind the cliff. Below, the valley floor and its far wall steamed in an early light, but the forest would stay dank and somber until the cloud above his head had burned away.

Weaklekek moved on to a point where the wood ended

in a clearing between great boulders; the wood edge leapt with plants of light and shade, the most striking of which was a great rhododendron, its white blossoms broader than his hand. In the shadows and clefts of the boulders, wood ferns in wild variety uncurled from among the liverworts and lichens, the mosses and silver fungi. The ferns were the triumphant plant of the high forest, with species numbering in the hundreds, but Weaklekek was oblivious of the ferns, of all the details of his world which could not immediately be put to use. The ferns, like the mist hung on the cliffs, the squall of parrots echoing on the walls, the sun, the distant river, were part of him as he was part of them: they were inside him, behind the shadows of his brown eyes, and not before him. He would see a certain fern when he needed it for dressing pig, and another from which pith was taken to roll thread, but the rest withdrew into the landscape.

The experience of his eye was not his own. It was thousands of years old, immutable, passed along as certainly and inevitably as his dark skin, the cast of his quick face. These characters were more variable than experience, for experience was static in the valley; it was older than time itself, for time was a thing of but two generations, dated by moons and ending with the day in which he found himself. Before the father of Weaklekek's father was the ancestor of the people: his name was Nopu, and he came from the high mountains with a wife and a great bundle of living things. Nopu's children were the founders of the clans, with names like Haiman, Alua, Kosi, Wilil, and they had opened the life bundle against Nopu's will, releasing the mosquitoes and the snakes upon all the people, the *akuni*, who came after.

Nopu was the common ancestor, but perhaps he was also that first Papuan who, one hour in the long infinity of days, from the forest of the mountain passes, saw the green valley of the Baliem River far below him in the sunny haze. How many years, or centuries of years, this man had wandered out of Africa and Asia may never be known, for he traveled lightly, and he left no trail.

Before the coming of Nopu, in the millenniums of silence, the greatest of the valley's creatures was a bird, the cassowary. Birds of paradise, red, emerald, golden, and night-blue, fluttered, huffed, and screeched among the fern and orchid gardens of the higher limbs. Hawks and swiftlets coursed the torpid airs, and the common sandpiper of Africa and Eurasia flew south like a messenger from another earth to teeter on the margins of its streams. In stands of great evergreen araucaria, in oak-chestnut forest and river jungle, a primitive fauna of small marsupials, with a few bats and rodents, prospered in habitats long since pre-empted, elsewhere on the earth, by the cats and weasels, dogs, bears, hoofed animals, and apes: the marsupials, stranded on these mountain outposts of the Australian continental shelf by the wax and wane of ice-age seas, became carnivores and insectivores and, in the wallabies and kangaroos, strange herbivores of the high grasslands.

Then that first man—perhaps Nopu, perhaps another —reached the coast, and eventually the inner mountains; he occupied the valley, with his women and children, his bow, bamboo knife, and stone adze. Like the mountain wallaby, the cuscus, and the phalanger, he had cut himself off from a world which rolled on without him. The food in the valley forests was plentiful, and he had brought with him—or there came soon after—the sweet potato, dog, and pig. The jungle and mountain, the wall of clouds, the centuries, secured him from the navigators and explorers who touched the coasts and went away again; he remained in his stone culture. In the last corners of the valley, he remains there still, under the mountain wall. His name is not Nopu, for he is the son of Nopu's son, but he is the same man.

So now he paused to take in his surroundings, standing gracefully, his weight balanced on his right leg and upright spear. His right hand, holding the spear, was at the level of his chin, and the spear itself, sixteen feet long, rose to a point which drew taut, as he stood there, the stillness of the forest. The spear was carved from the red wood of the yoli myrtle, and a pale yoli, its smooth bark scaling like reptilian skin, stood like the leg of a great dinosaur behind him.

Weaklekek was darker than most Dani, a dark brown which looked black, and the blackness of his naked body was set off by the white symmetries of his snail-shell bib. He looked taller than his five feet and a half, lean and cat-muscled, with narrow shoulders and flat narrow hips. At rest on the long spear, he gave an impression of indolent grace, a grace by no means gentle but rather a kind of coiling which permitted him to move quickly from a still position.

He stood there watching, watching. The landscape as it was, had always been, his eye shut out. The stir of change, the detail out of place, was what he hunted: a distant movement, a stray smoke, a silence where a honey eater sang, a whoop of warning. Across the valley other men stood watching at this moment, under the long spear, for today there would be war.

From where he stood, still as a snake, the southern territories of Kurelu's Land spread before him. The narrow gully of the upper Aike dropped away on his left hand, the hill brush of its edges giving way as the land leveled to a riverain forest ruled by casuarina. Before him rose the smoke of morning fires, though the villages themselves—Abukumo, Homaklep, and Wuperainma—were not visible. On his right hand the cliff curved outward from the valley rim; it declined rapidly to a rocky hill, and finally a steep grassy slope, which plummeted for several hundred feet into a stand of giant araucarias at its foot. The three villages lay in a kind of pocket in the mountain flank, between the steep hill and the Aike River.

The araucarias were straight and tall, well over one hundred feet, with tiers of branches curving upward, and needles clustered in great balls, like ornaments. The araucaria was an ancient tree, disappearing from the valley, from the world; each needle of this tree grew very old, refracting the sparkle of the dew for forty years and more.

Directly below Wuperainma a small wood surrounded lowland brooks. The far part of the wood could be seen from where he stood, and beyond it a fringe of long-grass savanna, scattered with bushes, sloped to the bottom lands and drainage ditches of the sweet-potato fields. The bed of purple, veined by silver water, spread unbroken for a mile, ending at a far line of trees. Beyond the trees a marshy swale marked the frontier; it continued into no man's land, surrounding a low rocky rise, the Waraba, and the near face of a pyramidal hill, the Siobara. The Siobara stood in Wittaia territory, and Wittaia fields and villages lay to both sides of it. Behind the Siobara a hairy spine of casuarina marked the course of the Baliem along the valley floor, and beyond the river a subsidiary valley mounted steeply to the cloud forest beneath the western walls.

The trail wound down the slopes toward Wuperainma, passing alternately through low woodland and open brush; the bare feet of many years had beaten away the grass and the thin topsoil, laying bare the chalky white of a fine quartzitic sand. When dry, this sand was as soft as powder, but in the rain it glazed to a smooth hardness. The white sand erupted in great spots across the valley, and from where Weaklekek walked three patches of it could be seen, like snowfields, at the base of the Siobara and on the farther hills to the southwest.

The limestone soil supported many plants in various stages of new flowering. Flowering and fading occurred in the same plant at once, the blossoms and burning leaves, for there was no autumn in the valley. The leaves died one by one and were replaced, so that the foliage of each plant was brilliant red and green against the hillside. The equatorial monsoons which brought a rainy season to the coasts had small effect here in the highlands; from moon to moon, the rainfall varied little. Winter, summer, autumn, spring were involuted, turning in upon themselves, a slow circling of time.

Weaklekek moved swiftly down the mountain. At a certain point he paused and called out toward the cliff—*We-AK-le-kek!* And when the voice returned to him, *AK-le-kek,-le-kek,* he grinned uneasily, for this was the voice of his own spirit. On the lower slopes the pigeon, *yoroick,* called its own name dolefully, and from far below, where the sun was shining, the bird was answered by the high voice of a boy.

■ At dawn that morning the enemy began chanting, and the chant, *hoo, hoo, hoo, ua, ua,* rolled across the fields toward the mountains. The fields were tattered still with mist, and a cloud hung on the valley floor, submerging the line of trees at the frontier. A man ran past the wood of araucaria, called Homuak after the spring which, rising silently from among the bony roots, flows out and dies in the savanna; Homuak lies at the foot of the steep hill near Wu-perainma. He cried out urgently, his voice a solitary echo of the wail from behind the mist. The call was taken up on the far side of the hill and trailed off northward to the villages of Kurelu.

The wood of Homuak was strangely empty. The black robin chat and a yellow whistler sang in the evergreens, in the rich voice of new nesting, and the night's rain fell in soft drops from the needles. High behind the still village of Wuperainma the sun rolled up onto the rim, and the mists creeping on the fields slowly dispersed. Still the Wittaia chanted, and the answer grew in all the villages.

A puna lizard, two feet long, with dinosaur spines and heavy head, crept out along a branch of araucaria, seeking the sun; its long whip tail, trailing behind, slid silently on the rough bark.

Small bands of warriors were moving out toward the frontier. The men carried their spears and bows and arrows, and the boys ran behind them. A figure climbed slowly to the top of a *kaio*, one of the many lookout towers visible from the wood; the kaio is built of tall young saplings bound into a column by liana thongs, and rises to a stick platform some twenty-five feet above the ground. The kaios, erected in defense against raids upon the gardens, march across the distances like black lonely trees. At the base of each kaio is a thatched shelter, and here the warriors assembled, leaning their spears against the roof.

Beyond the kaios and gardens lies a thin woodland, then a swale of cane and sedge, and at the far edge of the swale a solitary conifer. The tree marks the edge of the Tokolik, a grassy fairway nearly two miles long, paralleling the frontier. The Tokolik is the high ground of the swamp of no man's land; on its far side a brushy bog occurs, scattered with dark tannin pools and reeds and sphagnum. The bog extends to the base of a low ridge, the Waraba, and beyond the ridge is the sudden pyramid, the Siobara, like a great fore bulwark of the enemy. In the middle of the Tokolik, just southward of the tree, lies a shallow grassy pool. Small streams have been diked to form the several pools on the frontier; black ducks with striped cinnamon heads frequent the pools, and the people know that the clamor of their flight might betray a raiding party of the enemy.

From the foothills at the south end of the fairway the smoke of a Wittaia fire curled, to lose itself at last against the roll of cloud which cut the valley floor from the dark rim. Near the fire Wittaia warriors were ranked, their spear tips clean as lances on the sky. A larger group, convening on the Tokolik itself, raised a new howling, broken by rhythmic barks. Before the sun had warmed the air, three hundred or more Wittaia had appeared.

At the north end of the Tokolik there is an open meadow. Here the main body of the Kurelu were gathering. Over one hundred had now appeared, and at a signal a group of these ran down the field to the reedy pool. On the far bank a party of Wittaia danced and called. The enemies shouted insults at each other and brandished spears, but no arrows flew, and shortly both sides retired to their rear positions. Because the war was to be fought on their common frontier, the majority of the Kurelu were Kosi-Alua and Wilihiman-Walalua—the southern Kurelu. The northern warriors were not obliged to fight, but the best men of even the most distant villages would appear.

The sun had climbed over the valley, and its light flashed on breastplates of white shells, on white headdresses, on ivory boars' tusks inserted through nostrils, on wands of white egret feathers twirled like batons. The alarums and excursions fluttered and died while warriors came in across the fields. The shouted war was increasing in ferocity, and several men from each side would dance out and feign attacks, whirling and prancing to display their splendor. They were jeered and admired by both sides and were not shot at, for display and panoply were part of war, which was less war than ceremonial sport, a wild, fierce festival. Territorial conquest was unknown to the akuni; there was land enough for all, and at the end of the day the warriors would go home across the fields to supper. Should rain come to chill them, spoil their feathers, both sides would retire. A day of war was dangerous and splendid, regardless of its outcome; it was a war of individuals and gallantry, quite innocent of tactics and cold slaughter. A single death on either side would mean victory or defeat. And yet that death—or two or three—was the end purpose of the war, and the Kurelu, in April, were enraged. Two moons before, three wives of the Haiman *kain* Maitmo, with another woman and a man, had gone off to a pig feast held by clansmen in a nearby tribe; on their way they had been killed by the Wittaia, and though the Kurelu had come off best in the wars since, the score was not yet evened.

Toward midmorning a flurry of arrows was exchanged, and the armies, each three or four hundred strong, withdrew once more. But soon a great shout rose up out of the distance, and the Kurelu answered it exultantly, *hoo-ah-h, hoo-ah-h, hua, hua, hua,* like a pack cry of wild dogs. From the base of the tree the advance parties ran to the hillock at the edge of the reed pool, mustered so close that the spears clashed. More companies came swiftly from the rear positions, bare feet drumming on the grass. Here and there flashed egret wands, or a ceremonial whisk; the whisk was made of the great airy feathers of the cassowary bound tight by yellow fiber of an orchid. The wands and whisks were waved in the left hand, while the spears were borne at shoulder level in the right. Four men had black plumes of the saber-tailed bird-of-paradise curling two feet or more above their heads; at the bases of these plumes shone feathers of parrots and other brilliant birds, carmine and emerald and yellow-gold, fixed to a high crown of fur and fiber.

All wore headdresses of war. There were thin white fiber bands, and broad pandanus bands with the brown, gray, or yellow fur of cuscus, opossum, and tree kangaroo. There were crowns of flowers and crowns of feathers, hawk, egret, parrot, parakeet, and lory. Feather bands were stuck upon the forehead, black and shiny with smoke and grease, and matched pairs of large black or white feathers shot straight forward above the ears. Most common of all was a white solitary plume, bound to the forehead by its quill.

On the black breasts lay bibs made up of the white faces of minute snail shells: the largest bibs contained hundreds of snails. Most of these were fastened to the throat by a collar of white cowrie shells, and some of the men wore, in addition, a section of the huge baler shell, called *mikak;* this spoon-shaped piece, eight inches long or more, was worn with its white concave surface upward, just beneath the chin. Over the centuries, the shells had come up from the coast on the obscure mountain trade routes; they were the prevailing currency of the valley, and a single mikak would purchase a large pig.

Few of the men were entirely without decoration. Even the youngest warriors, the long-legged *elege* of fourteen to eighteen, wore strings of snails, or a lone feather in the dense wool of their hair. But here and there were naked men—naked, that is, but for the basic dress of every day, worn by all warriors in addition to the shells and fur and feathers: the tight armlets of the pith of bracken fern, braided beautifully upon the wrist or just above the elbow; black fiber strings, one or more, worn at the throat; and the *horim,* an elongated gourd worn by all but the smallest boys upon the penis. The horim is tied in an erect position by a fine thread of twig fiber secured around the chest; a second thread is looped through a small hole in the horim and down around the scrotum. The horim is often long enough to extend past its owner's nipples, and is sometimes curled smartly at the tip; many are decorated with a dangling hank of fur.

The advance warriors swept forward past the pool, reflections writhing on the windless water. The clamor increased as the Wittaia came on to meet them, led by a figure whose paradise plumes swayed violently above a head from which white feathers sprayed; he wore a boar's tusk through his nostrils, hanging down like a white mustache. Both mikak and shell bib gleamed upon his breast, and staring white circles were painted around his eyes.

Two armies of four to five hundred each were now opposed, most of the advance warriors armed with bows, a few with spears. They crouched and feinted, and the first arrows sailed high and lazily against the sky, increasing in speed as they whistled down and spiked the earth. Shrieks burst from the Wittaia, and a wounded Kurelu was carried back, an arrow through his thigh; he stared fearfully, both hands clenched upon a sapling, as two older men worked at the arrow and cut it out. Soon a second man returned, astride the shoulders of a comrade, for this is the way those wounded badly are taken from the field. The battle waned, renewed, and waned again; the fighting was desultory. The day was hot and humid, and as war demands a great amount of heroic leaping and running the warriors very much dislike the heat. But soon the Wittaia began a chanting, heightened by shrill special wails used little by the Kurelu—

dtchyuh, dtchyuh, dtchyuh—woo-ap, woo-ap
woo-r-d-a, woo-r-d-a—

and the Kurelu ran down the Tokolik to battle, in a flying avalanche of feet, spears balanced at the right shoulder, tips angled down. Fighting broke out in the swampy brush toward the Waraba, and, as the line swayed back and forth, the bush fighters remained where they were, crouched down in ambush. A Wittaia low behind a bush, thinking himself unseen, leapt high with a screech as a long spear arched through the bush and caromed off him; he darted away, too shaken to retrieve it, for it had nearly run him through.

Now a shout of derision burst from the Kurelu. On the crest of the Waraba, two hundred yards away, above the battle ground, thirty-odd warriors stood in silhouette. These were men of the Huwikiak clans, from a country two hours distant, on the far side of the Baliem. The territory of the Wittaia borders on the river, and the Huwikiak are Wittaia allies. These men had walked far for the fighting. They streamed down the bank into the swamp to join the battle.

In the early afternoon there came a prolonged lull. The number of warriors was still increasing on both sides, and massed legions were spaced back along the Tokolik for nearly a mile in both directions. Rainstorms, like dirty smoke, filled the high mountain passes, but the clouds hung back along the walls. At the edge of the field a young warrior sighed in agony as an arrow with a long, toothed tip was worked from his forearm with a bamboo sliver.

A wind sprang forward from the east, and the sky darkened. As if caught by the suspense before a rain, the warriors by the pool grew tense, and a Wittaia whoop, breaking the silence, was hurled back on waves of sound. A harrier hawk with a black head, coursing the battleground, flared off and away.

The men assembled in their war parties, and the rear groups closed behind them. A warrior passing the wounded boy seized the bloody arrow as it was twisted free and ran with it toward the front: ordinarily the arrow is kept by the wounded man, and the old man who had removed it shook his head, as if shocked by this breach of custom, moving off toward the rear. The boy, deserted, stood up shakily, staring at the blood running away between his fingers. At the same time, he was proud, and the pride showed.

A man without valor is *kepu*—a worthless man, a man-who-has-not-killed. The kepu men go to the war field with the rest, but they remain well to the rear. Some howl insults and brandish weapons from afar, but most are quiet and inobtrusive, content to lend the deadwood of their weapons to the ranks. The kepu men are never jeered or driven into battle—no one must fight who does not choose to—but their position in the tribe may be determined by their comportment on the field. Unless they have strong friends or family, any wives or pigs they may obtain will be taken from them by other men, in the confidence that they will not resist; few kepu men have more than a single wife, and many of them have none.

A kain with long hair in twisted cordy strings stalked forward, followed by another whose shoulders were daubed with yellow clay. U-mue came, in his huge mikak and tall paradise headdress, black grease gleaming in the hollows of his collarbones: the miraculous pig grease, blackened by the ash of grasses, is applied by all warriors whenever it is available, for it is sanctified by ceremony and contributes to morale and health as well as good appearance. It is worn by most men in their hair and on their foreheads, and sometimes in a broad bold band across the cheekbones and the nose, but U-mue smears it all over his head and shoulders, producing a black demonic sheen. He moved separately from the rest, for he claims to be a solitary fighter, with a taste for the treacherous warfare of the underbrush. In truth, he is rarely seen in action, and his claim to five kills is treated with more courtesy than respect. Among the warriors the numbers of kills are well established and are an important measure of degree of kainship.

Despite his claims, U-mue is not thought of as a war kain: he is the village kain of Wuperainma and the political kain of the clan Wilil in the southern Kurelu. The positions of war, village, and political kain are quite separate, though all may be combined in the same man: Wereklowe, the village kain of Abulopak, is also political and war kain of the clan Alua, and one of the most powerful men in all the tribe. Above the kains of all the clans is the great kain Kurelu, and below them are the lesser and younger men with varying degrees of kainship, based on property as well as valor, family as well as worth. U-mue, with four wives and eleven pigs, is a rich man, and his wealth, in company with his ambition and a rare gift for intrigue, has brought him power.

The fighting was closer and more vicious than that of the early skirmishes. More than a hundred men were actually in combat, as opposed to the twenty or thirty who had previously run out in the brief forays: the cries resounded to a strange, monotonous rhythm of twanged rattan bowstrings. The lines remained some fifty feet apart, but a few warriors moved out on the middle ground, crouched low, or down into the brushy swamp, stalking with spears. This is the dangerous fighting, for few men are killed by the thin bamboo arrows. Some may die afterward, but it is the spear which usually accounts for the rare kills made on the battlefield itself. The spear fighters in the brush beneath the Waraba kept low, for an arrow sailed at every upraised head. On the Tokolik, the battle line wavered back and forth, and at one point the Kurelu were swept back to the pool. Kurelu himself came forward then, and his men rallied. When the former line had been restored, the old man returned to the rear companies.

Seated among the taller kains, Kurelu looks shrunken and obscure. The scars of an ancient fire burn have pinched his chest, and his dress is old and brown and simple. His face is intelligent and reflective, almost shy, and its power is not readily perceived. But Kurelu's gentle smile is private, and his eyes are cold and deep, like small holes leading to infinity.

Each little while a wounded man was carried back. One of these was Ekitamalek of the Kosi-Alua, with an arrow in the breast. Ekitamalek would die. The battle flew back and forth until, toward midafternoon, another long lull occurred. An hour passed, and the warriors of the far villages started off in single file for home. But on an instant fighting broke out again. It was led this time by Weaklekek, who was a war kain of the clan Alua and one of the great warriors: Weaklekek, with his broad brow and mighty grin, was presently in mild disgrace, having missed a fine chance in the last war to kill a Wittaia with his spear. As it was, he had found himself cut off and was saved at the last moment only by a wild foray and flurry of arrows shot by two of his men.

A number of warriors had now been wounded, but no one had been killed on either side, and the fighting continued until dusk. The warriors whooped and ducked and came up grinning in an access of nervous ferocity, much like the boys with their grass spears on the homeward paths of twilight.

■ The four wives owned by U-mue do not all live in Wuperainma, partly because one or more must tend his pigs up on the mountain, and partly because Hugunaro and Eka-puwe fill the village with their fighting. In consequence, Ekapuwe, who is pregnant, has been sent to the pig village of Lokoparek, while the other three work in their husband's fields.

U-mue's wives and their small children share two con-ical huts called *ebeais*. The ebeai, or woman's round house, is perhaps ten feet in diameter and eight feet high. The lower floor is built a foot or so above the ground, and the sleeping loft about four feet above that: the loft is entered through a square hole in the ceiling. Both floors are carpeted with grass straw but are otherwise unfurnished. In the cen-ter of the ground floor is a hearth, which is delimited by four wood uprights at its corners. The uprights, which help sup-port the ceiling, also prevent people from rolling into the fire: this a common accident among small children, and many akuni bear the scars of it, including Kurelu himself. The smoke of the fire must escape through a small doorway giving on the yard; outside the doorway, under the hanging fringe of the thatch roof, is a small area where two people, one on each side, may squat out of the rain.

The ebeais of U-mue's wives are two of five in the long yard: two others belong to Loliluk, and one to Ekali. Across from the row of ebeais is the communal cooking house, an airy rectangular shed with a peaked roof of thatch and sev-eral doorways; though only six feet wide, it is over sixty feet in length, with three supporting posts from ground to ridge-pole. The smoke escapes it through doorways, walls, and roof, rising with the steam of the wet thatch to mingle with the ground clouds of early morning.

Hugunaro crossed from her hut at daylight to prepare her fires. Morning *hiperi*—hiperi, or sweet potato, is the basic food, so much so that *hiperi nan*, the "hiperi-eating," is synonymous with "meal"—are roasted at the fire's edge, and the children are sent with them eventually to the men's *pilai*, a communal hut like a very large ebeai which stands at the head of the yard, opposite the entrance: the men ordinarily rise later than the women and remain in the pilai by the hearth until the sun is well up from behind the cliff and the dank morning chill abated.

Their meal finished, Hugunaro sent her daughter with the other children to tend the pigs, which dwell in low sheds divided into separate stalls: the pig sheds may open into the rear wall of an ebeai, with the nearest stall reserved for piglets or sick animals in need of special care, but in U-mue's yard the two sheds are separate structures in protected corners, with one end of each facing directly on the yard. Each yard normally contains one pilai and one cooking shed, five or six ebeais, and one or more pig sheds, depending on the prosperity of the inhabitants, all of these facing on a common ground and surrounded by a fence of palings; the village fences, as well as those surrounding outer gardens, are crested invariably with straw, designed to protect the raw fence wood from rot. Small plots or borders of tobacco, sugar cane, gourds, ginger, and other special plants are kept within the fence, where they may be guarded.

The entire enclosure, with its own entrance from outside, is called a *sili*. Sometimes an entrance is boarded up and the fencing between two silis taken down, establishing a common yard; in this case there are usually two pilais and two cooking sheds, with a corresponding increase in the dwellings of pigs and women. A village may be composed of one or more silis, depending on its age and its importance, though there are rarely more than three. Wuperainma, an important village, can boast four, but one of these is presently abandoned. As is often the case, the fence of the abandoned sili has been maintained, and the grounds have been turned to small garden plots as well as a grove of banana trees. Bananas are also grown, sometimes in company with pandanus, in weedy corners between silis, which tend to be erratic in their alignment. The warm green of the great banana fronds, wavering on the colder greens of the mid-mountain landscape, may signal the presence of a village even when the gold thatching of the roofs is quite obscured.

The sun had burned away the mists, and the men had left for the lookout towers to mount guard; Hugunaro, with the other women living in the sili, went out into the fields. Aneake, the birdy old mother of U-mue and Yeke Asuk, usually goes also, but today she remained about the cooking shed, tending the piglets and the smallest children. Frequently these children accompany their mothers: they sit astride the women's shoulders, clinging to their hair. Infants are always borne this way, while new babies are carried in the bottoms of the nets extending down the mothers' backs: here in the dark folds, except when taken to the breast, they ruminate all day.

The nets are a series of overlapping bags, woven from brown fiber of an aquilaria bush, and decorated usually, though not always, with V patterns of dark red and purple dyes. They are attached by a headband at the forehead, and swing freely down the back, over the hips; a full load may and often does include a cargo of vegetables at the shoulder blades, a small pig upside down toward the middle of the back, and a small baby in the deepest net, jouncing along on the behind.

Empty or full, the nets are worn at all times by the

women, though they are not an article of dress. The women's clothing is a sort of skirt of fiber coils which circles the body well below the waist; it passes under the bare buttocks, sweeps upward to cross the hipbones, and dips down again under the belly in a kind of scanty pelvic apron. The coils are slung loosely except at the hipbones, where they are tightly bound together; it is the pressure here which just maintains an otherwise precarious arrangement. The new coils may be very pretty, for a gray base of palm fiber is overlaid with the hard shiny inner bark of two woody ground orchids, one with red blossoms and red fiber and the other with purple blossoms and a fiber of bright yellow. The women's skirts are woven by the men, who are the artisans of the akuni.

In the morning the nets are empty, swaying gracefully on the women's backs.

Hugunaro and the others walked in single file down through a wood of small trees and across the brook and out through the savanna to the ditches and the sweet-potato fields. A fairy-wren, a tiny scrap of black with bright white shoulders, chased another through yellow pastels of rhododendron. Each woman carried her digging stick across her shoulders and behind her neck, both hands raised to clutch it. The digging stick—the large oarlike stick used by the men and the smaller pointed one used by the women—is the only garden tool of the akuni.

U-mue's fields are far away toward the Tokolik, and the file of women angled back and forth along the path, which zigzags out among the ditches; the drainage ditches, which are crossed by bridges in the form of slim poles, serve also to deter the pigs from ravaging the gardens. Hugunaro carried a tight bundle of grass thatch containing fire: the fires are used throughout the day to burn dried garden trash. Arriving, she laid this on the ground and built it up with dry weeds and vegetable detritus. Each woman then took fire to the area which she was working.

Hugunaro began immediately, using her digging stick with sharp backhand strokes, like paddling, to slash the weeds; later she would break the ground in the same way. Her digging stick is about five feet long, pointed sharply at both ends; it is known as the hiperi spear, for it must serve also as a weapon in the event that the women are attacked. Though their spears would be no match for those of Wittaia raiders, the women in concert might defend themselves just long enough for help to reach them from the kaios.

The smoke rose slowly from the fires, and all across the gardens, on both sides, small white plumes broke the dark patterns of the fields. It was midmorning. In midafternoon the men would take up their spears and move back toward the villages, and the women would go too. There were only two meals in the day, in the morning and the evening, and the hiperi must now be cooked, for dark would come in a few hours. The women would take the vegetables harvested that day and load them into their nets, so that, trudging homeward, they looked twice the bulk of the skinny creatures who had gone out in the morning.

Hugunaro's figure is typical of the women, who, except when pregnant, are little fatter than the men. She is perhaps five feet tall, with small shoulders and full breasts, small hips, and short, thin, childish legs: these legs, which are characteristic, seem curiously out of place on female bodies otherwise well made. She is a pretty woman, with bright brown eyes and a quick mouth and a wry, strident manner; in her stridence and quick temper she resembles the pregnant wife, Ekapuwe, which accounts in part for their mutual ill feeling.

Koalaro is older than the other wives and without fire: she is of the mood and color of bare earth. The young wife,

Yuli, has no child as yet, though she looks strong and willing. She is taller than the rest, high in the breasts and heavy in the legs and hips, for her labors have not shrunk her to muscle. Yuli has tight little eyes in a large and stupid face, and her loose smile is playful. She looks as if she had a secret, and indeed she may: not long ago she was seized while in the fields and taken away to their own village by some men of the Kosi-Alua. After three days she came back of her own accord, and while it is assumed that she was not raped, and even that no intercourse took place, U-mue is nonetheless very angry with the Kosi-Alua and plans revenge.

■ In the evening fields below the grove of arau-caria, a man with a black dog was hunting a tiny quail. The dog, sharp-eared and bushy-tailed, was quick and small; it came with the akuni long ago and is peculiar to the high-lands.

The man, carrying a throwing stick, followed the dog. His arm was cocked. There were four boys with him, the fleet *yegerek* of seven to fourteen, not yet warriors and no longer children, the scouts and messengers, the swineherds and the carriers of weapons; the yegerek were armed with short sticks of their own. The dog pounced, and a quail flew. The place was surrounded, and two more quail flew out, the low sun gleaming through their wings as they whirred down the savanna. None were struck down, and the group trotted onward.

The boys soon tired of the hunt. They broke off small spears of a firm grass and staged a war, dancing and feinting with the spears, and whooping, before darting forward to throw, wrists quick as snakes. In the dusk their thin bodies were no more than silhouettes, outlined against the distant hill called Siobara.

■ The warrior Yeke Asuk of Wuperainma got his name when still a boy. Yeke Asuk means "Dog Ear" and refers to a gift for overhearing word of any activity which might lead to trouble, such as raid or pig-theft, and tagging along behind. Yeke Asuk, volatile and hot-tempered and a sulker, has not lost his taste for trouble and is often, these days, at the root of it. But, as U-mue's younger brother, he has influence, and he is brave.

Two days before, on the Tokolik, Yeke Asuk had received a scalp wound from an arrow. The wound was superficial and no longer bothered him, and he sat with the other men around the hearth in U-mue's pilai until the sun was high over the cliff behind the village. U-mue himself had been absent since the night before, on a visit to his pregnant wife up in the mountains.

Each morning, when their sweet potatoes had been eaten, the men smoked and talked in the dense warmth of the hut, and performed slow, peaceful work of manufacture and repair. Several worked together in repairing a shell bib: the shell strings lay coiled on a large leaf, and next to the leaf lay a supply of fiber from the spiny bamboo as well as some soft aquilaria. The aquilaria was woven across strands of bamboo to make the tough bands on which the rows of snail shells would be sewn.

In the sleeping loft above, Ekali turned softly. The ceiling of thin bamboo shafts supported by crossbeams of wood creaked vaguely with his movements. Soon a leg appeared out of the ceiling hole; it probed blindly for the wooden step which, polished with long use of callused feet, gleamed in the pale light through the doorway.

Ekali took a place behind the other men, who squatted near the door to use the light. At the hearth, as well as in the loft above, one is closer to the front according to one's status—in a crowded hut, the kepu men and younger boys move to the rear. A tall, smiling man with a confident air, Ekali is kepu, but the others greeted him politely, their soft voices passing around the circle. *Ekali, narak-a-laok,* they said, taking his hand. *Narak, narak.* From the shed adjoining came the bumping of U-mue's pigs, the consternation of each morning's meeting with the children.

Yonokma is an older boy, an elege, sixteen or seventeen; he took from the wall an arrow shaft of cane and fitted it with a long tip, but the binding of vine needed repair, and Yonokma, with the shiftlessness of his age, replaced the arrow without really working on it. As the young brother of U-mue's wife Koalaro, Yonokma stays frequently in this pilai. Because his movements are indefinite—he stays as often at his father's pilai in Abulopak—his name signifies "the Wanderer."

Yonokma's friend Siloba began to sing. Siloba comes from the village of Mapiatma, on the far side of the wood, but he usually sleeps in Wuperainma, for U-mue is his *nami.* All akuni have namis, or men favorably disposed toward them in a protective and generous way; the nami is most often the child's maternal uncle, though the relationship is not automatic, and a boy may have more namis than one. The nami relationship is the warmest of all family ties. A child will also have ceremonial fathers—the brothers, often, of his real father. Such a father would claim Siloba—*An-meke*, he would say, Mine, grasping his horim—with as much authority as Siloba's own parent, and, in fact, the distinction between true and ceremonial is thought quite unimportant—in a sense, the head of the clan is the father of all in it. The ceremonial father, like the real one, is apt to be remote and strict, while the nami is indulgent.

As a house of warriors—in addition to Yeke Asuk, there are Hanumoak and Loliluk, and the boy Yonokma is already a fierce fighter—the pilai is stocked heavily with arrows and bows, with an arsenal of spare bowstrings, bindings, and new arrow points. The latter objects are wrapped in neat packets of straw or banana leaves and stored in the rafters or hung along the walls. Bundles of feathers, packets of fibers, a gourd calabash containing small fetish objects, a net bag of tobacco, some stone adzes, a bird-of-paradise headdress belonging to Hanumoak, some spare horims, and a men's digging stick are stacked or hung against the walls toward the rear. Attached to the fire frame, near the ceiling, are a set of boar's tusks for the nostrils, a boar's-tusk knife, a cane mouth harp, and Yeke Asuk's armlets of brown dog fur. By the side of the fire, which was now reduced to embers, lay long bamboo holders for the tobacco, and a small wooden tongs. The tobacco, wrapped and smoked in a coarse leaf, is called *hanum;* Hanumoak, "Tobacco Bone," is named after the holder.

The sun had pierced the mist at last and gleamed in the puddles in the yard. One by one, the men left the dense warmth of the hut. Taking their spears—the spears are too long to be brought into the pilai, and are kept outside—they wandered toward the entrance of the sili.

U-mue's wife Hugunaro, squatting in a doorway of the cooking shed, watched the departure without interest, for she watched it every morning of her life. As Siloba slipped past her, Hugunaro hissed at him. *Siloba,* she said softly. She beckoned him with the characteristic gesture, arm extended, palm down, folding her fingers down and back, down and back. *E-me, eme.* Come. She handed him a blackened hiperi. Siloba smiled, a quick, shy smile of thanks.

The warriors went down through the wood and out across the fields toward U-mue's kaio. The path angled back and forth among the dark green leaves and violet trumpet flowers of the sweet potatoes. Every little while it crossed one of the drainage ditches, from which a coarse calla lily erected its large stalks; the corm of this lily supplies the vegetable of Oceania known as taro. Beside the taro plant floated leaves of its wild relative, a small water lily. Orange dragon-flies zipped up and down the ditches, clashing in mid-air with a small dry, harsh electric sound, or poising suddenly on a leaf, their long transparent wings cocked forward. Like the drab mountain swiftlet which coursed the air above them, they were hunting insects.

U-mue had come down from the mountains and was already at the kaio. He wore a new crown of white feathers, taken from the wing linings of the black duck; the quills had been punched through a strip of papery pandanus bark to form a crown. Ordinarily the men do not wear such decorations to the kaio, but the crown was a new one and U-mue is vain. To go with the crown, he wore his large mikak and fine shell bib, with a string of cowries hanging down his back. A fresh band of black grease was drawn across his face, and his brow was also greased and shiny. Otherwise his dark skin was clean; he habitually looks cleaner than the other men, who do not always remove the fine gray scale of their own grime, nor the mud flecks on their lower legs. With U-mue was Apeore of Lokoparek, a taut-faced warrior with cold browless eyes.

The men crept beneath the shelter and hunched around

the fire. On most days they would have rested here all morning, but today there was men's garden work: though the women tend the gardens, the men do all the heavy work of creating and rebuilding fields and ditches.

Soon all but U-mue left the shelter. They had on the short horims worn at work, and the few wearing shell bibs turned these around so that they hung down behind. In a ditch a hundred yards away other men had already collected, standing in water over their knees. They reached down and dug double handfuls of mud and threw these up upon the banks, where older men packed the mud around each hiperi plant. Soon nearly twenty were splashing in the ditch, heaving and sweating. Hanumoak, who is quick-witted and handsome, paused for a while to daub some gray clay on his shoulders; he craned his head around, taking pleasure in his own appearance. The lame man Aloro came along after a while: he planted his spear butt in the earth and, sidling clumsily, joined the others in the ditch. Aloro was greeted with deference, for despite his twisted leg he is a fanatic warrior; it was Aloro who, with Yeke Asuk, saved the life of the war kain Weaklekek when the latter was cut off by the enemy. Though both Aloro and Yeke Asuk are young warriors, they have each killed two.

Beyond the men rose a pall of women's fires. This morning the women had avoided the garden where the men labored, for though a man works sometimes with his wives, the two sexes never mix in larger groups. Once in a while the women, in apparent approval of the spectacle in the ditch, would laugh loudly among themselves, for in their cheerful way they are in league against the men.

U-mue climbed slowly and sedately to the top of the kaio tower and sat himself upon the platform, his feathers gleaming as he turned his head against the sky. U-mue was worried about his new crown, for though many of the people broke the taboo, the use of the wild duck in any way was considered *wisa*. Certain plants, animals, acts, localities, and other phenomena were wisa—invested, that is, with supernatural power. A wisa thing was not necessarily good or bad, but neither was it to be trifled with without due ceremony.

U-mue knew that the great kain Wereklowe, for one, had been angered by his use of duck feathers. A man who touched this bird, according to Wereklowe, lost much of the keenness of his sight and would thus be unable to spy out a raiding party of the enemy.

■ Just south of the village of Homaklep a small spur of the mountain, in the form of a low wooded ridge, slides out onto the valley floor and disappears. The village of Abukumo, half deserted now, lies on this ridge, and below Abukumo is a small wood. The wood gives on a grassy knoll, with a small grove of trees shading gray boulders; the knoll is called Anelarok. Below the south flank of Anelarok flows a small brushy stream, the Tabara, and to the west lie the open grasslands and the gardens.

Anelarok lies at a crossing of the paths, and because it commands a fine view of the valley there are often people, and a fire. The paths lead from the villages to the Aike, and from the fields into the mountains; the least-used is the one which plunges down into the undergrowth of the Tabara, crosses the stream on large flat stones, and climbs again on a steep slope toward the land of the Siep-Kosi. This path was used one afternoon to take a wounded Siep-Kosi home to his own country.

In former times the Siep peoples fought separately with both Wittaia and Kurelu, and though this practice proved too costly, their warriors still wished to go to war. The tribe divided into factions, one of which—the Siep-Elortak—fought henceforth at the side of the Wittaia, and the other —the Siep-Kosi—at the side of the Kurelu. This warrior had been wounded in the upper chest, fighting on the Tokolik. Too seriously hurt to be carried across the hills, he had lain for many days in Mapiatma. Then one day his people came for him and took him home.

Two poles were lashed parallel with vines, and the man was slung between them, supported under the arms and knees. His body was swathed in leaves and lashed securely; even his head was covered, leaving him just air enough to breathe. He was borne by seven men across the fields in front of Homuak, down through the woods, and up over the knoll of Anelarok. The journey homeward was a long one, but the men did not pause at Anelarok to smoke. Some Kurelu were there, and a fire burning, but the Siep-Kosi passed through quickly. The Kurelu and the Siep-Kosi, enemies in the past, could readily become enemies again.

The stretcher jolted down across the Tabara and climbed again on the far side. The paths were steep and rocky and slippery with the rains, and the seven bearers struggled with their load. The man sat still as a green mummy, as if he were long dead. Only once, when the caravan faltered, high on the far slope, did a slow hand rise toward the green head, hover a moment, and drop away again. The bearers moved onward, picking their way toward a sky gray with coming rain, until the figures were as small as ants hauling a dead cricket.

The journey was watched from the kaios of the Kurelu. The men at the kaios knew about the journey, as the akuni know of all things in their world. An event in the lives of the Kurelu is known as fast as a boy can run the ditch logs with the news, but no boy is ever sent. The word bounds straight across the fields like the flight of the brown finches, from village to path to garden—the men's heads turn in the shadow of the shelters, the women straighten to rest a moment on their sticks—in a series of small whoops as pure and unmistakable as the flight signals of the birds. The people know the course of things, for the course of things may be thousands of years old, and all they really need to hear is the one word which changes; the event does not. The man's name is called, with the high whoop which relays it onward.

The wounded man had come of his own accord because he wished to fight, and he was wounded because he was too brave or too careless, or because the power held in the holy stones of his people had not worked for him. This too was in the course of things. The Kurelu would be sorry if he died, and they would weep because weeping was expected, but a large part of the sorrow would be brought about by the satisfaction given the Wittaia. The Wittaia knew about this warrior, in the same way that they knew about each enemy struck in the body: they knew his name and village and his clan, and they hoped that he would die. But it now seemed that he was going to live, and in a short time they would know this too.

■ In the morning, when the sun appeared over the valley, the warriors trotted along beneath the mountain, bound for the northern wars. Among those who did not go was Yeke Asuk. He was not quite recovered from the head wound suffered on the Tokolik, and he had private business to attend to.

Some time ago a man from a village in the northern Kurelu had trespassed in his gardens. This is a most serious offense, and Yeke Asuk had stolen three of the man's pigs in compensation. Two of the pigs had been speedily consumed, but recently the third had been restolen by its owner.

To redress this outrage, Yeke Asuk traveled to the village to demand the pig's return. He was accompanied by his friend Tegearek, a violent man who shares with the lame man Aloro the war leadership of the clan Wilil. The color of both Yeke Asuk and Tegearek is golden-brown, markedly lighter than the average though by no means unique, and as both are also very short and powerful, they made, as they set off, a distinctive pair.

Yeke Asuk, less than five feet, is probably the shortest of male akuni. Limo, a kain man of the Kosi-Alua, is among the tallest. Limo is probably five feet nine, but his small shoulders and lithe body, more typical than the stumpy shape of Yeke Asuk and Tegearek, make him appear well over six feet tall. Many other warriors seem taller than their height: this is especially true when they are holding, as they often are, spears three times their own length.

The pig was not returned to Yeke Asuk, and, as circumstances did not encourage either seizure or re-theft, he and Tegearek went home. The complaint had been registered, to justify in advance any action that might be taken afterward. There was, in the valley, all the world and time.

■ Uwar and Aku came down along the wooded ridges, carrying on their heads bundles of fagots for the sili fires. When the steep slope fell away toward Wuperainma, they rolled the fagots down the hill, and the bundles leapt and sprang through the green hill shrub, starting the yellow white-eyes and quick wrens from their low shade.

The children, black motes on the white cumulus, strayed on the afternoon's high horizon, sad to descend out of the sky. From where they stood their whole world and their whole life lay before them, all the northeast corner of the valley. The Elokera slid away beneath their feet, forsaking the mountain near the village of Takulovok, which lay invisible under the crest. The river entered a woodland of albizzia and emerged a slow brown grassland stream, unwinding along the mountain wall. Then it curled off westward, through the Kosi-Alua and the Wittaia, to come to an end in the smoke-misted distance, the Baliem.

The Baliem lay in the countries of the enemy, and though it was less than four miles distant, at the far end of the Siobara, the children would never know more of it than the fringe of casuarina which hid its waters from their sight.

Above the children's heads three brown hawks circled, shrieking in tight, ratchety vexation in the high blue day. Other birds came rarely to the crest, which was no more than a jagged outcropping of limestone karst, heaved up out of the sea in other ages. Lichen and bracken ferns clung to sparse soil, with dwarf shrubbery in the niches, but songbirds rarely paused there; the insects were scarce, and the dry lizards stayed away. Only the hawks came, riding the updrafts from the valley warmth, and the fierce blue-gray hunter of all continents, the peregrine: the falcon dove down the steep hill like a shard of falling sky, its passage booming a half-mile away.

Below the hill, on the south side, was their own village of Wuperainma: Uwar is the son of Loliluk and Aku the daughter of U-mue. The children could spy down on the silis and watch Aku's grandmother, Aneake, pick her way along the cooking shed. This was the still time of the afternoon, when all the people were in the fields; Aneake was too old to work steadily in the fields and rarely left the village now except to hunch in the near weeds or gather twigs.

They came down slowly, caught in the grave immobility of time, the sun and grass; the crests of the araucarias which shaded the spring of Homuak were still far beneath their feet. Now they could see Abulopak, the bare yards gleaming through the pale green of banana trees, backed up against the hill's northwestern flank. Between the children and the villages, the slope was broken by round limestone sinkholes, and in one of the holes the wall sheltered a grotto; there was a fireplace, and long ago, before the children had first gone there, akuni had drawn pictures on the wall. Almost everywhere that people had sheltered beneath a rock and built a fire, such drawings had been made. They were

made still, with charcoal sticks, for no other purpose than the amusement of the artist, for there was no language of symbol. There were men and women on the soft, pale stone, and a large crayfish, and some lizards.

The children sprang down the grassy hillside, quick as black dancers. Their voices called out to the people passing on the trails below, but the voices came from another world and went unanswered. Uwar sang vaguely, sadly, without sadness, and the song wandered on the airs of afternoon.

■ Early in the morning, when the pigs of U-mue's sili are herded out into the fields, they are apt to consort briefly with a herd from the sili adjoining. The animals of U-mue's sili are tended in rotation by the numerous children, while those of the sili of Asok-meke are tended invariably by Asok-meke's stepson, Tukum.

Like all the swineherds in the Kurelu, Tukum conducts his pigs each morning to a predetermined pasture, usually a sweet-potato field gone fallow. Here the pigs eat greens and the stray vegetables which have escaped the harvest, and root for grubs and mice and frogs and the small skinks along old ditches. In the afternoon he escorts them back to village pens, where they are fed hiperi skins and other offal from the fires. Each pig is marked almost from birth for a certain fate—a ceremony, a marriage gift, the payment of a debt—but until the day of its demise it leads an orderly and pleasant life, prized and honored on all sides.

Despite the great worth of the pigs and the prestige they bear, little husbandry is practiced, though piglets, very small or ailing, are usually carried in the women's nets and receive special attention. Should a sow reach breeding age, she may be escorted to a noted boar, lest one of her own scraggy kin should work his way with her. The daytime haunts of these illustrious boars, like the haunts of every animal in the villages, are common knowledge, and, while permission may sometimes be asked of the boar's owner, the decision is more often left to the stern animal itself.

As Tukum is thought of as incompetent, even for a child of seven, such a delicate matter as sow-breeding would probably be left to his mother. Tukum's mother is a shrill, cheerful woman, the gat-toothed bane of her young son's existence, who, with her infernal pigs and her incessant shouting, reduces Tukum almost daily to bitter tears. Not only is Tukum smaller than the children of U-mue's sili but his pigs are larger. The pigs take advantage of Tukum's forgetful nature by losing themselves in the low wood or barging into gardens where they do not belong, and as they are far stronger, better coordinated, more numerous, and more intent than he, they make of his days a series of small emergencies. His only weapon is an extraordinary voice, both loud and gruff, and hoarse with use, which signals the presence of Tukum and his charges from great distances away.

■ Ekapuwe lives presently in the hill village of Lokoparek because she cannot abide Hugunaro. According to Ekapuwe, her rivalry with and dislike for Hugunaro was born of U-mue's insane love for Ekapuwe, on the one hand, and Hugunaro's disgusting jealousy on the other.

Ekapuwe is a Wittaia woman, married formerly to a Wittaia. In those days, perhaps seven years ago, the Kurelu were at war not only with the Wittaia but with those Siep-Kosi who are their neighbors to the southeast; the region of the upper slopes where Lokoparek now lies was then wild forest, a part of the frontier no man's land.

One day Ekapuwe and her husband came to the forest to gather fiber, and there the beautiful Ekapuwe was spied by U-mue. It came to U-mue on that instant that he must have this woman above all things in life; at the same time, he was not prepared to attack her husband single-handed. The love-stricken man ran down the mountain to summon reinforcements, and returned not long thereafter with a well-armed band. Ekapuwe's husband was driven off, and Ekapuwe herself became the prize of U-mue.

The romantic tale of Ekapuwe and U-mue is anathema to Hugunaro. Her terrible jealousy, in Ekapuwe's opinion, makes the idea that U-mue should sleep with other women unbearable to Hugunaro, and it is for this reason that she resorts to an abortionist, for otherwise U-mue might neglect her in time of pregnancy. Hugunaro has made a habit of having herself aborted, four or five times, it is said. The abortion is effected by certain skillful women using techniques of pummeling and massage; the fetus is dropped in a special pool in the small stream called Tabara. Among noted abortionists is Asok-meke's wife, mother of Tukum the swineherd. While abortion is more or less accepted among unmarried girls—as most girls are wed within a year or so of puberty, the event is rare—it is frowned upon when practiced by married women, and the likelihood is that U-mue and Hugunaro have quarreled on this account. On the other hand, the husbands are rather ignorant about abortions; there is a song of the akuni in which the women gloat over their husbands' innocence,—*but we, the women, know the truth!* Many women dislike having children, and abortion is quite common.

It was the passionate Hugunaro who gave her husband the mildly derisive name that he now bears—the name U-mue means "the Anxious One." With his intrigues and maneuverings, U-mue has every reason to be anxious, and a group of wives which includes, besides the rivals, a big, sleepy girl like Yuli cannot add very much to the Anxious One's peace of mind.

■ When a man enters a sili which is not his own, his spear is left against a tree outside; otherwise, he rarely goes without it. The cheerfulness, even gaiety, of the people is the more remarkable for the fact that never in the whole course of their lives can they be certain that death does not await them down the path; after each peril, like the small mice which dart or flatten in the grass at a hawk's passage, they continue as though nothing had occurred. Nevertheless, a man travels armed, not only in the vicinity of the frontiers but on his home trails; quite apart from the enemy, he may need his spear in the disputes which occur constantly within the tribe itself.

One fine day, down by the river, a man of the Kosi-Alua was badly injured, in part because he had left his spear at home. The wife of this man had left him for a man of the Siep-Kosi, and he had reason to believe that her flight had been assisted by Tegearek of Wuperainma. He came to question Tegearek, who denied all part in it, and when he came several times again, suggesting by his insistence that Tegearek had not told him the truth, the latter became woe-fully annoyed: whether or not the man's suspicion was well founded, Tegearek felt himself insulted.

One morning the man came to the Aike, accompanied by several tribesmen; they were bound not for Wuperainma but for the lands of the Siep-Kosi, to inquire after the missing wife. The husband, foolishly unarmed, had wandered from his friends, and near the river he encountered Tegearek.

Tegearek is the young war kain of the Wilil, an innocent man of violence: his name derives from *tege warek*, or "Spear Death." He is strong and stocky, with two black front teeth and the wistful expression of a man easily confused. He is hot-tempered in the way confused people often are, and he had with him Yeke Asuk, whose hot temper is more complex. These factors, in combination with the fact that his tormentor was alone and unarmed, persuaded Tegearek that an attack was timely and, after a brief and violent ex-change, he launched it. No cowardice on Tegearek's part was involved in this, for according to Dani codes a man who so forgets himself as to run afoul of an antagonist while un-armed and alone deserves no mercy and receives none.

Tegearek did not intend to kill the man but simply to punish him a little. To this end he jabbed him twice, once in the thigh and a second time in the head. His victim seized hold of the spear and tried to wrest it from Tegearek; when he managed to turn it in Tegearek's direction, he was speared in the stomach by Yeke Asuk. Yeke Asuk did not wish to kill him either, and the spear was withdrawn after having penetrated two or three inches. The two friends left the man where he lay, not knowing how many Kosi-Alua might be along, or when they might appear.

The group of Kosi-Alua appeared soon after. They car-ried their friend home across the open fields, avoiding the brushy trails under the mountain. The wounded man sat astride the shoulders of each friend in turn, supported by two others at the arms. He was slumped, head hanging, and his head had been bandaged in vegetable leaves; in the sun, his back glistened with heavy sweat. The women straightened, watching in silence as the group made its way across the fields; it entered the brushland west of the dancing-field called Liberek and disappeared.

Since this episode Tegearek and Yeke Asuk have moved with caution, for they expect reprisal.

■ One morning on the way to his kaio, Weaklekek, the great warrior of the clan Alua, startled a large bird from the base of a rhododendron. The bird flew to the low limb of a chestnut tree overlooking the lower Tabara. Weaklekek took a hunting arrow from the bundle he carried with him and laid the rest in the grass; he ran silently down a slope on the far side of the tree, beyond the bird, and crept up on it through the bushes. The bird sat uneasily on the limb, a soft, rufous brown bird with a very long, wide tail. It was a mountain pigeon, the call of which, *hoo-oik, hoo-oik*, hollow and mournful, is imitated by the warriors in time of war. Weaklekek crept up too close, as he did not wish to waste his arrow. The bird flew as he raised his bow, and the arrow skittered across the empty branch.

A man's voice called to him, *We-AK-le-kek, a-oo.*

Weaklekek went on down toward the Aike, stepping over a tribe of biting ants which, oblivious of his feet, dragged a dazed grasshopper across his path and into the grass jungle. He was the first man at the kaio. Other men, bearing their spears, arrived in a few minutes, and Weaklekek left his kaio and went down into the gardens. His wife Lakaloklek and their daughter Eken were breaking up stale earth, turning and splitting the old lumps with hiperi spears. Weaklekek had the men's digging stick, and he set rapidly to work, panting rhythmically and hoarsely from the start. Behind him the girl, whose name means "Seed" or "Flower," burned the dried weeds, and a light air out of the east carried the smoke toward Weaklekek and shrouded him. With Lakaloklek, he surged and vanished in the fumes. Feet planted in the black-brown earth, the man and woman were the exact color of the soil, as if they had sprung out of the smoke and earth, like trolls. Weaklekek's great strength and energy were of the earth, infusing him, as if one day he might leap free and climb the sky.

Except when in the act of love, in wayside grass or the night darkness of an ebeai, a man and wife are entirely undemonstrative; this is prudishness, not lack of warmth. Weaklekek and Lakaloklek are no exception. Nevertheless, and despite the fact that Weaklekek has other wives, he is plainly closest to Lakaloklek. Lakaloklek herself, a slim, spirited woman with a pretty, elfin face, took upon herself the disapproval of the community by rushing to Weaklekek immediately after the death of her first husband: her name means "She Who Would Not Wait." More than any other man and wife in the southern Kurelu, they seem a pair. There is an air of strong communion when they are together, of wild and unarticulated tenderness.

Weaklekek worked relentlessly, his dark body gleaming in the pall. The dirt flew, tumbling in clods. From one clod wriggled a bronze ground lizard; it writhed down to the water of the ditch.

Weaklekek cried gleefully at the sight of it, for the fact

of it. Some water spiders flew before the falling clods, and he called out softly, *Pilili, pilili*—Be quick, be quick. Behind him, Lakaloklek laughed, as affectionately as wives of the akuni ever laugh, but she did not cease working. She turned the earth slowly and steadily, bent over her stick, breasts swaying.

When Weaklekek first came to live in the southern Kurelu, he was called simply We-AK, which means "the Bad One." He brought this name with him from the northern countries, where he had had a wife. One day, not long before he came to Homaklep, this wife told him that she had been raped by men of a near village, and Weaklekek went immediately to confront them. The men were absent, and Weaklekek, as was his right, seized a number of their pigs and took them back to his own sili.

The next day his wife confessed to him that she had not been raped at all; apparently she had lied to him in the simple hope of making trouble. Weaklekek has a dark temper, and he became enraged. Nevertheless, he retired into his pilai, attempting to control himself. Some hours later he emerged and, finding his wife before him in the yard, struck her a terrible blow along the jaw. She dropped senseless to the ground, and before the next morning she was dead.

Weaklekek was grief-stricken, for he had loved this wife; certainly he had not meant to kill her. He could not forgive himself for what he had done, and meanwhile his own life was in danger. Custom demanded that she be cremated, but her kinsmen were infuriated by her death and swore that they would kill Weaklekek; he could scarcely invite them to the funeral. Furthermore, he had no support from his own people, who were shocked by his act and would not go near him; they referred to him from that time forward as the Bad One.

It was characteristic of Weaklekek that he made no attempt to excuse himself, to mollify the akuni by inviting them to feed upon his pigs. On the morning following the death, when the funeral would ordinarily have occurred, Weaklekek went out into his yard. In a passion of grief and anger and remorse, he tore down the fences of his sili. All alone he hurled the laths together in a mighty pyre, and all alone he carried forward the body of his wife and laid it on the flames.

When this stark funeral was finished, Weaklekek left his village and walked off to the southward. There was no life left for him where he had lived, and he knew that sooner or later the kinsmen of his wife would try to kill him. He went to the village of Homaklep, on the far southern frontier, bringing with him a heavy heart and a bad name. Homaklep lay in the shadow of the enemy, and its people were glad to have a man such as Weaklekek, even though he was an outcast.

Not long thereafter his wife's kinsmen ambushed Weaklekek along a trail. He killed one of her brothers with an arrow, fighting furiously—so furiously that the attack was never again repeated—but in doing so he worsened his own reputation. Nevertheless, in his new village he worked hard, earning respect, and became one of the great warriors of the region. Over the years, the name We-ak was lengthened to Weaklekek, to wipe away the sense of it, though the killing of his wife and her brother have maintained his reputation for violence.

The akuni still fear Weaklekek on those rare occasions when he loses his temper, and Weaklekek himself, despite his generosity and kindness, gives frequent sign that he is a burdened man. Always solitary, he retreats at times into a somber silence, as if in dread of his own strength. His broad back to the world, he hunches over a long shell belt, weaving, weaving.

■ Not long ago both wives of a man named Werene were raped in the fields by men of the Kosi-Alua. Werene stole two of their pigs, the normal compensation, and gave them to Weaklekek for safe keeping. But the Kosi men did not recognize his right, having small respect for Werene. They came to Homaklep and, failing to find the two animals in question, made off with Werene's entire herd.

A man suffers offenses according to his inability to defend himself, and Werene suffered both of the most common ones, which are pig-theft and wife-rape. In principle the offender is paid back in kind. Should he be found out—and as these acts are usually an expression of power, he is almost invariably found out—and should he accept the theft of his own pigs or the rape of his own wife, the matter is then closed. But more often the victim of the offense is chosen in advance for qualities of cowardice or impotence and suffers his injury to go unpunished.

The great kains, though wealthy in both pigs and women, are not often sinned against, for it is one of their prerogatives to kill a man, or his subordinates or children, when he has done them harm; indeed, the demonstrated willingness, and even eagerness, to take life is an important asset in establishing a great kainship in the first place. But a man who is totally kepu soon loses to stronger men any pigs he may have acquired, and his wives, when not raped, are taken outright. This is the law, and, should he resist it, he may die or be cast out.

Werene's main asset was his friendship with Weaklekek, who is kain of Werene's village. Weaklekek is a loyal and generous man, and he heeded Werene's request that he intercede. It was arranged that the two original pigs be returned to their first owners, whereupon the pigs of Werene would be returned to him. This much was accomplished, but Werene, in the end, had two raped wives without a compensating increase in the number of his pigs, while Weaklekek was much resented by the Kosi-Alua.

■ One night in late April the young warrior Ekitamalek of the Kosi-Alua died of a wound from a Wittaia arrow; this wound had been suffered in the recent war on the Tokolik. Ekitamalek had not been a very good warrior, spending most of his time in the second line, and he had been in the second line when the arrow struck him. The arrow entered his breast on the left side, and the shaft broke off. The old men could not locate the tip and assumed that only a small piece was still inside, and within a few days Ekitamalek was walking around in the village of Kibitsilimo, where his father, Yoroick, lived. He did not feel well enough to work, but he was not in pain. One morning two weeks later he felt strange. He went to his mother's ebeai, complaining of his wound, and was helped into the sleeping quarters in the loft. He started to cry, and the men came to see him. Within three hours he was dead.

The village of Kibitsilimo lies southwest of Homuak, across a savanna of abandoned fields and weedy ditches. On the morning after the death the women on their way to mourn Ekitamalek stopped on the banks of a stream just south of Kibitsilimo and daubed their faces and bodies with ocher clay. In single file they then resumed their way, yellow and leprous, bent beneath brown nets of hiperi. From the river the moaning in the village could be heard, rising and falling like a dull wind.

Near the outer fences of the village the women paused in silence while a group of men passed ahead of them. The women's faces were set and cold, and in the yellow clay they looked possessed. When the men had gone they moved onward again, into a little grove on the south side of the village. Arriving, they climbed slowly, one by one, through the narrow entrance stile. Seated facing them, on a high chair in the hot sun, was Ekitamalek.

The sili is a large one, laid out in an L, with the entrance at the top of the letter: the chair stood in the long part of the L, not quite at the angle, looking toward the mountains. On the right hand of the women entering stood a long cooking shed, and by its wall the women laid their nets and offerings of sweet potato. Then they went forward to sink among the massed brown female backs hunched on the earth before the chair.

The women rocked and groaned, hands to their faces or forearms across their brows; some scrambled awkwardly to touch the dead man's feet and rub his legs. Two women stood before the chair with leafy branches, brushing the black flies from the dead man's face and wounds. All the women cried, and at the same time they moaned in rhythmic response to the litany of the dead man's father, who stood behind the chair. Yoroick's voice quavered with grief as he called out his elegy of his son, in phrases.

The only woman behind the chair was the dead man's mother. She clung to the chair post, hands clasped around its top, and sometimes she sank down at its foot, boneless with grief.

A pathway was kept clear among the ranks of women, and the incoming men passed through in single file. Kains from the nearer villages had brought pigs; those from farther off had with them ornamented belts of cowries. The animals were not brought in, but were left in the pig stalls of adjoining silis; the cowrie belts were taken into the men's pilai, which occupied the corner of the L, beyond the chair.

The visitors were important warriors and men of property; the few young men were relatives, or of the sili. None of the men had brought their spears or bows, and none wore ornaments; they were dressed as simply as the dead man himself. Because of an old quarrel, neither Werene nor Hanumoak, younger brothers of Yoroick and uncles of the dead boy, had felt welcome. Among the kains were Nilik of the Walilo, Polik of the Halluk, and U-mue of the Wilil. Weaklekek was also there, but he was received coldly by the Kosi-Alua, owing to his intercession on behalf of Werene, and left the village before the funeral had begun.

The men paused a few minutes before the body, standing in the pathway among the women: they joined in the lament, rubbing their right thighs with their right hands and wiping their eyes with their left. They sniffed and grunted dutifully, and most, after a few minutes, were able to summon tears: the tears flowed down their faces and mixed with long strings of untended effluvia from the nostrils. *Eghl Eghl Eghl Eghl* After a time this was given up, and the men moved to a second position, behind the chair. There they stood quietly, under the harsh gaze of the female body. Most bent their heads, an appropriate expression on the face, and one or both arms folded behind the back. The hand behind Polik's back held the tight brown roll of his tobacco. Then they retreated from the vicinity of the chair, to join the other men seated on leaves and ferns in the yard before the pilai.

The newcomers passed among the rest, taking and squeezing each hand in turn, with quiet greetings—*Narak-*

a-la-ok . . . Narak . . . Ny-ke. Narak-a-la-ok, the basic
form, means "I eat your feces," but it is said in vainglory
rather than deference, as if the speaker, in accomplishing
such an act, could only be quite a fellow.

Close friends and relatives embraced without kissing,
patting each other on the back and murmuring, *Wah, wah,
wah, wah, wah,* in a kind of rapid panting. The old men,
who are treated generally with great affection, are embraced
more often than other people and at greater length. The
greetings done, the men sat and talked and smoked, joking
quietly and answering casually the cries of Yoroick.

Yoroick is very tall, and he had a small amount of yellow clay stuck on his shoulders. Hands folded across his
lower stomach, he recounted imaginary deeds of the mute
presence in the chair in front of him, in short ascending
phrases: the response of the women began on the high note
and descended softly, like a sigh.

The warriors went to the Tokolik

> *Ai-i-e-eo*

And moved slowly past the ponds.

> *Ai-i-e-eo*

He, all alone, went forward.

> *Ai-i-e-eo*

Now he is gone

> *E-eo*

Our child is dead
And this is very sad.
Our land can be here no more
We will go far away.

Shall we go northward, to the spring of Elesi?
Or south into the Southern Valley?
Shall we go to the peoples in the west,
Or shall we start a new life, far away?

From behind, the chair looked ponderous and out of

place. The chair had been built especially for the funeral and while it stood was the only piece of furniture in the village. Straight-backed as a throne, its seat high off the ground, it was a makeshift of split laths and saplings lashed together with lianas. The back and seat were lined with fronds, and Ekitamalek's body sat in a semi-fetal posture, legs folded over a lath secured across the front of the rough chair arms beneath the knees; his knees were at the level of his chin. His lower legs were bound together with strips of fiber, and his head was secured to the back of the chair by another strip passed under the jaw. His hands rested palms downward on the chair seat.

In a humid heat the dead man sat, attended by the flies and sun. There grew from him, as the day passed, that infinite silence which, despite its mourners, surrounds a dead body like a great drop of dew. Strands of his wild crest of curly hair caught glints of morning light, outlining the head against the pale straw thatching of the huts. His body was naked save for its horim, still tied erect, and the black fibers at the throat, worn by all warriors for good luck in war. His head was inclined softly to the right and, as the day went on, appeared to sink gradually toward his breast. His face looked less martyred than pensive and sad; his mouth, hung slightly open, was still firm and strong. He looked mortally tired, and at the same time relieved that he had sunk into sleep at last. Like most of the men of the Kurelu, he had been given a second name when his life was well started, in recognition of a characteristic quality or act or manner. The name Ekitamalek meant "Empty Fist."

The war kain Husuk, who is the owner of the sili, moved quietly among the mourners. Black-skinned and straight-backed, with a small step almost delicate and a gently sardonic smile, Husuk attended quietly to the progress of the ritual. Like most akuni men, he wears a short neat beard the whole length of his jaw. In the middle of the day he brought from the pilai the long shell belts: these are woven belts, five or six feet in length, to which are sewn large cowries. The shells are spaced an inch or so apart, and between each pair is a cross band of bright red or yellow fiber; sometimes the belt is edged with tiny snails or tufts of fur. The cowrie belts are a form of currency; as ornament, they are worn only at birth, at the time of initiation, and in death.

The kains came forward and draped the belts around the forehead and down across the shoulders of Ekitamalek. A fine fur headpiece of tree kangaroo was hung on the chair post above one shoulder, and a mikak shell was fastened at his throat. On the arms of the chair, as the only offering they could make, the women draped new nets.

Three young pigs were brought into the sili. Each was hoisted by two warriors, one holding it by the ears and the other by the haunches. The pig was held at chest height, and Yoli, village kain of Hulibara and Yoroick's kinsman, took up a bow and arrow. The arrow's tip was a half-shaft of sharp bamboo, sharpened at both edges to the tip; this is the bleeding arrow, used invariably for killing pigs and as an auxiliary weapon in the wars. Arm shaking, Yoli hauled upon the bowstring. From a distance of a few inches, he drove the arrow into the pig's lungs. The pig writhed, squealing, to the ground and trotted around the sili, pumping blood. When it had weakened, it was caught once more, and a man worked the blood from it with his foot as it gasped upon the ground. This process was repeated twice.

Banana fronds were brought and stretched on the ground before the pilai. The three dead pigs were laid there on their bellies, legs extended forward and back, in a neat row. Their tails and ears were lopped, to be put aside as ornaments and fetishes, and leaves were heaped on their hindquarters. Other men, off to one side, were digging a cooking pit with the long digging sticks. The pit, when finished, was three feet deep, and narrow at the bottom, an inverted cone, and the black mud of its sides and edges was stamped smooth.

Husuk appeared, bearing a large charred log. Another log was brought, and a fire built between them. The pigs were singed upon the flames; they turned a blotchy black and white as the mud and bristles were scraped free. They were then returned to the banana fronds, the seared lips sucked back upon their teeth in a taut snarl. The bright leaves of a blue-flowered spiderwort had been heaped upon the fronds, and eight of the elder men, using stone adzes and bamboo knives, dressed out the pigs and cut them to small sections.

The fire was enlarged. A man with a heavy ax, more like a club, from which the stone protruded like a nose, split long laths; the laths were placed across the two original logs, and others were tiered above them. Stones were piled into the fire, and damp leaves heaped upon the flames to hold the heat. The heavy smoke poured out across the sili, filming the crouched bodies of the women.

All morning the chanting had continued, but it was gentle now, like the breathing of small waves on a quiet shore: the old man's scratchy voice was the water sucking back among the pebbles, and the response was the soft falling forward of the wave. *Tik, tik, tik, tik, tik, tik—aie-ee-o-o. De-e-o.* The dead boy's mother still clung to the chair, draped down its back like an old net, as if her wrists had been lashed to the rude post. For the moment she was quiet. The sun was bright and the air windless; the southeast trades have not yet come, and in this season the corner of the valley is all but windless, strangely so, except just before a rain. Dragonflies and small gaunt wasps and a solitary butterfly, coal black with white spots on its wings, hovered at the sun-shined mud where the night's rain was fading. High above, a wind of the upper atmosphere moved clouds out of the east, and dark small swiftlets hurtled down the sky. Then a vague breeze turned the air, rattling the fronds of the banana trees which stood in ranks around the village.

A line of men came across the fields, framed by the tattered fronds. At the fences of the sili they passed to the older men lashed bundles of fresh leaves and ferns, which were banked into the cooking pit. The hot stones were carried from the fire, one by one, in tongs made from split staves, as hiperi and pig meat were brought forward. Bound in a grass cone by a coil of rattan, the leaves and ferns were piled above the surface of the ground. Vegetables, stones, and ferns were placed in layers.

Some of the pig meat had been hung on a crossbar between two huts, and more had been stored in the pilai; this part of the sacramental pig, *wam wisa*, would be saved for the next day. The rest was placed in the cooking pit with the vegetables. A small smiling girl stood near the women, looking on. In her hand she held a gleaming strip of tripes, like a toy necklace.

The great war kain Wereklowe came to the funeral late; he stayed out of sight in a hut near the entrance. Kurelu himself was there but took no part in the ceremony. For a while he remained outside the fence entirely, looking obscure and humble in an old brown head net. Later he entered, crossing a back fence, but he sat quietly with some lesser kains around the corner from and out of sight of the ominous ranks of women. Sometimes the women much resent the men who call for war and have been known to rush upon them and beat them severely about the head and shoulders.

The food baked slowly in the rock fire, and big drops of rain fell through the sunlight. Small children, bored, rubbed flies from the damp of their eyes and nostrils, using fat spread fingers; they stood framed in the doorways of the huts, and when they cried were withdrawn into the shadows. Through big chinks in the back walls of the cooking shed the hiperi fields were visible, rolling away toward the Baliem River and the valleys which climbed beyond. An old man tottered about, crying out empty instructions in a thin, long-range voice; he was gazed at briefly, without rancor, and then disregarded. Other old men, in a file of eight, appeared belatedly at the entrance. They came to stand among the women, as the others had, and paid their respects to the dead man. Though they wore no decoration, one old man had dried pig testicles tied above his elbows as an evidence of wealth. In their honor, the chanting strengthened briefly, and the new mourners sniffed and quavered fulsomely in unison.

In the silence of his chair, Ekitamalek became more and more a presence. While his people, awaiting the cooking food, sank into a kind of torpor in the rain, he himself appeared to vibrate with a special life, as if the spirit which possesses all akuni in their lifetimes was only now attempting to escape. Littered though he was with ornament, he maintained an invincible dignity; with his dark face framed by the rich belts, he looked more regal and far wiser than he ever had in his timeless days as boy and man in this same sili.

Below him the rain and sun gleamed on bare backs and large mute haunches, which seemed to grow from the earth on which they crouched. Even his mother, behind the chair, had sunk away in resignation. One woman still stood before him, crying soundlessly, with open, untwisted face. This was the sister of his nami. The nami himself lived far away, but the sister lived among the Kurelu and represented the nami at the funeral. While other women came and went, clutching at him, scarcely looking, she had stood there all that day, gazing straight into his face. The leafy fly switch in her hand was long since bedraggled, but still she moved it aimlessly, as if transfixed.

In midafternoon the leaves were taken from the rock fire, and people stirred. A very old woman in yellow clay picked her way along the fence as careful as the thin-shanked heron picking its way along a ditch. With her small back and tiny breasts, she looked curiously childlike, shy and knock-kneed as a little girl. Younger women came and went, fetching the food; these were big-breasted, with a heavy stride and a determined air, and many carried babies on their shoulders, in their bellies, or invisible at the bottoms of their nets. The women would content themselves with tubers, for all the pig was taken by the men.

Steadily and softly, like a breathing in deep sleep, the chanting continued while the people ate. As afternoon waned, the light rain ceased. The chanting grew once more, and Yoroick led it, on his knees, tears pouring from his eyes; his grief, like that of the woman before the chair, was deep and clear as water of a spring. Yoroick had moved some years ago from his home village of Abukumo, after a dispute with his brother Werene; he had taken his three sons with him, but two of them had now been killed in war. The third, a young boy, watched him unhappily from the doorway of a hut. Ekitamalek's young sisters were also in the sili, in their little girls' rush skirts: their part in the funeral would be played the following morning, in the ritual mutilation.

While Yoroick grieved, the kains went forward and stripped the body of its ornaments, and women came to take away the nets. The offerings, like the grief itself, had been part ritual; a funeral was an occasion of exchange, and those who had brought offerings expected something in return. The cowrie belts were stretched on the banana fronds, and the men gazed upon them avidly, oblivious of the denuded corpse in the chair a few feet away. The Walilo kain Nilik, hawk-faced and ambitious, held up the shell strands one by one and announced who would receive them; the strands were awarded according to the size of the pig brought to Kibitsilimo that morning, and the former owner of the strand received that pig. A strand given to old Asisal was seized violently by another claimant, and Asisal struggled for it, screeching in dismay. Asisal, a greedy, troublesome old man, was formerly called Hup, after a bird, because of a nervous habit of peering about in time of war in search of a safer position. When at last he was too old to go to war, his name was changed to Asisal, which means "Extruded Rectum." All the akuni laugh over this name, even chagrined Siloba, his son, who lives with his nami U-mue in Wuperainma.

But Asisal was in the right and got the belt: the women, who took the funeral more seriously than the men, groaned loudly in disapproval at the disturbance. One woman received a strand in the name of the absent nami; this was she who had stood with the dead man all day, under the sun.

From Ekitamalek's nose black blood began to drip, more and more rapidly, flowing over his lips and down his side. Soon men came forward and cut the body free, and a loud wail arose, the loudest of the day—o-woo-oo—and the panting egh! egh! egh! of pain. O—woo—oo. The body was supported from behind as the chair was dismantled around it; the grieving mother got to her feet to assist in the dismantling.

The body was carried back to the fronds before the pilai. It had stiffened in its seated position, paper-skinned from the heat of the sun. The swelling of the wound had spread all over the left side. A warrior held Ekitamalek from behind, while two old men kneeled at his side; the mother clambered forward, on her knees also, and bent over to embrace his feet, which were pointed in toward each other; for one instant, in the dramatic light of a sinking sun, she completed stark harmony.

On the site of the dismantled chair a pyre was being built, a wide, strong tier, left hollow in the middle.

An old man, holding a bamboo sliver, attempted to cut the arrow tip from the body. Though the arrow had entered the left side, it had apparently worked upward and cut the lung; he widened a large incision already made on the upper breast. The arrow was deep and he could not exract it. Another old man cut farther and at last, by inserting his fingers into the body, was able to wrench free the wood; it was a large piece, the length of his hand. This enemy arrow would be placed with other fetish objects in the recesses of the pilai.

The withdrawal of the arrow had brought with it a strong rush of dark dead blood, and with it a stink of putrefaction; the blood drew a cry of anguish from the mother. She remained kneeling, back to the pyre, as the body was lifted once again and borne toward the flames. There an old man held high a banana trunk wrapped in straw; as the body was carried under it, a warrior shot an arrow into the bundle. The arrow released the living spirit, which now became the ghost; the ghost would go off into the enemy countries, where, by causing trouble and dissension, it would abet the cause of its former comrades in the wars to come. The bundle would be stored with other bundles in a small shelter in the woods.

Ekitamalek was lowered, face upward, onto the flames. The fire was very hot, and his bearers were forced to bend his legs in hastily; even so, one of the legs, from the bent knee to the foot, protruded from the pyre throughout the cremation, turning the same blotchy black and white as had the pig. Other logs were laid on top of him, and a woman stoked the fire with a pole when the flames lessened. Smoke carried the smell of the scorched flesh throughout the sili, but the chanting had died quickly as the first flames sank, and the men were talking once again; already women were leaving the sili, filing out into the twilight fields.

The mother crouched close at the fronds, by the puddles of mixed pig and human blood. Yoroick had disappeared into the pilai. After a time, all but unnoticed, she crawled painfully on all fours across the yard toward her ebeai. There an ancient crone, shrunk up in a tiny bundle like a dead spider, reached out a feathery hand to her and drew her in.

■ In the gathering darkness, the few yegerek who had come to the funeral fled homeward, darting and flitting down the paths and across the precarious log bridges at the sinkholes and weedy ditches. *Pilili, pilili*—they called and regrouped like swift, late-flying birds—*selimeke*. Hurry, hurry—the enemy. In a fit of nerves, Tukum the swineherd stopped to urinate, leaping off into the savanna grass to do so; he crouched modestly in the grass as the yegerek always do, even among themselves. The others cried to him, and he ran after them again, jerking and twisting through the dark bushes, like a bat.

■ On the morning after the funeral the men of Kibitsilimo, arriving at their kaio, called out to the enemy. They called the dead man's name, adding a long whoop at the end so that the name would carry—*Ekitamalek, a-oo*. The whooping was answered by the Wittaia passing the news back through their villages, and the voices rolled across the valley, *hu-a, hu-a, hu—a-oo*.

The dead man's ghost, hearing this sound, would stay in the Wittaia land and work its harm. After a season there, it would return to the village of the dead man. Ekitamalek's water calabash would be wrapped in a wisa bundle; the ghost would remain in the vicinity of the calabash, which was the last vestige of the dead man.

To lay the ghost, a pig would then be killed and a piece given to his young brother. The boy would take both calabash and meat to a place near the frontier. There he would eat the meat and, leaving the calabash under a tree, return. The ghost, unwilling to leave the calabash, would remain at this place forever.

The Wittaia knew about the coming of the ghost, but their joy was stronger than their dread, and they whooped all that day. In the afternoon several hundred warriors appeared on the Waraba, where their celebration might best be observed by the Kurelu. Two large groups danced and stamped upon the ridge, howling and waving spears, while before them young warriors whirled and pranced with the white egret wands, erratic as butterflies in the distance. Soon the Wittaia streamed down the slope onto the Tokolik, where the performance was repeated. A huge fire had been built on a ridge in their own lands, and they moved toward it; there they danced again. The next day they would stage the formal victory celebration, called *etai*.

The skull and large bones of Ekitamalek had not been consumed in the fire. They lay in the yard where relatives and friends arriving late from distant villages could mourn over them. The following day the bones were gathered and carried outside the village. There they were buried, and a stick shelter constructed around the place to keep away the pigs and rats and dogs. On this day too there took place a mutilation. Though a few older men cut fingers in time of grief, it is usually the smallest girls who are selected for this ceremony, and a woman in the valley whose left hand is not a stump is very rare. On this same day the first two joints of the two outside fingers were hacked from the left hands of Ekitamalek's small sisters, in sign of mourning.

■ Yeke Asuk and Hanumoak, with their friends Asukwan of Homaklep and Walimo of Hulibara, are wild young warriors of the southern villages, moving restlessly from place to place, seeking diversion and avoiding work whenever possible. They are irreverent and obscene, though of the four only Yeke Asuk is noisy. Yeke Asuk, who has been married more than once, each time quite briefly, is older than the others and their leader, a squat, powerful, bandy-legged warrior and hoarse comic whose voice is recognizable at any distance. Yeke Asuk is a malcontent, whereas the other three are only mischievous.

Walimo, Asukwan, and Hanumoak are all three hand-some—Asukwan, with a huge head of hair and a bold black band of charcoal across his face, and Walimo, languid and feckless, with faun eyes and the sudden smile of a small child, and Hanumoak, supercilious as a hawk. Asukwan is a cautious fighter, though he lingers at war's outskirts, and Walimo fights erratically, in gallant fits and starts, but Hanumoak, in his casual way, is one of the first warriors of the Kurelu.

Hanumoak is mercurial, as prone to affectionate silliness as he is to bored disdain. Hanumoak's face is a series of masks—love, terror, outrage, idiocy, grief—through which his cool eyes shine. The roles are played in comic exaggeration, and he is truly funny, miming everything taken too seriously by others; only his sudden moodiness seems real. At these times he is deep-eyed and silent. But in a moment his face will begin to twitch as if he were about to throw a fit, and he will squeal with infectious laughter. The akuni laugh with him in bewilderment, for they are never sure that he will not stop laughing suddenly and stare at them.

On the day after the funeral, at the fire site above the spring at Homuak, Yeke Asuk pretended terror of the dead man's ghost. *An nai-UK*, he squealed, biting his knuckle—I am afraid. The others laughed, but Hanumoak slipped quietly into an impersonation of the dead man in his chair, then of the ghost itself. Pressing his palms to the sides of his face, he cocked his ears forward with his thumbs. With his little fingers he flared his nostrils wide. His eyes he squinched to wrinkled slits, sewn up by death, and, rolling his tongue, he pinched its protruding tip between his teeth, at the same time forcing his head back on his upraised shoulders, like a man stabbed in the neck. Thus prepared, he tottered forward, blind, on tiptoe, and despite themselves the akuni drew away from him in alarm. The men grinned nervously at one another, pointing their fingers at the distorted figure that had been Hanumoak as if to assure themselves that they were not alone with this hallucination; a few, despite themselves, tapped their horims with their fingertips in awe. Tukum the swineherd stared wide-eyed from one face to another, and the older boys howled out their fear and laughter.

Hanumoak, who as Yoroick's younger brother is an uncle of the dead boy, forsook his role as suddenly as he had begun it and contemplated their simplicity, unsmiling.

■ Weaklekek of Homaklep had gone to honor Ekitamalek at his funeral. But Weaklekek felt uncomfortable at Kibitsilimo and left the sili after midday, traveling homeward over the fields alone. Like all the other men, he had gone to the funeral unarmed.

Weaklekek's plan was to go to his kaio, on the knoll above the Aike River known as Puakaloba. But when nearly there he changed his mind, deciding to pass by way of Homuak. This decision probably saved his life. The story, as he pieced it together from signs and footprints the following morning, was approximately the following.

A band of Wittaia, observing from the ridge called Turaba that the kaio was deserted, staged an ambush raid into the territory of the Kurelu. Unlike the wars, with their fanfare and heroics, the raid has as its sole purpose the stalking and killing of any smaller party or unwary individual. No distinction is made between man, woman, or child: the spearing of a little girl or an old woman is ample reason for a victory singing. The kaios are the consequence of such raids, for without these sentry towers and the squads of armed men which, during the day, are always in the thatched shelters below, the women working in the fields would be defenseless.

But today the women were in mourning, and the kaio at Puakaloba was deserted. The Wittaia descended from the ridge and crossed the Aike upstream from the kaio, where the river plunges under a wide bridge of rock. They came downstream again, to the path which comes to the river from the villages, and here, in the undergrowth and cane, they lay in hiding. They could not go farther for fear of being surprised and surrounded; the ambush of a raiding party is almost as common as the raid itself.

They waited all that day, but no one came. The Aike frontier is a favorite raiding place of the Wittaia, and the people, knowing this, take care to avoid it, especially when there is no guard at Puakaloba. In the late afternoon, for want of a better plan, the Wittaia attacked the empty sentry post, putting the shelter to the torch and toppling the watchtower itself. It lay there the next morning, broken in a tangle of lianas, like a dropped bundle of giant twigs.

Weaklekek, inspecting the ruin of his kaio, knew very well that, had he come there in the middle of the day before, he would now be sitting in his own yard at Homaklep, in a wooden chair.

Puakaloba is spoken of as the kaio of Weaklekek, but in fact it is the common property and responsibility of those men living in Homaklep and Wuperainma whose fields and women it helps to guard. Nevertheless, Weaklekek is the chief warrior of the kaio and had to see to it that the kaio was restored as rapidly as possible.

Work on the kaio began almost immediately. Asukwan, who lives in Weaklekek's pilai, went down to the Aike River, fifty yards away. He entered the river and angled across the swollen current which seeped over the banks, shoulder high out of the water in the stiff sidestroke of the akuni. On the far side was a place in the riverain forest where he could find the long liana used to bind the thin poles of the tower.

In the wood south of Puakaloba, Tegearek and Asok-meke cut the new poles. Asok-meke is head of the warriors' sili—Tegearek, Siba, Tuesike, Tekman Bio—which adjoins the sili of U-mue in Wuperainma; it was U-mue who gave him his strange name, which means "Outsider." For some reason Asok-meke had not bothered to attend a pig feast given by U-mue, who dismissed him in anger, saying, He is not one of us—he is *asok-meke*. Since then the men of the two silis have been distant with one another. Asok-meke, a reflective man of middle years, is the stepfather of the boy Tukum; at the tip of his horim he wears invariably the great spiny cocoon of a drab woodland moth.

The hollow tock of the stone adze echoed along the silent river like the call of a lost bird. On the rise itself, Siba and Weaklekek dug a new foundation. Aloro the lame man sat in the shelter, observing: this was not his kaio, and he took no part in the work.

The spears were leaned against the sides of the shelter, sharp and clean against a bright blue sky. Some of these, of a light white wood, were imported from the Yali River tribes four days to the eastward, but most were of a heavy reddish myrtle wood, from the eucalyptus-like yoli. Some spears were eighteen feet in length, with an ornamental sleeve below the flat, sharpened blade; they were tapered to a dull point at the butt so that the spear might be stuck into the ground.

In the corner of the shelter lay the bows and arrows. The bows are small, about four feet long, scarcely longer than the arrows, and cut usually from a woodland rhododendron or from laurel. The bowstring is not a string at all but a flat, hard strip of rattan. It is perhaps a quarter-inch in width, too wide to permit the use of arrow notches, and this factor, in combination with the fact that the arrows are un-feathered, makes the accuracy of men like Aloro the more remarkable.

The arrows themselves are thin spears of hard cane and differ chiefly in their heads. For war, the preferred head is a myrtle shaft, unbarbed, about a foot in length: most of this length is inserted in the cane, and it is bound at the junction by fine strands of ground vine. Another arrowhead of war is notched with one to three files of jagged teeth; its advantage is that it must be cut out from the flesh. Sometimes the notches are reversed close to the shaft, so that the arrow cannot be drawn on through an arm or leg. Both of these arrows are weakened at the base of the point, to insure that they will snap off inside the wound, and both are wrapped, more often than not, with a loose strand of sharp fiber from the woody ground orchid; when the arrow is withdrawn, the orchid fiber slides off and remains inside. It is believed to cause unusual pain and inflammation.

There is also the bleeding arrow, and varieties of hunt-ing arrows, with heavy heads knobbed with two to five sharp prongs; these are designed for birds and the small mammals. A few of the cane arrow shafts bear decorative scratchings, and the wooden points may be engraved with crude designs cut into them with a mouse tooth: the marks on certain arrows represent the sole decoration practiced by the Kurelu.

Asukwan returned from across the river, dragging a long coil of liana. He had lost his horim in the Aike and for the rest of the morning kept his back and side to all the others. Asukwan, who is much admired by the women, is very conscious of his appearance: without his horim he felt himself indecent and was very upset and embarrassed.

New poles had been brought and were inserted in the

hole; the poles were lashed together at intervals of five feet, or wherever a man standing on the fresh band of liana could comfortably start the next binding above. Where the poles began to taper, smaller sticks were inserted down between them, to build the kaio at a uniform diameter. Moving slowly up the tower, Tegearek and Weaklekek and Siba, all powerful men, worked in sure harmony, with neither haste nor rest; they braced their feet and hauled on the lianas, leaning out against the dark horizon of the mountain rim, the hard muscles of their arms and buttocks corded with effort.

The binding finished, short lengths of stone-hewn board were passed to Siba, whose husky form, with its tattered crown of soiled green parrot feathers, gleamed black on the hard sky of noon. Above his head a goshawk, its reddish breast washed to pale pink by the sunlight burning through its wings, circled in tight-brained curiosity.

Siba bound the boards into a sturdy platform, two or three feet below the sapling tips. White puffs of cumulus, sailing south on the high winds above the valley, seemed frozen in the air, while Siba, grinning wildly on his flying platform, rode northward against the sky.

In the shelter, Aloro played on a small mouth harp. This sole musical instrument of the akuni is made in two different keys, one high, one low. A half-section of cane is scraped out with chips of flint, then polished smooth with a fibrous grass used as a sandpaper. A reed is cut free down the center of the section, and a fiber thread attached at the base end. The mouth harp is vibrated with short tugs of the thread, the cavern of the player's mouth giving it resonance.

The lame man, playing, stared abstractedly at the fields. There was no melody, but only a series of rhythmic notes up and down a foreshortened scale. The frail sound he produced was eerie, scarcely audible in the bright noise of daylight, like an ominous echo from remote regions of his mind.

A few feet behind Aloro, outside the shelter, stood a small arbor of the horim gourd; stone weights had been attached to the gourds so that this vegetable, shaped naturally like a water drop or tear, would assume the fine elongate shape required by the warriors. Beside the frame a boy built a fire. Into this fire, tied in a small bundle, he placed stalks of a heavy grass. When this had scorched a little, it was taken from the fire, and the leaves were strewn in a small circle on the raw earth around the kaio. This grass is a symbolic offering to the great company of friendly ghosts who would keep watch with the kaio's men, as sentinels.

Weaklekek now fashioned a toy bow and three arrows of twigs and sticks. These he inserted among the kaio poles, about two feet from the ground. The bow and arrows symbolize the area's defense, insuring that any enemy who ventures within sight of the kaio will be struck down.

Finally, all the men who had participated in the rebuilding of the tower underwent a purification ritual. The new materials of the kaio were considered wisa, and, until the wisa ban had been removed, the men involved could not indulge in food or drink, tobacco, or copulation. Near the center pole of the shelter a tuft of red parrot feather affixed to a small straw had been stuck into the ground. The feather was presently taken by Weaklekek and passed back and forth an inch or so above the hands that had done the work.

The kaio ceremony is wisa because of the importance of these towers in the life of the akuni. The kaios must guard a frontier with the enemy which extends several miles; there are twelve of them in the southern fields alone, and each of these may post a guard of four to ten warriors at a time. Visiting warriors come and go, and the kaio, the great part of the time, is little more than a kind of outdoor pilai. Here the men gather to talk and smoke, to weave shell belts and mend arrows, while around them the women labor in the fields. High on the tower at Puakaloba, one of their number watches for movement in the river forest.

Weaklekek's kaio must guard against any approach by way of the Turaba; it guards as well a segment of the main frontier just off to the westward. It is well situated on a high grassy bank, commanding a view not only of the gardens but of the low river woods.

At Puakaloba, a few years ago, there took place a great victory of the Kurelu. From the top of the tower a raiding party of Wittaia had been observed; the enemy were sneaking through the river woods, intent on a surprise attack against the outnumbered guard. The men signaled the next kaio for assistance, and the word was passed along, while the Wittaia completed a roundabout maneuver. The Wittaia crept stealthily into the trap, and before they could extricate themselves five of their warriors had been killed.

Across the Aike is the steep ridge, Turaba, which rises abruptly just behind the wall of the river forest; the foot of the Turaba is scarcely two hundred yards from the kaio itself. The ridge is an inhospitable array of limestone, jagged and tumbled, haired over with low scrub. Because it is uninhabitable, and because of its location, it serves as a natural barrier in a corner of the valley where lands of the Kurelu, the Siep peoples, and the Wittaia come together. It is also a natural path of ambush and surveillance, and, as such, is generally avoided. On one occasion Weaklekek and a companion went up onto the Turaba to scout, and the other man, ahead of Weaklekek, was waylaid by hiding enemy. They killed the man and very nearly caught Weaklekek, who managed to escape across the river.

Like the hill above Homuak, the Turaba is a salient of the mountain wall, though it begins but halfway up the wall rather than at the crest, and extends much farther outward, dying at last in forsaken country now thought of as no man's land. The Turaba, like all the no man's land of the frontiers, is known as Place of Fear.

Today the Wittaia women could be seen dancing on a hillcrest to the westward. In the morning the men of Kibitsilimo, going to their kaio, had chanted of the death of Ekitamalek, and the men at the Wittaia kaios had raised a whoop of triumph. The afternoon the Wittaia came in war regalia to the Waraba, dancing and singing.

The men in the new kaio watched the enemy without comment. Ekitamalek was the first man they had lost since the last full moon, while the Wittaia had lost four; the Kurelu had learned this from a Siep man who was friendly with both factions of his tribe and had spread the news. The Wittaia had not announced the names, and, until they did, no etai could take place. But sooner or later the names would come, and the Kurelu would hold an etai of their own.

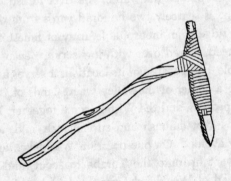

■ In late April the rains had come each afternoon. The Aike was very high, and the sandpipers which, a few short weeks before, were common on the river logs and mudbanks, had disappeared.

The Aike in its upper reaches is the southern frontier of the Kurelu. It slides down off the mountain wall in a steep narrow rush, only to plunge beneath the rock once more at the head of the riverain forest. Fifty yards below it bursts forth once again, forming a pool already as wide as the river will become. Less than a quarter-mile beyond, it passes the kaio at Puakaloba, and a mile below this point disappears into the lands of the Wittaia.

Unlike the Wittaia, who build villages on the Aike, and who have spanned it with rickety pole bridges, the Kurelu go near the river seldom. They can swim the Aike if they have to, but their solitary bridge, built downriver close to the frontier, is sagging with disuse. No native boats are known in the Baliem, and the Kurelu lack even the crude rafts used by most other tribes; they cannot travel safely on the river and have nothing on the farther side but the Place of Fear.

Nor does the river bring them food. The Baliem system, if and when it formed a lake, lacked native fishes, and its present gorge at the south end of the valley has prevented the passage into the mountains of fish from the southern marshes. The valley is without fish of any kind, and the one valuable creature found in all its waters can be taken more easily and safely in the streams. This is a fresh-water crayfish, which in the small streams attains a length of four or five inches: the boys feel for it with their toes, walking the mud.

Of the three terrains open to the akuni—the valley plain

which they have farmed, the cloud forest rising behind them, and the river forests on their southern border—it is the latter where they feel least at home. Sometimes they go down to the Aike for a drink, or to gather lianas and certain woods, but otherwise the river is avoided. It lies too near the Turaba, and the natural bridge where the river roars underground, overhung by jungle trees and dark, dripping limestone grottoes, is considered a place of ghosts. This is a dank world of air plants, crowding for space on every limb, of myrmecodias with their colonies of ants, of fleshy orchids and pale-bellied ferns. Below, in the clefts and shadows, the fungi thrive in the slow seepings, clematis trails across the rocks, and miniature begonias, white and pink, flower in secret in the rotting shades. In the motionless air, only the silent woodland butterfly takes wing, skipping its delicate trail of filtered sunspots. The insects of the rain forest gnaw stealthily under leaves and behind wood, the huge horned beetles and great papery cicadas, the armored millipedes and dusty moths, and the spined crab spiders. In the earth beneath the insects and the spiders, its soft body protected by the detritus of the forest floor, there stirs an earthworm four feet long. The skinks, so common in the sun, are missing in the shadows. In the crevice of the grotto rock is wedged the skeleton of a dead dog.

This forest is not silent. Honey eaters come and go with chortlings and shrieks, and a flock of parrots, gold and red and black, and the tiny brilliant myzomela. The parrots and parakeets scour the canopies of the river forest and the forest of the upper slope and rim; they are seen in the valley's open air but fleetingly, in high, swift flocks, at dawn. They shatter the dank air with their screeching and vanish into the mountain mist which seeps each morning down the ridge, thinned out by the pale, cataracted eye of the climbing sun.

■ Tukum the swineherd, elf-faced and pot-bellied, shouted gruffly at his pigs while his mother shouted at him. He was followed on his way not only by pigs but by small girls and women; they went along through the low wood to the fields in front of Homuak.

Tukum's horim is forever askew, tucked sideways under his belly; there is straw in his hair and gray dust on his skin. He marched along, a half-hiperi in his hand, and now and again he stifled his own growling by plunging his round face into it.

Tukum hated pigs, and though he tended them nearly every day, the very idea made his huge eyes overflow. At these moments he looked more like an elf than ever. Tukum is nearly four feet tall and looks, not full grown, but complete. In his way, Tukum is spiritual; his natural haunt is not the pigsty but the toadstool. Tukum, with his wild brown eyes and portly evanescence, does not belong among the flies and swine, nor even in the sun, but in the ferny glades of distant woods.

■ In the night before a sunny day of May, in the hill village of Lokoparek, Ekapuwe had a child, a little girl. The birth was a simple one, assisted only by an older woman of the village. Ekapuwe took the baby in her stride and by midmorning was sitting up in her ebeai, smoking tobacco in her long holder and chattering with her usual good-humored petulance.

On the occasion of a birth the child's nami usually comes and wraps a ceremonial cowrie belt about its head. But Lokoparek is a long way up the hill, and girl children are not important, and for one reason or another—the akuni are often informal about minor ceremonials and waive them readily when it is expedient—this little girl was suffered to embark upon her life without a shell belt. She will pass a week or two in the darkness of the ebeai, after which she will take up a residence of indefinite length at the bottom of Ekapuwe's nets.

The new baby was U-mue's third girl child—he has no son as yet—but even so he was anxious and solicitous and gave a great many senseless orders, interspersed with fits of shouting. U-mue dearly loves a drama, the more tempestuous the better; the joy he takes in the passions of the mind is childlike in its abandon. Wracked with grief or rent by rage—it is all one to him, he is in his element.

I will go off into the mountains, U-mue cries, striking a pose, Never to return again—and his quick, sly face collapses in comic grief. For he enjoys himself hugely at these moments, though he tries heroically to muster tears, eked out with dreadful sounds, part grief, part laughter. When outrageous, he caws and swirls like a bird of paradise, but in his way he is a kindly man; he is often with his small Nylare, walking and talking, holding her hand. Like most of the men, he treats his little girls with the same gentleness that boys receive only from their namis.

U-mue is both charlatan and buffoon, but he is intelligent, perhaps the most intelligent of all the akuni, a statesman and deft intriguer who, for all his frailties, is a true leader, demanding and receiving strict obedience from his people. The people respect U-mue's intelligence, his pride in and exhaustive knowledge of akuni ways, akuni ceremonials and family lines. U-mue has whimsy in his face; he seems to be laughing, from time to time, at insights that his people will not ever understand, but this laughter is veiled and rueful, as if he did not know the source of it himself.

■ The time of dawn and the first sun is called the morning-of-bird-voices, and is quite distinct from the ordinary morning, which comes later. Today a pigeon called in the high araucaria all through the morning-of-bird-voices, and the warriors, as if stimulated by this sound, went to war when morning came. The great war kain Wereklowe strode out toward the frontier, and behind him trotted Yeke Asuk, decked out in fierce red clay. The armies would take some time to form, and in the next hours, as the sun gained strength, a silence lay upon the fields. Only the black robin chat sang its sweet liquid song: this bird appears to have an affinity for war, for it perches commonly on the tips of spears implanted on the ground, or on the tops of kaios, and sings even in the midday hours, at the outskirts of a battle.

The older men moved gradually toward the Tokolik. Embracing, two bony elders stood together in the green-purple leaves, gazing outward at the Waraba. Few Wittaia had appeared on the far crest, and there now seemed doubt that there would be a war.

An hour more passed by as tension slackened, and the enemy did not appear. The kains returned across the fields and gathered at a fire in the araucaria grove. This fire site, on a ledge of needles under a deep bank of fern, is often used for councils, for it lies between the two main groups of southern villages, overlooking the cool spring of Homuak. In a hollow trunk above the ledge dried graybeard lichen, which tatters the araucaria, is stored as tinder, and with it a small bundle of long tobacco pipes.

Several warriors and yegerek loitered in attendance, but Wereklowe himself clambered up onto the slope above to gather dry sticks and grass: this is partly because Wereklowe cannot contain his energy and must see to it personally that all matters proceed as rapidly as possible. But it is also true of the great kains that nobody is asked to do what they will not do or have not often done themselves, whether going to the fore in battle or picking lice from a child's head.

The men talked quietly and quickly in their low sweet voices: every little while one would reach forward and place a twig or fagot in the flame, the hand seeming to know by instinct just where the twig should lie. The fire neither grew nor faltered. They moistened the dried lisanika leaves for their tobacco and talked and talked, for it is at these fires that news is passed and war discussed and the affairs of the valley regulated. The sound of smoking—a soft, implosive *phoot* made by pressing the tongue to the roof of the mouth as the smoke is taken in—was a rhythm of the conversation, which was gentle and deferential, little more than a murmur, and at the same time rapid and intense.

Limo, the tall war kain of the Alua, ground his teeth in a loud, ruminative manner. All men of the akuni grind their teeth habitually, in pauses between speech, but few as powerfully and rhythmically as Limo. Also expert are the young warriors Huonke and Asukwan; these men are audible at thirty feet. Loud Huonke with his hard, furtive face was present at the outskirts of the kains, his expression insolent and cornered; Huonke has never killed an enemy warrior, though he once took the life of a woman of the Siep-Elortak found wandering near the frontier.

Wereklowe and U-mue led the talking, and once the other men rapped their horims with their fingernails in a fast staccato racketing, saying *u-yuh* in quiet exclamation, and a soft, explosive *f-whe-oosh*. The horim is invariably tapped at moments of astonishment or awe, and when a number of men are astonished all at once a sound rises like a gust of chattering finches in tall dry stalks of cane.

At the edge of the circle the men and boys squatted in silence; though some were kepu, they were neither disregarded nor dismissed. With few exceptions, the kains do not brandish power or maintain distinctions of a social kind between their akuni and themselves. Any strange boy or halt old man, except in the most urgent councils, may sit at the side of Kurelu himself, or Wereklowe or Nilik, and may even have his head picked by his betters. Generosity and simplicity of manner are marks of the great kain and are regarded as such by one and all. Of the chief kains among the Kurelu, only Maitmo of the Haiman clan, north of the Elokera, keeps his people at a distance; he is a small belligerent man, with a shrill, distempered voice when he is angry, and the awe in which all kains are held is in this case tinged by fear. While Nilik of the Walilo is also fierce, and Wereklowe and Polik indulge fits of violence, these men do not abuse their power; the young war kains Husuk and Weaklekek, like Kurelu himself, are almost invariably soft-spoken. Kurelu listens and listens, watching, watching, and, though he is a harmless-looking man, he is the most powerful of all.

The Kurelu, perhaps twelve years ago, were split into two warring tribes, separated roughly by the Elokera River. In those days the north was already led by Kut-ilu, the Wise Egret. His name, from which was taken the name of the eventual alliance, referred not only to his intelligence but to the light color of his skin. In those days too the southern Kurelu were allied with the Wittaia: the patterns of old ditches rolling beneath wild grass, with the banana trees of abandoned villages now grown up in woods, are skeletons of distant days when the area of the Waraba was not a Place of Fear but peaceful garden.

Thus the alliances in the northeastern valley are transient and uneasy, and it is never certain from one season to the next which group will represent the enemy: a child protected fiercely as a member of one's own people may become an enemy overnight, to be killed on sight, without ever being old enough to know the difference. In the Kurelu, though many clans have intermingled in the villages and are well represented north and south of the Elokera, the bad feeling between the groups persists, and men fleeing the wrath of one side may still find sanctuary in the other. Weaklekek and the cold-eyed warrior Apeore are among many who have taken refuge in the south, where their respective clans— Alua and Wilil—are more strongly represented.

A feud, which could occur at any time, is feared by the great kains, for it could lead not only to a weakening of the alliance against the Wittaia but to a merciless civil war, fanned by old grudges. Those most likely to cause trouble are Maitmo and Amoli, war kains of the clan Haiman, who go out of their way to take offense.

The Haiman kain Amoli, whose village of Hulainmo lies just across the Elokera, shares with Weaklekek the reputation of hunuk palin, which refers to fits of manic bravery in battle, joined with a capacity, when in temper, to take life among one's own people. Hunuk palin men, few in number, are very well known and are treated prudently; in the southern Kurelu, besides Weaklekek, the hunuk palin are Apeore, Polik, Tegearek, Limo, Asikanalek, and Husuk.

Asikanalek and Husuk are both warm, quiet men, and their reputation as hunuk palin is as surprising as the exclusion from this category of a fanatic warrior like Aloro.

All of these men but one are war kains, and most lead their own villages. Even Tegearek, though young and without great wealth, shares with Aloro the war leadership of the southern Wilil, due to a reluctance to fulfill this role on the part of U-mue.

The exception is Apeore, who is an exception in many ways. Of the best Wilil warriors, only Aloro and Apeore do not live in Wuperainma. Aloro lives in Abulopak, which was formerly the central village of the Wilil and where his father still maintains a sili, but Apeore has withdrawn to Loko-parek, under the mountain wall; he has no family, for his only wife was stolen by the Wittaia. Unlike Ekali and U-mue, who go to Lokoparek to see to their pigs, Apeore remains there. He is slashing a field out of high forest to the southward and works relentlessly, day in, day out, like a man possessed.

No other man resembles Apeore, who is yellow mongol in his color, whose forehead slants back to a scalp drawn tight beneath a head net so that his skin seems stretched, whose browless eyes are flat and cold in a face as hairless as a skull. Apeore's skin gleams with fresh grease, and his muscles slide powerfully beneath it.

Apeore is seen rarely at the kaios, and he is rarely seen at war. When he comes, he comes to fight. His legs are painted with gray clay, and he appears suddenly out of no-where, stalking quietly, alone, at the edge of the underbrush near the front line. Apeore fled long ago from the northern Kurelu, and his full name, Apearole, which commemorates the murder by the northerners of his best friend, means "Killed by Strangling."

■ In the middle of the day the yegerek Supuk and Tukum, Uwar and Kabilek, were gathering firewood by the small stream which flows in front of Abulopak. The air was gold and humid, and the three kites which haunt the crest of the ridge above jeered at each other in the heat. By Abulopak a small myrtle tree had come into pink flower, and the finches with their black heads and blue bills droned like fat bees in the high brakes of cane.

Supuk climbed into an oak to knock down old dead limbs. One limb, breaking open on the ground, revealed a tiny twilight bat, torpid with sleep, and a hidden clutch of large white snake eggs, thirty-five or more. Some of the snakes had already hatched and gone, making their way down the great tree on its rough bark, but most of the eggs were still intact, and a few were hatching in slow reptilian silence in the moment that the limb had struck the ground. In the slime upon the eggs, the thin dark baby snakes lay like dead nerves.

Snakes are not common in the valley, owing perhaps to the numbers of foraging pigs. A small bronze-colored skink is plentiful, as are tree frogs and a large tree lizard, but there are no salamanders, toads, or turtles. No reptile or amphibian is used for any purpose by the akuni, though many insects and any sort of bird or mammal, including rats and cormorants, are eaten cheerfully.

The yegerek are afraid of snakes and left the broken egg mass where it lay. The insect bat is smaller than a mouse, but it is good to eat, and they wrapped it neatly in a leaf and took it with them.

Running home by way of Homuak, Tukum stubbed his

toe upon a root. Tukum is at odds with his own reflexes and is constantly stubbing his toe or stepping on bees; when he shows someone something he has found, he is apt to open the wrong hand in his excitement, permitting the escape of a huge cicada, or a beautiful hesperid moth with a scarlet silken head, or one of the lovely tropic butterflies with bright metallic wings, or some other, earlier prize he had forgotten that he had.

Discomfited, Tukum growls in his deep voice, talking fiercely in a series of sharp breaths, his large eyes flashing. He lives in a state of perpetual astonishment, and his words come in gasps, so that, when excited, he sounds like a small bellows.

Mel . . . mel . . . mel, he stammers. *Mel* is an interjection, uttered as a stopgap while the correct answer to a question is being considered. Tukum rarely arrives at the right answer, and at the end of a long series of *mels,* he usually says his favorite word, *welegat. Welegat* means "any old thing," or "just for the hell of it," or "how should I know?"

When his injured toe permitted him to walk, Tukum marched straight out to the fields and plucked a long blade of grass; bringing it back to the offending root, he tied it there in a sort of forlorn bow, to indicate to other passers-by that a dangerous root existed.

■ Some time ago the men of Amoli's village on the north bank of the Elokera accused U-mue of having stolen and eaten a pig. Though pig-stealing is a time-honored practice among the akuni and is not considered shameful, one must make compensation if one is caught. U-mue protested that he had not taken the pig, but he was not believed, and, as he has a strong dislike for violence, he relinquished an animal of his own.

In recent days U-mue has decided that the theft had been committed by the Wittaia, and early one morning he set off, accompanied by Yeke Asuk and Hanumoak, to request the return of his pig. His request was refused. In the next hours, however, a pig was removed from the environs of the village, and the identity of the thief was common knowledge, as it often is, within hours. The thief was Yeke Asuk, assisted, in all likelihood, by his friend Hanumoak.

A raid on the Wittaia took place on the following day, in revenge for the death of Ekitamalek. Warriors from Wuperainma went along, but as Amoli's men went also, Yeke Asuk and Hanumoak remained at home.

■ When the sun was high, a party of men under the leadership of Nilik, kain of the Walilo, went west quickly and quietly to the albizzia forest in the country of the Kosi-Alua. From there they moved toward the north side of the Waraba, slipping through low woodland. From the wood they crept down along the banks of a small stream which flows between the Waraba and the Siobara. They were nearly a hundred, including Husuk and his men and a band of Wilil under the leadership of Tegearek. Siba was there, and Tuesike, reserved and quiet, and Aloro, the lame man.

Sometimes their women weep when the raiders go, for the raid is very dangerous, and on hearing the women, the men may sing this song:

See, we will set an ambush in the gardens of the Wittaia,
But we are afraid,
For if caught, we shall be killed.

The raiders slipped through the brush and sedge grass, crossing the deep sloughs of the April rains in water to their chests. A Wittaia lookout outlined on the crest of the Siobara failed to see them, for they kept close to the bottom of the hill, and they were hidden as well from the sentries on the grassy ridge off to the southward.

It was a quiet morning, overcast. The Kurelu women worked stolidly in the fields, and sentries climbed into the kaios. In the woods of Homuak a dove called dolefully. Dull light reflected from the smoke of fires, from the leaden water of the ditches, from the banks of white quartz sand on the hills of the Wittaia. On the savanna between the gardens and Homuak the yegerek fought noisily with spears of grass, but the men were nowhere to be seen. Two egrets which frequent the Place of Fear sat still as white flowers in the distance, just west of a tall bush which, in the few days past, had burst into orange flame.

In the early afternoon the Kurelu crossed the frontier of the Wittaia. The main party had been left in hiding in the wood by the Waraba, while thirty or more young warriors led by Tegearek crept forward. They were stalking a kaio and the surrounding fields of a village south of the Siobara.

There was a sentry in the kaio tower; he did not see the attackers until they were at the field edge. There were no warriors in the shelter, and but a solitary man, named Huwai, working in the gardens. The man on the kaio scrambled down and fled, shouting the alarm. Huwai was not fast enough. The war party surged out of the brush and rushed upon him; he was run down and speared to death by the wild-faced, shaggy-haired son of the war kain Wereklowe.

The raiding party returned quickly through the woods and climbed onto the rocks of the Waraba. There they were joined by the others, and the rest of the Kurelu came forward from the kaios, prepared for war.

The Wittaia came quickly, shouting out their rage, and challenged the Kurelu to a battle on a grassy meadow just below the Waraba and to the south of it. Though badly outnumbered, this advance party of the Wittaia fought with ferocity and drove the Kurelu back among the rocks; a man of the Kosi-Alua was speared through the calf, and Tuesike of Wuperainma caught an arrow in the stomach, just one inch to the right side of his navel. The Wittaia moved into the rocks of the Siobara, awaiting reinforcements, while the Kurelu perched on the gray boulders which lie tumbled along the crest of the Waraba. The spears of both sides wavered on the sky like spines.

Tuesike was carried back on the powerful shoulders of Siba and put down in the shelter of some bushes on the north flank of the ridge. He was in terrible pain and in a little while passed into a state of shock. Siba supported him from behind, grasping his hair to hold his head upright. Tuesike's horim was gone, and his blood ran down his stomach onto the grass. The wound was not bleeding badly, for the arrow shaft had broken off inside, and the point was in too far to be withdrawn on the field. Tuesike panted tightly, harshly, as his brown face, draining, turned to gray. He was half conscious, and the others stared at him like awed children who have hurt one of their friends by accident. Tuesike, whose name means "Bird Bow," closed his eyes.

The Wittaia continued to gather on the Siobara and in an open area between the Waraba and the kaio near which Huwai had been killed. There a grass fire had been lit to burn away his blood. Wereklowe and other kains sat on the highest rock, observing, and now the Wittaia called out to the Kurelu across the way, confirming that Huwai had died. At this the Kurelu raised a shout, rushing forward to mass in a large body at the west end of the ridge. Some went farther, down onto the middle ground, and danced and shouted insults at the enemy. The Kurelu wanted war, but, strangely, the Wittaia now refused it. They sat in dead silence on the rocks and would not take up the challenge. Opposite, on the knolls and boulders of the Waraba, the Kurelu awaited them.

The Waraba, shaped in an L, is a rock garden of strewn boulders, set about with ferns and orchids and shining islets of wild sugar cane. Old gardens dance in the wild flowering below its flanks, for in the corner of the L, in years of peace, had been a village; banana fronds gleam in the low forest, a sparkling varnished gleam which turns to silver in the western light.

The horizon beyond is a dark mid-mountain landscape,

dark with cloud shadows, distant thunderheads, dense tropic greens of montane forest, high black walls. But the darkness is muted by the soft colors of the gardens, by the green velvet of low marshy swales. The gold grass of the old fields draws the light, and rays of white break the green weight of the distances—a sprinkling of vivid whites, like snow patches. In the dawn of certain days true snow is visible, a scraggy outcropping near the peak of Arolik at fifteen thousand feet; for a few moments, on these days, the peak casts back the clouds. Soft white smoke rolls from the garden fires, soft as the mists on the horizons of far rains. And there are the blaze of sands on the flanks of Siobara, the alabaster statues of egrets, the shower of rhododendron. . . .

The Wittaia rose out of their silence, filed away.

At this the shouting was renewed, more strongly than before. The wild dancing of etai began, a whirling and prancing in which the men leapt high in the air or in a circle, driving both heels against the ground, or performed an odd taunting shuffle in which the feet are still, the knees pushed in and out, the hips and shoulders cocked in turn, and the arms darted snakily forward; the effect is one of lewd, jeering enticement, though it is a joyful dance, performed out of the wild high spirits brought about by a death among the enemy and the knowledge that no further risk will come that day.

Only the Aloros and a few others enjoy the risk, though all enjoy the war. At the first shout Aloro, alone among the warriors around Tuesike, had seized his bow and hobbled desperately toward a battle not destined to take place.

In a forest of spears the Kurelu were streaming back along the ridge, their stamping thunderous, their voices soaring. *O-o-A-i-i-A-y-y—WU! O-o-A-i-i-O-o—WAH!* Other voices, in simultaneous high counterpoint, howled, *WUA, WUA, WUA!* The egret wands and whisks of cassowary twirled like bright maddened insects, and the white of plumes and shells and boars' tusks flashed in the surging brown. At the edges of the tide ran yegerek, setting fire with thatch torches to the grass tops. Here and there bobbed a spot of brilliant red—the feathers of a parakeet, or a crown of the red ginger flower. These colors spun, and the weathered grays and greens of the ancient land lay still.

There came a shout, and Weaklekek with two of his men ran from the Waraba. They crossed the swamp and plunged through the reeds on the far side of the Tokolik, sprinting across the field toward Puakaloba. Once again the Wittaia had set fire to the shelter, which was burning fast. Apparently the enemy had been scared off, for the kaio itself still stood.

The warriors stopped to dance again. Some of them charged in a great circle, while others swayed and shimmied, *way-o-way-y—YO, lay-o-lay-y—AH!* to an answering din of hootings and wild high shrieks. In the middle of one group U-mue, resplendent in his clean bright ornaments of white, stood looking off into the distance, leaning on his spear, for he keeps his own counsel even in time of celebration.

A few women had collected from the fields, and these had begun their own slow sensual dropping of alternate knees, a swaying of the shoulders, while their arms shivered in and out, palms upward. One tall woman danced alone, far out in front of the rest, wearing a mikak shell above her breasts; in her splendor, she dominated a grassy hillside between the men and the women. This was the wife of Wereklowe's son, who had killed Huwai. Wereklowe came and danced beside her, but in a little while he went away again, and she swayed on, as if rooted to the landscape.

Soon the warriors ran down the slope, passing the bushes where Tuesike sat upon the ground and moving into the swamp of brush and sedge grass which separates the Waraba from the Tokolik. At the Tokolik they assembled to dance again, before moving on to the etai field called Liberek.

Tuesike was lifted painfully onto a stretcher. Siba and Asok-meke and Tegearek—the men of his pilai—were helped by a few elege like Siloba and Yonokma. Siloba winced himself, for, in the curing of an arrow wound which he carried at his left collarbone, his stomach had been lanced in several places and blood drawn; while the arrow wound had healed itself, the places of his cure had become infected and still hurt him.

Together the men hoisted the stretcher and entered the low ground. Tuesike was unconscious, and his body and face had been covered with green straw. The procession wound slowly through the black water of the swamp and, crossing the Tokolik, entered the home territory. It disappeared once more into the heavy swale of reeds and in a little while emerged, near the kaio which guards the outermost of the fields. Already, at the Liberek, dancing had started, and the chants of triumph did not cease at dark but rose and fell throughout the evening, from all the villages below the mountain.

■ The next morning U-mue's men adjusted their appearance. This was a slow and careful process. Yeke Asuk and Hanumoak, both single men, took the most pains, not only because both were vain but because the etai was traditionally an occasion for showing off one's beauty to the women and thus laying the groundwork for liaisons or wife-stealing. The women would dress too, to the best of their ability, especially those discontented wives amenable to the idea of being stolen.

Yeke Asuk, though still quite young, had already had three wives and was not in haste to find another. The first three had left him, less because they did not like him than because he had paid no attention to them, pursuing the single life to the best of his ability. Hanumoak, on the other hand, had never had sufficient property to obtain a wife; he had lived in U-mue's pilai ever since a quarrel with his brother. But he did own a fine headdress of bird of paradise, the black plumes of which rose three feet from the fiber head-band of pandanus. He arranged the plumes upon his mass of hair, very careful that a certain amount of hair should show beneath them. He then smeared his face and shoulders with a gray wad of fresh pig grease and singed in the fire some straw from the pilai floor; the ash of this he rubbed into the grease, using his thumb. In this way he blackened his forehead, which was naturally blackish-brown, and drew a clean black line about an inch in breadth across his cheek-bones and the bridge of his nose. Hanumoak is handsome, but his face is rather soft, and the hard black band, making his eyes more fierce, became him.

Yeke Asuk is not handsome, and the hair on top of his huge brow is nondescript. Of late he has worn a spray of cassowary plumes, but this has not pleased him, and today he replaced it with seven white egret feathers. Like Hanumoak, he greased his face and drew a black line across his cheekbones, but his forehead, beneath which his pug face is squashed, he treated with special attention. He took a dried piece of red clay and rubbed it on a stone; the dust he moistened with water, producing the dye he needed. His red eyes, when at last they passed inspection, gave him a remarkable look of choler. Both Hanumoak and Yeke Asuk put on their snail-shell bibs, and Yeke Asuk also put a boar's tusk in his hair. To his rattan stomach hoops, behind, he fastened a long green leaf of spiderwort which lay on the cleft of his buttocks and, thus adorned, he scrambled on all fours out of the pilai.

With other warriors, Yeke Asuk and Hanumoak went with their spears to a hillside above Abukumo to stage a preliminary celebration: the location was chosen to provide any Wittaia not at Huwai's funeral with a clear view of the celebration of his death. From this point, early in the afternoon, the warriors would move on to the Liberek.

At the Liberek, during the morning, a few young boys and women had collected. Husuk and his men, passing through from the villages of the Kosi-Alua, went on to a frontier kaio, where they staged a small dance comparable to that being held above Abukumo. The sun boiled a damp close air, and a large black harrier with gray tail feathers quartered low and lazily above the bushes.

The sun had already reached its crest when a large company of women came, led by the tall young wife of Wereklowe's son. She is a handsome girl with a strange abstracted gaze, and for the etai she had dressed herself like a young warrior. In addition to the mikak she had worn the day before, dancing alone in the twilight of the Waraba, she had red and black plumes of birds of paradise. Snail shells in separate strings rather than the close bib favored by the men swayed gracefully between her breasts as she began to dance. In a small circle on the grass of the etai meadow she moved slowly, as if feeling for her rhythm, and as she did so she began to call, *We-Re-A Re—WAY! We-Re-A-Re—WAH!* Another woman answered with the high, pure hoot of chorus, and the rest joined them, moving forward. Most of the women had confined their decoration to a thick coat of yellow ocher or gray clay, but a few had feather crowns or shell bibs or inferior small mikaks. From the masks of clay their dark eyes glared, depthless and spectral. Led by the girl, they moved back and forth in a massed body, wheeling sharply at the end of each phrase, *We-Re-A-Re—WAY! We-Re-A-Re—WAH!* the turn being made on the *WAY* or the *WAH.* Periodically they would screech, breaking into a heavy run, breasts flying, faster and faster and faster in a tight, driven circle, like creatures fleeing pain. Small girls in their reed skirts pattered hopelessly along on the fringe of the bodies, until exhaustion spun them away from their mothers; they sank in little heaps into the grass.

Then the women would stop, getting their breath and laughing, until one of their number, softly and slowly at first, would renew the chant and begin to sway, moving her arms languorously in and out. The others would take it up, and the dance would be repeated, up the field and down, around and around, the nets sailing on the turns to bare hard buttocks pinched tight by the coil skirts. At the side of the field the oldest women swayed in accompaniment, their mantis arms outstretched, their long feet twitching. U-mue's old mother, Aneake, was one of these, calling out fiercely.

At the west end of the meadow the boys and old men sat in the shelter. Some of the men performed on each other's faces the plucking of hairs from the upper lip and the neatening of beards, using the pitch of the araucaria and araucaria-twig tweezers; while almost all men wear short beards, the mustache is considered very ugly. The legs were also cleaned of hairs, and the hips and pubis, until the dark skin gleamed. One old man appeared from the bushes with the lost smile of uncertain eyesight: he was greeted with affection, and a young warrior barbered him. Other warriors had gathered, and now the Kosi-Alua at the kaio in the distance were mustering for their entry upon the Liberek.

The women danced on, for this was the last hour that

■ *89*

they would have the meadow to themselves. Two carried infants on their shoulders, and the head of one of these was submerged in a man's white egret crown; with his mother, from behind, he formed a giant, rushed along by the lesser creatures underneath.

We-a-AY   O-o-Aia-OH

The men came in midafternoon, arriving from two directions simultaneously. They massed at the end of the field, then charged across it, spears held high against the clouds and long plumes tossing. Immediately they turned and thundered back again, *AY-A-Wo-AI*, then broke to form a roaring circle. Some women rushed in from the side to mingle with the fringes of the men; as the speed increased, they ran more like men than women, the sulphurous colors of their bodies blotting out without obscuring the female breasts and hips. *Ay-HOO, ay-HOO,* the women wailed, their voices remote in the men's tumult. Just as their grief was deeper at the funerals, their joy was fiercer in etai, as if all of their emotions, accumulating in their long brown days, must find release in this abandon.

As the father of the man revenged, Yoroick was the guest of honor. He wore no decoration but the yellow clay, which was daubed thickly on his head and shoulders. Even his hair was yellow-white, patriarchal, and, with his great height among the men, he looked like some mad hermit, naked and glaring in the wilderness. He crouched down at a small fire near the shelter, mourning his son among the older men; the soft, wailing wind they made rose with strange force against the storm of victory. The old men, bony-spined, sat with bent heads over a clear flame invisible in the sunlight.

Yoroick rose suddenly with a hoarse shout. Seizing his spear, he bolted down the field through the startled dancers.

The dancing stopped, and a deep moan arose. The men of the Kosi-Alua took up their spears and followed.

The cause of the outcry was the soft-walking U-mue. Approaching the Liberek from the field above Homaklep, U-mue had come upon one of the men who had seized his youngest wife not long before. U-mue was accompanied by four of his best warriors and perceived an excellent opportunity to avenge the outrage. A melee started up just beyond the etai field, but, before anyone was hurt, Yoroick got wind of it and ran forward.

Yoroick is ordinarily a peaceable man, so peaceable that his reticence in time of war is a matter of common knowledge, but on this day he was the important person, full of noise and fire. Already in an excited state of mind, he was greatly offended that U-mue should have caused a distraction on this epochal occasion. Yoroick was anxious to kill U-mue, but he was prevented from doing so, not only by the people who caught up with him but by U-mue himself, who took his leave. The men calmed Yoroick and escorted him back to the etai.

The Wuperainma warriors trailed behind, but they were uneasy and remained on the outskirts of the celebration. Yeke Asuk, particularly, moved up and down with uncustomary diffidence, Tegearek and two others at his side.

Over five hundred people were present, all of them dressed to the best of their resources. Tukum the swineherd wore a thin, battered mikak and some shell strings; he bounced the shell strings on a round belly taut with sweet potato, producing a hollow sound which made him laugh. Some other boys carried their bows and arrows; they had drawn white patterns on their bodies. Five yegerek wore crowns of blossoms from the yellow rhododendron.

Wereklowe's son, who had run down the Wittaia and killed him with his spear, caused a quiet stir of greeting and respect as he moved about; in his hair were silver streaks of clay. A man with a headdress of red ginger flowers sat beside another with red feathers, in a pair, jutting out from his temples like low horns. Limo wore the long barred feathers of a large hawk; he sat in silence, watching, his handsome face, like that of Kurelu, gentle and merciless by turns. Nilik swayed, facing the dancers; he had armlets of thick fur of a rich brown luster, and a red and black wig of tiny seeds strung in cordy strands like hard, long hair. Nilik, as the political leader of the successful raid, was anxious to assert himself and did so.

Rain drifted from the mountains in the wake of a soft sun of twilight. Some older people moved onto the savanna paths toward home, but the dancers surged and chanted back and forth, undiminished. To one side of the central bodies a girl dyed red pranced back and forth with a girl of dead gray color; on the far side the tall wife of Wereklowe's son, with two men and another woman, formed a line apart, moving ceaselessly up and down the field with loose-limbed fervor. She had danced all afternoon, in a kind of trance, and was still dancing when Yoroick, perhaps fearing that he had lost his world's attention, cried out again: he wished that the men of the Kosi-Alua fall upon U-mue's men and kill them. Hanumoak, though he is Yoroick's youngest brother, moved out toward the brush uneasily, joining his friends. But the men of the Kosi-Alua were not prepared to act on Yoroick's wish, and the shouting died.

Aloro stood alone and watched the dancers. He stood on his good right leg, still as a heron, supporting his left side with his spear. He too wore the barred feathers of a hawk, and he had painted white circles around his eyes. He seemed to avoid the looks of others, as if ashamed that he could not dance.

Aloro's eyes slant back into his forehead, and his mouth

hangs open in a way less slack than wolfish; without taking his eyes from the dancers, he turned his head slowly, as a predator will, to pick up sounds from behind and from the sides. The white eyes and the toothed grin which is not a grin gave him an air of madness.

■ The day after the etai Tuesike was brought down from the sleeping loft of his pilai. The pilai belongs to Asok-meke and is inhabited also by Siba, Tegearek, and Tekman Bio, as well as by Asok-meke's small son, Tukum. Tuesike was helped to a sitting position against one of the frames of the pilai fire, and rattan was strung from one post to the next to support his head. He breathed slowly and poorly, and it was thought that he would die.

Tukum slipped in and sat down next to him, holding a piece of hiperi. Over a period of time he nibbled at it, chewing slowly, intermittently, to avoid the pain of swallowing. From time to time he coughed, a taut, dry cough that caused him to turn and stare at the other men in surprise and pain.

Tuesike's eyes looked glazed, and he did not respond to the friends who had come to sit with him, but remained with his back to the ashes of the morning fire, staring into the dark recesses of the round house.

Asok-meke, who was in tears, was crying for Tuesike, but he also cried with pleasure because a friend whom he had not seen for a long time had come to visit him from the Siep-Kosi. At these times, crying was the custom.

Thunder rolled out of the mountains like an avalanche, and the rain came down. An old man wove ceaselessly at the cowrie belt used in funerals, and in the darkness by the wall Aloro drew unearthly sounds from his cane harp. The other men, fourteen in all, sat smoking. They gazed stolidly outward at the mud forming in the sili yard, absorbed by the brown certainties of their own lives.

A few days later Tuesike was much improved, and in the early afternoon he sat alone, facing the doorway. Though he was not comfortable, he was not really in pain. Blood had been let from two cuts in his stomach, near the hole made by the arrow, and the long red point of the arrow itself was there above his head for any visitors to admire, on the rack over the fire frame. With it was an arrow point removed previously from the body of Tegearek.

Tuesike had felt much better since the capture and cutting of a field mouse and a rat. The cutting was done by Aloro. The belly skins of the animals, still alive, were slit open with a bamboo knife: if the stomach wall had been pierced and entrails spilled, Tuesike's own wound would have been mortal, but the entrails of both animals had remained intact, as his own must therefore be. The rat ceremony was only performed when death was close, and everyone had been much reassured; more likely than not, had the hand of Aloro been less steady, Tuesike would have given up and died. At the moment the animals hung from the fire rack behind him, strung up by the throat. The teeth of the rat were bared and its tail hung in a stiff curl, as if it had tried to climb or gnaw its string.

That morning Siba had made a fetish. This fetish was a piece of cane three or four feet long into which feathers had been inserted, in the end and along the length. Tuesike had crept outside, and the cane, with a bundle of *lukaka* grass, was waved over his head. Once Tuesike had been treated, it was planted on the path in front of Wuperainma; the grass was laid at its foot, wrapped in *pavi* leaves. Pavi is a word which also means both enemy and excrement, but the choice of this leaf was purely fortuitous, the pavi tree, in this spot, being the closest growth at hand. The grass bundle, on the other hand, is almost invariably used in any such communication with the ghosts.

A man badly wounded, and thus troubled in body and spirit, is especially vulnerable to the wiles of ghosts. The fetish was placed between Tuesike and enemy lands to show the ghost of Huwai that the Kurelu were aware of its intentions and had taken suitable precautions; the grass bundle, like the bundle placed around the base of a new kaio, was there to indicate that a close watch was being kept.

Siba was confident that his warning would keep the ghost away, and Tuesike felt much better for it. He touched with his fingers the leaf poultices on his wounds and coughed a little. He had gotten very thin. In the silence of the afternoon he listened to a pig—the sound was more like a hollow thump than a live grunt—and to the peaceful droning of the flies, the flies of summer, in a summer which would never end.

■ In a war of the yegerek Uwar was struck beneath the right eye by a grass spear; this accident is a common one and accounts for the large incidence of boys and men among the Kurelu who are blind in one eye. Uwar barely escaped blinding. Though he was badly hurt and crying, he found the shaft of reed which struck him and took it to U-mue's pilai. Unless he is very lucky, he will do this again some other day, in the wars with the Wittaia. The arrow will be of hard, sharp cane, and, more likely than not, it will be carried back for him by another warrior.

■ In the village of Abukumo, which lies on a low spur of the mountain between Homaklep and the Aike, there is a sili abandoned after an argument between its owners. The small garden of the sili is sadly overgrown with amaranth and daisies, and the huts, weighted down by rotted thatch, sag slowly among the weeds.

The sili was owned formerly by three brothers. The eldest, Yoroick, left Abukumo and went to live with the Kosi-Alua, outraged by the seduction of one of his wives by the second brother, Werene: Yoroick's name means "Pigeon," and Werene's name means "Parrot," and Pigeon had previously done to Parrot what Parrot was subsequently to do to Pigeon. Since physical retribution is usually avoided except by the kains and the violent ones, the fitting revenge is thought to be the identical offense.

Before long Werene left the sili too. He moved down the slope to Homaklep, taking with him a third brother, Hanumoak, at that time no more than a child. One day, a few years later, Hanumoak refused Werene's command that he go out to work in the gardens. After the quarrel which occurred, Hanumoak left Werene's sili and moved to the pilai of U-mue in Wuperainma.

Another old sili adjoining the abandoned one is occupied by a kepu man and his sick father, and a third is being restored by Asikanalek: Asikanalek, a solitary man, is a very brave young war kain of the clan Alua whose name, "No Sound of Bow"—literally, Sike-Ane-Lek, or "Bow Voice Not" —refers to the cessation of the wars with the Siep-Kosi. Already a new pilai has been constructed, where his old father can blink away his days, and in early May, Asikanalek started work on a new cooking shed. Assisted by his neighbor, he turned the dogged earth. The earth was hard-surfaced, baked to rust-colored ceramic by old fires, and with his digging stick he chunked into it, foot by foot, while the other man spread the raw hunks of clay on the old yard.

When the foundation of the new shed was completed, two hollow trunks of the pandanus were laid parallel as sills. The ends of the structure were erected, followed by the front and back. Each side was a double wall of oak and beech slats pounded and worked into the ground. Cross slats were wedged down between the uprights, knocked tight by a heavy wooden knout, and the whole affair was lashed with strong rattan: to tighten the bindings, Asikanalek would place one foot high on the wall and haul on the rattan with his whole weight.

In the wall at each end a central post had been installed,

and a ridgepole was laid down the length of the shed. The slat roof was laid against the ridgepole, forming a peak, and the slats were covered with a loose layer of cane strips, before the whole was thatched. Air spaces had been left at the ends of the shed, between the wall top and the peak, and the structure was nowhere tight, in order that the smoke of the fires could readily escape. The fires were placed between each of three posts supporting the roof. By the time of the new moon the shed would be in use, and it would shortly acquire the interior smell of all the buildings in the valley.

In the pilai, sitting before the fire, Asikanalek's old father supported his rotted frame by clinging to a rattan strung between two posts. At one time a warrior who had killed three, he had now reached extreme old age and had shrunk away to nothing. His skeleton, casting off its long disguise of flesh and blood, asserted itself indecently, and the long nails grew untended, as nails grow in a grave, an inch or more of yellow horn scratching fitfully among the few leaves of lisanika scattered between his feet. His skin, long dead, contrasted with the gleam of the cane ceiling greased black by the fire smoke. It was encrusted with hard scabs, as if his pores were to close over, one by one. His eyes, drained of all depth and luster, were two flat, rimless wet places on his face.

But still he heard and saw and smiled, and he could stir. He lifted a lisanika leaf toward his mouth, for his hands recalled tobacco; the lisanika leaf is always moistened before the tobacco is rolled into it. The yellow nails scratched dryly on the leaf, a mousy sound, as his gums lost it. There was no moisture in his mouth, and when the leaf escaped him he forgot about it. His feet were cold, and very slowly he lifted the bone club of his right heel toward the flame.

Asikanalek's child Namilike came in. Though girls and women are forbidden to enter the pilai, small children of either sex are at times tolerated, and Namilike cannot be more than four. Like all the other little girls, she wears a miniature grass skirt, a circlet of soft reed gathered at the water's edge, and she has her own small net. Namilike has large eyes and large eyebrows and a smiling mouth, and she is the prettiest child in the southern Kurelu. She sat next to her grandfather, her hand with its missing fingers on his dead knee, and at the same time unaware of him, as if he had assumed a final place among the dull brown packets of smoked straw and withered leaves which hung like bats from the dark rafters.

■ Woluklek is a wild-eyed man with an enchanted smile, and he is almost always by himself, Like Apeore, Tuesike, and Asikanalek, he is a solitary. But while Apeore and Asikanalek go their way alone because they like it, and Tuesike seems cut off from others out of shyness, Woluklek is alone because he is unique, and his solitude, though marked, is his condition. Unlike the others, he is not a respected warrior, but neither is he kepu, in the sense of cowardice. In war Woluklek is very often at the fore, but his activity is distracted, aimless, as if he had wandered across the battle lines on his way elsewhere and remained within the range of death out of bemusement. Yet he is not simple. It is as if, on the sunny paths of childhood, he had strayed out of his world into a dream and allowed the dream to waft him where it would, his life or death a matter of indifference.

So now he moved slowly through the world of shadows and hanging shapes which is the montane forest, squatting here and there to stare and pick, and passing on; he had no real errand, no real destination, a habitual circumstance which, by itself, had isolated him from others long before.

Woluklek wore no decoration on his head or breast: the whites of his large eyes excepted, he was dark as the earth beneath a stone. Behind, however, he had equipped himself with a strange fern, suspended from his horim string. The fern was bent from having been sat upon askew and stuck out to one side instead of hanging in the graceful way he had had in mind before forgetting it was there.

The morning sun filtered through the leaves in patches, alighting on red fruits of the pandanus. Single stems of giant bamboo shot toward holes of light or curved with languid stiffness back to earth, only to bend up again, toward the tip, like the head of a hunting snake. Large trunks of beech and myrtle loomed in the mass of foliage, to vanish into the green worlds of the canopy. Where a giant tree had fallen, an undergrowth of lesser plants fought for place in the new sun—rattan and scrambling fern and tall stalks of wild ginger with its scarlet flower.

Whistlers and honey eaters flicked quickly through the wood, their voices lost in the rush of a small stream. Woluklek squatted once again to eat gilled mushrooms. Woluklek liked to squat upon his heels and often did so even when the other men were standing, as if this angle gave him new perspective.

He moved onto the open slopes and down the white sand of the trickling stream bed, toward the valley floor. Along this path, in the sand beneath an overhanging boulder, some tribesman waiting out a rain had drawn the course of the Baliem River with sweeping arabesques of his foot. Woluklek investigated the sand drawing with pleasure and then, with his own foot, changed the course of the Baliem.

The boulder was one of an assembly of great rocks:

close by, the path detoured down through a steep cleft between two others. This place was rarely visited by the people. It was a dark, dripping niche of ferns and mosses, with a solitary pandanus, sprawling and twisted in a welter of its own leaves, as if defeated in its passage toward the sun. Here, on a narrow ledge, protected from the water drops of yellowish short stalactites, lay remnant bones of two Wittaia.

The enemy had been killed years before, and their bodies left to rot: eventually the bones had been placed upon this ledge so that the earth itself, in the slow fall of leaves and petals from the sun above, would not bury them and thus lay them to rest. Woluklek was vague about the story, though it was claimed that the enemy had not been eaten. The akuni did not eat people, but they knew that this was done quite frequently in the southern valley. Only a few months before, a raiding party of people living near the Aso-Lokopals had been cut off and wiped out by the Hisaro. There were more than twenty killed, and all of these men were roasted in a rock fire and consumed. The bones were placed out in the forest, in a wisa ground; this ground was considered very dangerous because of its great company of vengeful ghosts.

Woluklek skirted by the place of bones and went on down the hill into the sunshine. Passing a rhododendron, he plucked an unopened blossom. He bit off the tip and hollowed it and, by holding it pressed to his lower lip and blowing, was able to produce a shrill, thin whistle.

■ On the tower of his kaio, far out in the center of the fields, Wereklowe sat perched like a great bird. In the shelter below, his warriors mended arrows and wove armlets. Wereklowe, like Kurelu himself, dressed simply. Unlike the lesser kains, who were always in white regalia, Wereklowe was content with the flat black pig intestines at his throat and an armlet the color of pale gold braided onto his left wrist.

All the great fields to the north of the kaio belonged to him, and the women who worked in them, and even the men, and the kaio itself—he included them all with a wave of his arm. An-meke, he called them, Mine, grasping and shaking his horim. And Wereklowe smiled his ecstatic savage smile, a restless smile, constantly working, forcing great creases on his lean cheeks, a smile at the same time merry and without mercy.

Wereklowe's name means "He Who Never Works in Fields." It was given originally as a rebuke, but Wereklowe made no attempt to rid himself of the name. He has killed ten men, and the time is long since past when work in the fields would be expected of him: he is the leader of the Alua, and the great war kain of the tribe, with seven wives, a dozen pigs, and eight fine children. Only Kurelu himself, with ten, has more wives than Wereklowe.

Probably there is no man in the Kurelu who has killed more enemies than Wereklowe. But in the Hisaro clans to the southward there is a kain who is said to have taken more than one hundred lives. He is notorious throughout the valley, even among tribes like the Kurelu which have no contact with his own. In the course of an ordinary lifetime of tribal wars and raids it would not be possible to kill one hundred people, but this kain is not an ordinary man. A fanatic warrior in battle, he prowls as well on solitary raids into the countries of his enemies, killing quietly where chance offers. On one occasion he accosted a woman on a lonely path: the woman, assuming the stranger was bent on rape, lay down philosophically to receive him. His spear lay beside them, and, instead of raping her, he drove the spear inside her. Another time he entered a sili at midday, when only old women, infants, and sick people would be about. A sick boy in the pilai invited him to rest himself in the loft above until the men might return; when both had climbed into the darkness, the stranger strangled his young host and took his leave.

Despite the number of enemies to his credit, this man's need to take life is unfamiliar to the Dani and makes even his own people uneasy. The criminality of his acts is recognized; unlike Wereklowe, he is despised as well as feared.

Besides Wereklowe, the Alua kains include Polik, Weaklekek, Limo, and Asikanalek, village kain of Abukumo; the clan Alua, with its sub-clan the Halluk, is the strongest in the southern Kurelu.

After Wereklowe, the most powerful of these kains is Polik, leader of the Halluk. Polik is a tall old man with straight hair in stiff, cordy strings down to his shoulders; sometimes he wears a magnificent fur crown, and he is never without an enormous broad-bladed white spear eighteen feet long.

As a young warrior Polik behaved strangely and violently and is said to have killed more than one of his own people; because he was feared, he was given the name Mokat, meaning "Ghost." To this day he is commonly referred to by this name, with great respect: *Mokat kain kok-mekel* —Mokat is a great kain! His present name, which stems from

"He Who Came Up from Behind," recalls his bravery in a battle of long ago, when he circled back and saved the life of a man cut off by the enemy. Polik is never far from the front line, and his fierce shouts of encouragement and warning are a part of every war.

Polik is proud of his strong voice, which dominates not only wars but funerals. Above all else, he loves to sing. When Polik sings, a sleepy smile comes to his face, and he tosses his great head from side to side in his slow rhythm, so that his heavy hair flops on his shoulders. He sings songs of war and raids, of love and gardens, but sometimes he sings little wordless songs of sheer contentment, alone on a high rock on the sunny hillside.

> Ye-we-o   Ya wo-o-lo
>   Ma-ya-um
> We le-le-e   Ko-lo-lo

■ One night in late May, while the giant frogmouth, red-eyed and yellow-mouthed, called sepulchrally from the starry points of araucaria, the valley shuddered in an earthquake; the earthquake lasted only a few moments, two brief spasms, and then the earth was still again and the frogmouth resumed its lugubrious night song.

There are volcanic regions at both ends of the great island, but the central highlands are without volcanoes, and earthquakes are quite rare. In this equatorial climate, without seasons, where the steady pressure of the trade winds makes rain and sun constants of every day, nature is less violent than remorseless. High winds, drought, the torrential rainstorms of the monsoon coasts, are almost unknown, and perhaps this is why the akuni, taking for granted their mild, equable weathers, have not invested the rare tempests and earthquakes with supernatural powers; as a people they are notably unsuperstitious. Heat lightning is said to be the blood of a man killed by his enemies, rising into the sky, and the sky itself is thought to harbor other peoples; there was a rope leading down to earth, but, as the sky peoples stole too many pigs and women, the rope was cut. According to Asikanalek, the rope was cut by Kurelu himself, but U-mue says no, the rope was cut long, long ago.

On the night of the earthquake the men of U-mue's pilai descended from the sleeping loft and smoked; they talked uneasily of the earthquake and wondered at its origin and, after a while, returned above and went to sleep.

■ A full moon came at the end of May, and, as it filled, a fresh wind of the southeast trades, which prevail from May until October, cleared the humid airs. Buffy night herons had come into the valley and circled the landscapes with the blue heron and egret; the black ducks, now very numerous with the new birds of the spring nests, were joined by the solitary mountain duck, a rare small species, black and white, with a bright orange bill. Together they curved down in the afternoons into the ditches of the fields.

The mountain duck has flown these valleys for a million years and has never been seen anywhere but in the highlands; probably it evolved when the valley floor was still a glaciated lake traversed by limestone salients and ridges. The lakes and marshlands lay between the ridges, and the ducks gabbled in warm mornings never seen by man. But the limestone barriers eroded quickly, and the lakes seeped away. The Siobara, like a great pyramid in the center of the valley, is probably a remnant of just such a ridge, while high ground like the Tokolik may well have been lake shore: the lake-floor gardens, were they not drained by ditches, would still be part of the acid marshland which surrounds the Waraba.

The dry ground in those old millenniums, and the lower slopes to nearly seven thousand feet, were forested by tropic oaks and chestnuts interspersed with stands of araucaria. The oak-and-chestnut forest was a sign of arable land and, with the coming of man, was the first casualty; its destruction was hastened by the advent of the sweet potato, though whether this occurred three centuries or three thousand years ago cannot be known. The hiperi, and the large population which its cultivation permitted, encouraged extensive clearing; across the centuries the fields crept up the slopes, trailing the forest, and the drainage and development of the valley floor evolved. Each garden was short-lived: once the topsoil was cropped out and leached away by year-round planting, it was abandoned and a new plot slashed and burned and cleared.

The topsoil inevitably went quickly. Alluvial sediment, sifted down across the ages from the high massifs, it was a poor compound of limestone and quartz sandstone; the limestone, weathered, produced a weak, soluble soil and, in the end, dead white quartzitic sand: patches of this sand erupted long ago along the base of the Siobara and on the rain-leached hills, the bare bones of a limy, anemic earth.

In consequence, after a year or two or three, the gardens must be abandoned to savanna. The savanna is all but wasteland. Except for small rodents caught for rituals, there are no animals worth hunting. The grass shelters a tiny quail, a small gray rail, a scattering of songbirds like the robin chat and fairy-wren and black-headed weaver finch: the paucity of grassland birds which have occupied the open regions hints that the history of the akuni in the Baliem has been a brief one, for the grassland is of their making. But the time of their own coming the akuni cannot tell, only that it was long ago, with the father of their fathers. The villages rot, and the dead go up in fire, and their history decomposes in the soil.

In the clear days which accompanied the flowering of the moon, a new black patch appeared below Wuperainma, in the bottom of what once had been an ancient pond. Here Tegearek and Werene reclaimed a garden. The work was hard, for the shrubs had long ago established solid banks, even small trees, and the ground between was bound up tight with mats of roots. The sides of the old drainage ditches had fallen in, and the shallow water was choked off with weeds and rushes.

The two men worked adjoining plots and sometimes worked together. From day to day their helpers changed, in the intricate patterns of kinship and obligation. Each man had a heavy digging stick, which he drove into dark, grudging earth of purple-brown: the sticks made a dull biting sound and a muffled cracking as the roots were pried and snapped. The litter of fire-blackened stumps and roots on the scorched ground gave the whole scene an air of barren land, to be worked in vain by the black, panting bodies. Only a few yards away, across the ditches, the undergrowth stood in wait, as if ready to retake this ground at the first sign of negligence: beneath the blossoms and the bright green leaves, the roots were creeping forward, and the new seeds fattened with every sun in the receptacles of the flowers.

Werene the Parrot spat in the dry sun, a neat, quiet, and uneasy man who wears a string of pale blue grass seeds, the Job's Tears, across his forehead; like his young brother Hanumoak he is a handsome man, but his face is weak and sour, as if he knew that his ambitions must go unfulfilled for want of the power or courage to see them implemented.

■ A young woman of the Siep-Kosi came to visit the southern villages, and Weaklekek detained her as a wife; the girl was put to work in the gardens below Puakaloba, where he was able to keep an eye on her.

U-mue, hearing of this girl and wishing her for himself,

had demanded immediately to know if she were *wita* or *waia,* the two moieties or marriage groups into which all clans in the valley are divided, according to their patrilineal line. If Weaklekek, a waia, should make love to a waia woman, both of them might be put to death and their bodies thrown out into the fields to rot. The prohibition is an ancient one, so ancient that no explanation is known; it is not connected by the akuni with incest. Two associated clans are invariably wita and waia, so that marriage may take place between them, just as two men who share a sili are apt to be wita and waia, for, if both were wita, they could make love to each other's wives. The Wilil are wita, the Haiman waia, the Walilo wita, and Alua waia. Weaklekek had very soon determined the girl's moiety—it is the first question asked of any stranger who is not killed—which was wita. Since U-mue, as a Wilil, was wita also, he was thus ineligible. A few days later the girl herself resolved the matter by fleeing back to the Siep-Kosi.

■ This morning a party of Asuk-Palek people, led by a kain named Torobia, prepared an ambush in the gardens of the northern Kurelu. The Asuk-Palek lived formerly in the Kurelu, in the region of Wuperainma, but were driven out long ago. Many were killed and many others had their ears cut off; the rest settled among the Wittaia. At this time they were named, and are called still, the Asuk-Palek, or "Ears Cut."

While stalking the kaio, the Asuk-Palek were surprised by three Kurelu, then by two more, coming from an opposite direction. The five Kurelu saw immediately that they were outnumbered, while Torobia's band imagined that they had blundered into an ambush. Both sides fled. Polik and his men, who were nearby, pursued the party of Asuk-Palek. They wounded one man and they caught Torobia; while some held him, others ran him through with spears. From his head they cut some bits of hair. There is rarely time or opportunity to stop and strip an enemy body, and the hair is therefore a prized fetish.

Tonight the celebration started in Abulopak, where Polik lives with his kinsman, Wereklowe. The etai starts always in Abulopak, which is the largest of the southern villages; it is actually two villages in one, since it now includes the former Wilil stronghold which adjoins it. With few exceptions, the most important kains and warriors of the Aike region live in Abulopak or Wuperainma; the exceptions are Weaklekek in Homaklep, Asikanalek in Abukumo, and Apeore in Lokoparek. The other villages in this region are thought of as kepu, since they cannot claim an important kain or warrior between them.

The whooping was pierced by the ringing whistle of the huge cicadas; the cicadas cry briefly every evening just at dark, as time-bound as the folding of the ferns. The evening passed, and the whooping rose toward a moon in its final quarter, continuing on long after the insects had died away. To Homuak there came an owl, hooting uneasily against the din, and the great fruit bats, the flying foxes, on slow leather wings, quartered the evergreen silhouettes. An opossum coughed, and the nightjar with its great mouth and whiskers took up its sepulchral song, an odd tok—tok, like a shell rapped on a block of hollowed wood, interspersed with froggish mutterings. Sometimes the green tree frogs called, and sometimes the black dogs, crying: these strange animals never bark, nor do they howl. Their sound is the wail of a spirit trapped in the body of a dog, and its eeriness passes onward through the night villages in the moon shadows of the mountain wall.

At dawn Polik came to Homuak. Standing at the fire site above the spring, he called, *A-OH, A-OH*. The cry was taken up from the villages to north and south, and the long day of etai which would celebrate Torobia's death had started.

But the sun had not appeared above the rim when a troop of warriors, still heavy-faced with sleep, trotted swiftly through the grove, bearing their spears. One called out to Polik, and he ran after them, grunting fiercely; the Wittaia, still raging for revenge, had come in from the Tokolik and set fire to a kaio shelter of the Kosi-Alua. They had destroyed the tobacco patch and uprooted plots of sweet potatoes in the gardens nearby.

The warriors passed through the low wood below Wuperainma and Homaklep, and over the grassy knoll called Anelarok, where the women of Lokoparek, on their way to the Liberek, would stop that day to dance. They ran on toward the Aike, to guard against a raid from the Turaba, and a group of eight had crossed to the Turaba itself, to act as sentries.

The fair weather of the full moon had continued, and a huge blue day expanded above the valley. From southeast to southwest the rim was sharp as a black, jagged blade, with only the northern wall lost in the white cloud mountains. Thin wisps of mist drifted through the distant woods, like spider webs trailed out by the soft wind; this was the trade wind from the ocean, beyond the high horizons, which had dried the valley floor in a rare four days without rain. For the first time since the early days of April the sun rose cleanly from behind the cliffs, scattering small brilliant puffs of clouds: it gleamed on the rufous mantle of a white-headed kite quartering low across the gardens of Weaklekek.

Wittaia appeared on the Tokolik, and a shout arose from the villages beneath the wall; the warriors of the Kurelu streamed out across the fields toward the frontier. More Wittaia convened on the near slope of the Waraba, in silent wait. Polik went out with other men to the large central kaio, which stands on a wide belt of high ground traversing the main gardens. Tuesike was also there. He had done light work in the few days past and was slowly resuming his life as a warrior, but he moved uncertainly and was quieter than before.

On the Turaba, meanwhile, some Kurelu sentries huddled together against the early cold. They had not dared light the fire, for fear of revealing their position. Expecting that any Wittaia ought to come from the direction of his own country, they were facing westward, down the ridge, and were startled when a man appeared quite suddenly from behind them. At first they thought that the man was Tekman Bio, but when he called out to them, they recognized in dismay a fierce warrior who, some years before, fleeing the wrath of his own people, had been accepted by the Wittaia: he knew every stone in the land of the Kurelu and had crept up on the sentry party from behind. He also knew the sentries and their caliber, and, though he had but two men with him, they were good men, and he did not hesitate to approach boldly. He yelled at the Kurelu to get off the Turaba, that it was Wittaia land.

All the sentries except Hanumoak acted swiftly on the assumption that the Wittaia had many others in the rocks behind them; without pausing for their bows and spears, they got off the Turaba so rapidly that big Woknabin sprained his ankle. Hanumoak, the only true warrior in the party, had been sitting a little apart, among the rocks; the Wittaia had not seen him, and, instead of running, Hanumoak remained hidden, reluctant to lose his spear. A good spear was carefully carved and very valuable, and a half-dozen had been left behind. But the Wittaia found the spears and bows and bore them off in triumph. Meanwhile the sentries had raised the alarm, and a terrific howling echoed from the farther bank.

Polik and the rest ran toward the Aike, starting a frightened gray rail from the grass. Other bands led by Yeke Asuk and Weaklekek were strung out across the distance, coming fast. A large company of Wittaia, a hundred spears or more, sprang up suddenly along the crest of the Turaba, and the two tribes hurled insults at each other across the brown, swift silence of the river. In the confusion Hanumoak slipped down among the boulders and returned across the Aike at the land bridge, where the torrent dives beneath a wide ledge of rock.

The enemy, incensed by the recent raids, were clamoring for war. In the weeks past they had lost Huwai, Torobia, and at least four others, casualties of wounds suffered in the wars, while the Kurelu had lost only one man. Their bold appearance on the Tokolik and now the Turaba, with the disgrace of the lost spears, had excited the Kurelu, and war had become inevitable. The Wittaia moved slowly off the Turaba, filing, spears high, down the ridge, and the Kurelu moved out toward the frontier to wait for them. Men of the Kosi-Alua, assembling for the etai, were in war regalia; instead of going to the etai field, they went to the Tokolik. On the flanks of the Waraba another large company of Wittaia watched them come.

The Kurelu filed carefully through the swamp below the Waraba but remained within the cover of the sedges; when they outnumbered the advance Wittaia, the latter retired to the crest, awaiting reinforcements. The withdrawal brought a yell from the Kurelu, who surged onto the flank of the hill; in a short time they had gained the crest and driven the enemy to the west end of the L. In the brief skirmishing which took place Tegearek received an arrow in the small of his back, and a son of Maitmo, kain of the Haiman, was wounded also.

On the Tokolik the men were rallied by Nilik, kain of the Walilo. Nilik is a tall hawk-faced man with a harsh voice and darting eyes, and he was presently engaged in a power struggle with Kurelu. The dispute concerned the ownership of the ap warek—literally, "dead men," the booty—which came of the raid and resultant battle in which Huwai had been killed. The ap warek are held by the great kains, and in the past Kurelu would have received them, but this time Nilik had kept them and shared them with his kinsman Yoroick, in honor of whose son the raid had taken place; Nilik had also claimed the spoils taken from Torobia. Now he harangued the older men and lesser kains as they gathered and sat and smoked. He wore a tight brown head net, like a skull cap, but, shoulders excepted, he was otherwise undecorated: on his shoulders he wore a coat of heavy clay, yellow-sulphurous in color.

Midday came, in a dead silence. On the west side of the Siobara a large fire had been built, a signal to the Wittaia allies that a war was to take place. By the shelters of the frontier kaios the men waited in the languid drone of flies; most would have preferred the etai, and few went forward to join the warriors who had taken the Waraba. Beneath the great araucaria by the Tokolik, Asok-meke took his arrows, one by one, and scraped them sharp; Asok-meke is too old to fight in the front lines but is still belligerent in the reserves. A bird of the grasslands called now and again, a solitary wistful note which accented the stillness. The blue sky reigned, but the air turned heavy and lugubrious.

On an old man's shoulder, in the sun, a butterfly opened and closed its wings as if to the rhythm of his breathing.

A band came from the Aike, led by Weaklekek. They moved directly across the Tokolik and into the swamp, and their passage caused an unspoken stir: all but the oldest men rose to their feet and followed Weaklekek to the Waraba. The Wittaia held the long side on the L, and the Kurelu the short: the Wittaia side of the corner of the L would be the fighting ground. Fighting began almost immediately.

The corner of the L forms the high point of the ridge, a reed-covered knoll perhaps eighty feet above the swamp; the advance Kurelu were gathered here. Husuk was there, in shoulders of gray clay, and Limo and Weaklekek and a scattering of warriors good and bad: the main group of the Kurelu remained at the northern end, while a detachment of warriors, constantly replaced, fought on the forward line. The line extended from a grassy hollow in the corner of the L, below the knoll, up into the large rocks of the ridge crest. The fighting was still pantomimed, though a few arrows flew; men of both sides darted out in seizures of bravado, pranced and feinted with their spears, fled back again. The Wittaia warriors were more gaudy than the Kurelu: one man in feathers of black and red wore tusks in his nostrils which stuck straight out to the sides instead of curling down, and another had large white egret feathers in a cape which flew the whole length of his back.

All took chances to display their splendor, but the Wittaia took more chances than the Kurelu, whose apathy about the war was evident in their small numbers. The Wittaia had come in hundreds, and large parties of warriors were posted back along the ridge, with a reserve company of nearly two hundred men in a huge black spear-thorned phalanx at the base of the Siobara.

On the knoll the Kurelu laughed indulgently at the bravado of the elege Siloba, who took wild chances in the forays, glancing backward for approval. Siloba is feckless and frequently wounded. A roar went up when three brave warriors ran into the rocks to seize a Wittaia spear; Asikanalek, reaching it, was set upon by eight or more Wittaia who came at him from above, but he did not lose his head. He backed off slowly into the shelter of the rocks on his own side, holding the spearmen at bay until the moment for rushing him had passed. A cheer went up; the spectators on the knoll shook their heads and laughed.

Only Nilik and Maitmo were excited, the first because he was asserting his new leadership, the second because his son had been wounded in the morning: Maitmo had been the most fanatic of the kains ever since the day a few moons earlier when three of his wives had been killed by the Wittaia. But their fierce yelling failed to stir the warriors, many of whom had started to move back toward the swamp, in the direction of the etai field. Only a few among those at the fore fought with intensity, kept company by Woluklek and a scattering of leggy boys, brave and unfeathered, with small wobbly spears and scraggy bows. Siloba, wounded in the foot, limped back self-consciously, clutching the prized arrow tip where all could see it; he had chosen a look of worried modesty to conceal his pride, as if to say, I did only what I could. Woluklek, with the immunity of an innocent, took desperate chances aimlessly, gathering enemy arrows with a happy smile as if he were gathering up nuts, and forgetting to fire any of his own. Weaklekek, Apeore, Hanumoak, and Walimo gave spine to the Kurelu line, while U-mue, brandishing his spear in the second rank, shrieked menace. Walimo had smeared his lower half with reddish clay, like tights; he skipped frantically as a spear caromed off his thigh but returned again to the front line, leaping and bounding uselessly in the panic of his own bravado. But most of the Wilihiman-Walalua declined to join the battle, so much so that Maitmo, ranging up and down, shouted out at them his contempt.

Below in the hollow, Aloro, disreputable beneath a soiled white crown, fought beside some Kosi-Alua. Speared through the arm only ten days before in a war on the north frontier, he stalked and circled, aiming steadily and firing from the hip. With weapons in his hands he attains grace, as if the bow brought his body into balance. Aloro moved up the hill and down, hunting his chance; he remained forward all the afternoon, when even Weaklekek had returned to the knoll to rest. His arrows, sailing viciously across the tops of rocks, kept his opponents low and wary. In battle Aloro looks peaceful, almost sleepy.

But the Kurelu gravitated to the north tip of the Waraba, ignoring the catcalls of the enemy. In the late afternoon, they staged a preliminary etai, jumping in a circle as they chanted, and a few had already started through the swamp when the Wittaia howled out their frustration and surged forward. They outnumbered the Kurelu, and they seriously outnumbered the Kurelu who wished to fight: in a few minutes they had overrun the lines and taken command of the high knoll. A myzomela, strayed across the battlefield, bounded upward on the wave of noise; the sunlight caught on its crimson cordon as it vanished back into the dull greens of the land.

The Kurelu had backed into the swamp, all but a small company of warriors marshaled by Husuk and Weaklekek. A horde of Wittaia danced down from the hilltop. The howling was immense, seeming to swell, to fill the twilight like a thunder, and the Wittaia, white-tusked and feathered, shattered the long line of the hill, leaping and squatting with the glinting spears; their gleaming bodies, bending, weaving, stretched to throw a spear, were magnificent and grim in the strange light of the failing sky.

The Kurelu were also grim and struggled to withstand them. The fighting was suddenly in savage earnest, with neither taunts nor braggadocio. The arrows crossed one another in mid-air, dropping low and fast as the lines closed; a Wittaia and a Kurelu, nearly colliding by mistake, fought each other off with a clash of spears. All the warriors were crouching now, to avoid getting hit in the stomach or the chest, for the man thus wounded was more likely than not to die. They moved across the hillside, squatting low, swift as great spiders. Husuk moved among the men, touching and reassuring them, but the wounded were already coming back; a man clutched an arrow that protruded from his upper leg, and Wakilu of Sulaki held one that was buried in his inner thigh, below the groin. Wakilu had sunk down just beyond the fighting, and the men who operated on him peered warily over his shoulder: when the arrow sprang free, with a rush of blood, the men laughed in relief and hurried toward the rear. Wakilu's wound was not serious, but it became infected, and two moons later he would die.

A man came back with an arrow through the skin of his head, along the temple; the arrow protruded like a grotesque feather. Another sprouted foolishly from a young warrior's right buttock; he returned unhappily to the end of the ridge and sprawled on all fours while an old man dug it out. The warrior grunted with each tug and smiled thinly with relief when it was over. Other wounded hobbled back, and even loud Huonke had miscalculated; he had been speared in the upper leg, and he hastened rearward in consternation, his furtive face glancing back over his shoulder. Walimo was wounded in the shoulder, and Hanumoak caught an arrow on the hipbone, but neither wound was serious, and nobody on either side was killed outright, though a Wittaia was seriously speared and a Kosi-Alua was wounded badly in the breast. Siba had come late to the war, but in the final battle he was struck in the chest, just at the right nipple.

More than fifteen of the Kurelu were wounded, and the battle line fell apart. Another surge of the Wittaia drove the Kurelu entirely off the ridge. The Wittaia screeched and threatened from above, led by two fierce warriors who had been in the forefront all day. One of these was young and swift, with a fixed, quiet grin, the other a wild-mouthed man whose long corded hair flopped crazily on his shoulders as he leapt; from below, the two were silhouetted on the twilight sun, black spears shivering.

With a concerted hail of arrows, the Kurelu regained a foothold on the Waraba. But dark was near, and the Wittaia had already claimed the victory, moving off in triumph. Both sides held a brief dance of victory: the Kurelu, despite the defeat they had suffered, were proud that they had done as well with such small numbers.

Kurelu himself had come and looked morose. He sat

alone in the tall grass, taking no part, as if he had learned, just at that moment, that Nilik meant to claim the spoils of war.

■ Among those injured on the Waraba, the only man pleased with his wound was Walimo. Walimo's striking dress and warlike behavior, unremarkable in the past, have been encouraged by special circumstances: he has been warned by Husuk that such behavior might save his life.

Some time ago Walimo paid a visit to clansmen among the Huwikiak, on the far side of the Baliem. The Huwikiak are allies of the Wittaia, and the journey was therefore a very foolish one. Still, he returned safely, traveling by night. The kains were very angry, thinking it bad luck for a man to traffic with the enemy: treachery is punishable by death, and while Walimo's act was in no way subversive, his airy personality was not taken into account. Wereklowe and Maitmo wish to kill him, and either he must run away or try to redeem himself before it is too late.

Community punishment is rare and very serious, in the exceptional cases when it is not fatal. Some years ago a man of the Mokoko tribe on the far side of the Baliem was punished by his own village for setting fires in the fields. He had a taste for mice and rats, which he would catch by burning off the grass hiding their holes; when his fires endangered the crops of his neighbors, he was warned to give them up. But his appetite was too strong for him, and one day he was seized and held face down over a new fire of his own making.

This man is a familiar figure along the banks of the Baliem. He wears a fine mikak and an enormous headdress of white feathers, framing a hideous shrunk face with neither nose nor mouth. There is a small slit through which food may be passed and from which a muffled sound fights free, like a voice calling in a grave.

■ The etai for Torobia's death was held the following day. The men of Wuperainma did not go to special pains for the etai, especially since three of their best men had been hurt the day before. Hanumoak, by morning, only winced a little when he moved, though he would limp for a few days to come, and Tegearek sewed stolidly at a new shell bib, for he is not a man readily disconcerted, even by an arrow in his back. Behind him Siba sat, precisely where Tuesike had sat two weeks before; like Tuesike, he would survive, but he was in severe pain. His whole torso was wrapped in taro leaves bound so tightly with vine that he could scarcely get a breath, and his eyes bulged; his horim had been snapped off like the broken bone of a bird and had not been replaced. After a while he slumped onto one side, clutching himself, and began to groan. Then he crept painfully to the dark wall in the back, and crouched there, facing it. A second groan seemed less in pain than in fear, and his friends glanced at one another in discomfort.

Most of the warriors retained their decoration of the day before, including Weaklekek, who is the rare warrior without vanity. He is content with his old modest battered bib and rarely or never wears other decoration; as fast as Weaklekek acquires wealth, he gives it all away.

Weaklekek's dignity and generosity are important criteria for true kainship, and he ranks with Limo as an important war kain of the Alua. But Weaklekek is more fearless and less ruthless than is good for him, and he may not survive to take a place as one of the great leaders. His clansman Limo will survive, tall, classic Limo with very large eyes full of reserve power and contempt, who on the morning of etai sat eating hiperi in Weaklekek's pilai, not with the gusto and pleasure of his host, but with a sort of remote arrogance, pointed up by his long tobacco pipe and by the largest shell bib in the Kurelu. One is caught by Limo's face and drowns in the coldness of his eyes.

Around them sat Asukwan and other warriors of the pilai, all dressed far more splendidly than Weaklekek himself. Weaklekek squatted on his haunches, scraping potash from a sweet potato, delighted with everyone and everything. From time to time he took up a new horim, still green, and blew through it approvingly.

Weaklekek, trailed by Asukwan, went to the knoll called Anelarok for the preliminary etai. There the men had gathered in midmorning and begun to sing. Tekman Bio led the singing in his high, strange voice, as one man always does, and the others chanted in response. On Tekman Bio's head the strange blue-veined plume from the head of a bird of paradise was mounted on the long black tail plume of another. As he sang he plucked the hair from the buttocks and back legs of a warrior prostrate on the ground, assisted by a man seated on the other side. The Kurelu consider all body hair unsightly and pick ceaselessly at those parts of one another which are difficult for the owner of the hair to reach: the plucking of backs, like the neatening of beards and the reciprocal search for head lice, is an important part of the etai's morning ritual. Asok-meke, too cross and hairy to be bothered, has made himself an exception: he has strange little tufts like black woolly lint all over him. Asok-meke sang too, in a kind of exasperated groan, and even the man on his stomach sang, his buttocks rising and falling with the effort.

The singing was interrupted by a loud squalling from the women of Wuperainma. The wife of Tegearek had run away and was at this moment on her way to the Siep-Kosi; she could not have been popular among the women, who had decided to betray her.

Her path led behind Homaklep and Abukumo and up into the mountains, and Tegearek moved without haste to cut her off. He dragged her back to Wuperainma, where he beat her. She uttered a series of long, pure screams, which rang above the chant of etai, but the screams themselves were largely ritual, part of her shame and penance.

Nilik came early to the Liberek. He had brought with him the trophy bundle; there were seven or eight fine spears, some bows and arrows, a cassowary whisk, and a small grass packet containing the tufts of Torobia's hair. The "dead men" were lashed to a pole stuck in the ground at the head of the field, and Nilik sat beneath them at the fire, in the central place. He wore his wig of ten thousand seeds, red seeds and black, and over the wig a white crown of egret feathers. The wig flew when he stood up to shout, and when he danced; at other times it hung forward like a hood, and his eyes peered sharply from beneath it.

In a pause in the dancing, Polik's men—those who had killed Torobia—came to the fire and took up the trophies. With these they charged to the center of the field, where the trophies were held aloft. A great sighing shout arose, and the men rushed back again in a close avalanche of bodies, *O-way-y-O.*

Polik himself was present, in his monumental crown. He was smiling his strange smile, benign and absent-minded, but at the end of the afternoon he spoke rapidly and fiercely to Nilik, apparently disputing the "dead men." Nilik spoke fiercely in return, and at the end of the dispute he moved to the pole and untied the trophies: these he entrusted to two of his men, then wrenched the sapling itself out of the ground. The men went away with the trophies, and Nilik stalked behind them, the sapling on his shoulder, in the direction of the mountains.

■ Ekapuwe walked up and down the sili yard, alone in the village of Lokoparek; as she walked she sang softly to her new baby, who slept, invisible, far down in the bottom folds of her empty net. The net was a new one, dyed in a red and blue pattern. Ekapuwe was restless, and her walking served to rock the baby. When she was not singing, she would smoke, using the long holder which, despite her bony feet and hanging breasts, gave her a certain elegance. In the distance, under the cliff wall, some Kosi-Alua were cutting wood, and the tock of the stone adze echoed monotonously across the forest.

Before long the sound ceased, for war had been called on the northwest frontier, and the woodsmen had departed. Husuk had come that morning to fetch Wereklowe, and some other warriors had gone along. U-mue did not go: he was cutting a new field in the pandanus forest of Lokoparek. To break the silence, Ekapuwe yelled at her husband, but he did not answer.

■ Aku, who may have known eight springs, and her friends Eken of Homaklep and Werekma, the pretty daughter of Loliluk, wandered in the afternoon onto the hillsides. Each of the thin children picked a bouquet of bright flowers, mostly the blossoms of the yellow rhododendron, *nektamuk*, but also red ginger, *eroaloali*, the small white rhododendron, *wamasi*, with its sweet spicy smell, a burmannia, *le*, which is a strange pale blue, and two varieties of ground orchid, one small and purple, the other large and brown and white and lavender.

The girls carried their flowers for a little while, strolling down through the coolness of the evergreens by the spring of Homuak. Above, the war kains sat around the council fire, against the wall of fern, and the children stood apart, pressed to the trees. Small bellies and behinds sticking out, the flowers clasped in hands folded neatly on their skirts of reed, they stared at the fierce old men. Word had come that a woman of the enemy had drowned in the Baliem. Women's suicide in the Baliem occurs from time to time, but the cause of this death was unknown. The death of a woman was not the same as the death of a man, but it was glad tidings all the same.

The children went up onto the hill again. They did not know quite why they had picked the flowers, which were of no use or consequence, and, looking at one another, they began to giggle, putting their hands into their mouths. Then Aku and Eken and Werekma picked their bouquets to pieces, and, because it rained during that night, the fallen blossoms were still living the next day.

■ The time of the full moon is past, and a slow rain has come again, filling the valley sky with pale gray clouds. With the rain's return, the fresh air of the southeast trades has died away, and the yellow gardenia is all but gone. The Aike River, bony with derelict trees after the dry spell, is speckled with large flocks of fledgling ducks, and the wood swallows, their nesting done, come in small flocks to the araucarias.

Weaklekek and his wife went up into the mountains, to the oak forest and beyond, in search of fresh lisanika leaves for his tobacco. Most of the other men worked in the fields, though Tegearek, glad of the distraction, spent much of the morning chasing a small snake up and down the ditch of someone else's garden, shouting and thrashing as if his life depended on it. His own new garden, though begun at the same time, has fallen far behind the garden of Werene.

Ekali of Wuperainma left on a trading journey to the Yali people, four days northeastward of the valley; he and his companions carried with them nets and stone adzes and will return within a fortnight with fine bird feathers.

Ekali took the mountain trail which climbs from the

valley floor, two hours away in the northern Kurelu; it continues past the salt wells at Iluerainma, over the ridge, and into the Pass Valley, and from there in a three-day journey to the Yali Valley, called the Yalimo. The Yalimo, unlike the Baliem—the latter, in the dimensions of its broad, level plain, is unique in all the highlands—is steep and is still forested; therefore the Yali peoples have remained skilled hunters. Shifting agriculture is still the common practice: the gardens are less expert than those in the Baliem, and the pigs fewer.

The Baliem tribes depend on the Yali peoples for certain articles which have vanished, in their own lands, with the destruction of the forests. The Yali supplies the great bulk of the fine decorative feathers, including plumes of the various birds of paradise. The furs come also from the Yali: such creatures as the cuscus and tree kangaroo, whose pelts adorn the crowns and armlets and horims, are now so scarce even in the upper forests of the rim that only one old man of Sulaki still goes in the nights of the full moon to hunt them. Certain woods which must once have flourished in the Baliem are now imported from the Yali, including the *bial* wood of the beautiful white spears, the *wio*, a fine dark bow wood, and many others. The handsome spear laurel, though it still occurs in the Baliem, is cut as fast as it is found; it will soon vanish from the cloud forests of the rim, and already the best laurel spears come from across the mountains.

In exchange for articles of feathers, fur, and wood, the Kurelu bring stone adzes, shell goods, pigs, and woven articles. Yeke Asuk only quite recently has acquired from the Yali people an opossum crown and a fine spear sapling in exchange for an adze and other articles; the fur alone required an adze in payment. The green and black stone of the adzes, used also in the holy stones, does not come from the Baliem, where it is unknown; it arrives there by an obscure set of trade routes, probably over the mountains from the eastward, and may well originate some hundreds of miles and many years away, in the far volcanic ranges of Papua. The shells, in turn, pass along from tribe to tribe, over trade routes from the southern coast; the coast is far away, beyond the experience of the akuni, who have no comprehension of the sea. The shells are the chief medium of exchange and travel endlessly, in a series of slow transfers, pausing in a pilai here, a shell belt there, for a month, a decade, or a century, only to pass onward from brown hand to hand.

■ Uwar and Kabilek are expert at a game called *sikoko,* which is played with rattan hoops and small cane spears; the boys keep their own hoops among their few possessions in the pilai. Though games are numerous, toys kept by the children from one day to the next are few. They include a bull-roarer—a slat of wood on the end of a string, which produces, when whirled, a loud hollow noise—a simple swing in which a vine is lashed to the middle of a board, and the large purple bulb of the banana tree, also on a string: the latter may be twirled in the air below the hand or towed on the ground behind, a technique favored by Uwar's small round brother, Natorek.

The rules of sikoko are simple, but the game is difficult. One boy rolls the hoops one after another across a length of ground, and, as they pass, the other must hurl the spears through them in such a way that the spear sticks into the ground with the hoop spinning on it. The hoops are hurled at full force, so that they bounce high and erratically as they go, but even so, the boys do not miss often. Unlike most other yegerek, who crowd the hoop and try to punch the spear through at the last second, Uwar and Kabilek keep a distance and impale the hoop with a whipping sidearm throw: Uwar is the only boy who is left-handed. Sometimes they bounce the hoops over the araucaria roots at Homuak, and sometimes they play on a downhill path below Wuperainma; at these times they are watched by Natorek and Oluma, who work as a pair under the direction of the former. Both little boys are fat and strong and truculent —at three, they are as old as fat men ever get among the akuni—and do everything not only together but simultaneously. Today, when Natorek marched into the weeds and squatted, Oluma took up a position right beside him; shoulder to shoulder, they relieved their small bodies in unison, neat and quick as birds, the pair of heads glaring balefully at the world across the grass tops.

The nostrils and upper lips of both Oluma and Natorek, like those of almost all the children and a number of adults as well, are chronically encrusted with dried mucus—the symptom of the one common ailment, a respiratory infection, in an otherwise strong, healthy, and clear-skinned people. Suspended mucus, rising and falling casually, is a feature of the akuni face, since hawking and spitting and blowing the nose are considered very rude.

Unlike Oluma and Natorek, Uwar and Kabilek are beautiful, in the large-eyed, carved-featured way of certain akuni, though the wild brightness in Uwar's face is replaced, in Kabilek, by wistful sadness; Kabilek appears to long for something he will never know.

As the only yegerek in U-mue's sili, Uwar and Kabilek

are together often, but they are in no way alike and could not really be called friends. Each time they play sikoko the game ends uncomfortably, for while Kabilek is gentle and resigned, Uwar burns with a quiet ferocity and works himself to a pitch of intensity in which, smiling still in a cold, glittering way, he contrives to disrupt the game. He hurls the hoops when Kabilek is not ready, or plays carelessly, in languid contempt, and finally he may hurl the hoop at his opponent or at one of the children looking on. At these moments he is beside himself, there is no real communication with him. The other children, and the adults as well, greet Uwar with deference, for he is quite exceptional, but he is not well liked. Uwar was born to lead and has small need for friendship.

Uwar is named for the Uwar River, which flows through the land of the Siep-Kosi, where he was born; later his mother came to the land of the Kurelu and married Loliluk. The latter is deceptive in appearance, a small timid-looking man in an old brown head net, puttering about the sili. Loliluk never wears shells or feathers and moves quietly. Nevertheless, he is said to have killed five, two of these on the occasion on which he received his present name. The name, which means "Bones Ungathered," commemorates the day when, a daughter having died, he rushed away into the mountains even before the funeral was finished and there, in a region beyond Lokoparek, then in enemy territory, killed two people in a fit of grief.

Ekali, father of Kabilek, is also deceptive in appearance. He is a tall man with a strong voice, strong face, but in fact he is uncertain of himself, afraid in war, yet unresigned to his own fear, a blusterer. At one time Ekali moved away to the Siep-Kosi, where in one way or another he made himself so unpopular that he was called Lan-i—"Go There," in the sense of "Go on Back to Your Own People." His new name, awarded since his return, describes the reaction of his young wife to his habit of gobbling up the best bits of food before the food leaves the cooking shed, rather than sharing it in the pilai with the other men; Ekali means "Shame."

Though Ekali is intelligent, and has gained a certain wealth in pigs as a result of trading journeys to the Yali people, his ambiguous reputation may put his son Kabilek at a disadvantage in regard to Uwar.

■ Yesterday the Wittaia asked for war, but the Kurelu, anxious to work their fields, refused it. Today the enemy staged a garden raid, to revenge the one in which Huwai had been killed. By midday a large party of them had crept to the belt of woods which separates U-mue's kaio from the Tokolik. Women were scattered through the fields, but none came near the ambush point. In the late afternoon, exasperated, the Wittaia rushed out and set fire to U-mue's shelter, then retired to the Tokolik. Their jeering howl was answered by the Kurelu, and warriors ran for the frontier; U-mue himself was at Homuak and at the first alarm leapt to his feet, screeching maniacally. Somehow he had grasped from the discordant shouts that the shelter was his own, for the prospect of battle does not ordinarily excite him; he ran off to fetch his spear. Others were already on their way. The young warriors ran in files along the paths among the purple sweet potatoes, among them Yeke Asuk, whose pale brown form among the dark bodies of the other men was luminous in the failing light.

An audience of yegerek scrambled up the grassy slope behind the araucarias. Tukum, on the way, was stung on the foot by a bee. He sat down on a rock like a sad troll and clutched at the foot. Behind him, Uwar located the small beehive in the grass: it was gray and papery and had white larvae in it. Without giving a bite to its discoverer, Uwar popped the hive into his mouth and ate it, rubbing his stomach in satisfaction.

Against the dusk the fire plume of the burning shelter was bright, and its white smoke rose toward the wreath of cloud at the peak of Arolik.

The warriors picked their way uneasily through the wood toward the Tokolik; they knew that the reeds might conceal the waiting enemy. A *mokoko* heron rose like a gray shade, venting its grim croak, as other men came on from the Liberek. Fighting broke out immediately, to fierce howling, and from the distance the white feathers could be seen between the trees, spinning disembodied in the gathering darkness. There were nearly one hundred Wittaia, and though the skirmish lasted but a few minutes, they wounded four of the outnumbered Kurelu. At dark both sides withdrew, for dark is the hour of the ghosts; the Wittaia built a high, bright fire at the east end of the Tokolik but deserted it after a short while and continued homeward.

The man of the Kosi-Alua speared in the last moon by Tegearek and Yeke Asuk was speared again, this time along the side of his neck. Yeke Asuk, fighting nearby, was arrowed in the back. The arrow was removed by Aloro, but a short time later Aloro himself was wounded in the front part of his thigh. Aloro is wounded more often than any other warrior, not because he is careless or reckless but because he never leaves the battle line. One day he will be wounded mortally.

Two days later the Wittaia appeared in battle array again, having moved boldly to the wooded strip between the Tokolik and the shell of U-mue's shelter. Again the Kurelu went out to meet them, though not nearly numerous enough to fight. They gathered watchfully at the end of the Tokolik, while opposite them several hundred of the enemy massed in ranks. Weaklekek, Asikanalek, and Husuk circled apprehensively among the few young warriors who moved out to face the taunting party of Wittaia; more Wittaia lined the Waraba. A brief skirmish took place in which Husuk threw and lost his fine dark spear; annoyed, he walked around in the front line without a weapon, hands folded behind his back. Plainly the Kurelu were waiting for the rain, which swept in dense palls along the northeast mountains; the men gave way in spite of Maitmo, who ran forward to rally them, screeching with his usual belligerence.

A party of Wittaia had crept through the swamp from the Waraba and appeared suddenly on the flank; a roar broke out, and the Kurelu fled. The Wittaia did not press them. Light airs from the west swung around and freshened, bearing the rain out of the north; the north wind is a rare cold wind, and both tribes withdrew, hugging their shoulders.

Asukwan of Homaklep returned by way of Homuak. Like a little boy, using excited jabbing motions, he described to foolish Woknabin his own deeds of heroism. Woknabin, still lame from two arrow wounds suffered on the Tokolik, listened to Asukwan's tale with awe. Woknabin is a huge kindly man, blind in one eye and simple; he is a brave warrior and a poor one. Woknabin's name was given in childhood; he was terrified, each time his mother left the sili, that she would go away from him forever. His name, which suits the sad entreaty in his face, means "Take Me with You."

■ The arrow which struck Yeke Asuk entered near his right shoulder blade and penetrated toward the center of his chest, causing injury to the *etai-eken*—literally, the "seed of singing"—the life energy, the soul. The etai-eken, which occurs near the region of the diaphragm, varies in size according to the spiritual progress of each person, but it is always present except in smallest infants. Pigs also have etai-eken, but dogs and other animals have none.

The belly of Yeke Asuk was cut with a bamboo knife in several places to drain off the "black blood," and the vein of his arm punctured with a pig-bone needle, after which he was bound up tightly in a poultice of taro leaves. He slept well but this morning was in severe pain. He was helped down from the sleeping loft, and many men came to see him. Tuesike helped Yeke Asuk to a sitting position and, with loud Huonke, applied wet leaves of hiperi to the arrow hole and to the bleeding wound, binding him tight again with gleaming purple strips of fresh banana leaf. Yeke Asuk's wound is serious, but not serious enough to justify the catching and killing of small animals.

Outside, squatting in the smoke of a yard fire, U-mue made fetishes for his brother. Yeke Asuk was not well enough to come out, and Uwar and Kabilek, each holding a fetish high in the air, ran back and forth before the entrance of the pilai. Then they fled away down the yard, holding the canes high between them in a kind of arch. Both fetishes were planted outside the village, by the paths leading toward Wittaia land. Like the fetish made for Tuesike, they were intended to warn away unfriendly spirits.

The women's life, and that of the pigs and children, trudged ahead. Hiperi and *toa*, a large succulent grass, were cooking in the shed, and the smoke rose through the dark wet straw the whole length of the roof. Ekapuwe had come down the night before from Lokoparek and was greeting the visitors in a cheery manner. Holake, a little girl with rusty rag-doll hair, stood pigeon-toed and proud, hands clasped tightly on the headband of her net; in the net was Ekapuwe's new baby. From time to time Holake walked it up and down the yard, and the invisible child, which has passed most of its life to date within the net, murmured contentedly, a pale finger poking outward toward the sun like a small tendril. Beside Holake marched her small fat brother Oluma, who is Natorek's friend and double. Holake and Oluma are the children of Wereklowe; their mother came long ago to live in U-mue's sili, because of excessive beatings administered by her husband. The mother looks older than she is, but at moments she smiles the same shy merry smile as her ragtag little girl. Though she is said to be the woman of Yeke Asuk, she did not seem in the least upset about her lover's peril.

A yellow hog barged forth from the gourd garden. It snuffed, tail wagging, among the vegetable skins and husks cast out before the pilai and consumed a discarded butt of sweet potato with loud, chopping relish, contemptuous of all the world beyond its mouth. As it ate, it cocked a small evil eye, more like a sore, on guard against the man or pig who might attempt to interfere with its ingestion.

Some large hiperi were handed from the cooking shed, and the men returned into the pilai to consume them. Polik had come and took advantage of the visit to appraise a fine cowrie belt; he stretched it around the fireplace. In the corner Hanumoak, reaching for his shell bib hanging on the wall, saw the larger bib which belongs to Yeke Asuk and tried it on. He was watched by Huonke, who, caught watching, smiled his furtive smile, and Hanumoak returned the smile, though coldly. He removed the shell bib of the wounded man and tied on his own.

■ One afternoon Weaklekek obtained a fine small pig. Pigs are normally not eaten without ceremonial reason, but a reason was found, as it often is, and in the afternoon

Weaklekek drove an arrow into the pig's lungs. The pig ran squalling around the yard, but in a little while it was caught again, and Palek stood with his foot upon it until it died.

Weaklekek singed the pig on a fire in the cooking shed. He dressed it out, with the help of Asok-meke, on a bed of fern, cutting it up with a bamboo knife and a small stone adze. Asok-meke drew the tripes out from the viscera and handed them to the boy Supuk, who took them to the stream to wash them.

Weaklekek's wife Lakaloklek, farther down the long hall of the shed, had built a large fire to heat rocks. Lakaloklek's old mother sat alone in the dense smoke like a brown bundle, as if, after so many years, smoke had replaced air as her natural element; she watched the dressing of the pig with the slack avidity of old age. The women were joined by Weaklekek's youngest wife, just in from the fields; she swung her nets of gourds and hiperi into the corner. She also swung down her daughter, placing her next to the old woman. The little girl is the favorite of Weaklekek and wears two pretty cowries and a string of snails. The old woman stroked the child and showed to it a baby piglet which she carried with her in her own bottomless net. Then the young wife, returning, took the baby from her. While the child sucked at her breast, the mother smoked, using the long holder; her chin rested on the baby's head.

Supuk returned, bringing the tripe, but Lakaloklek sent him out again to put the pigs into their stalls; the child went promptly, without grumbling. Lakaloklek and the young wife, with the mother of Supuk, were whirling like three witches in the smoke, hair and breasts flying: they took up the heated stones with long stick tongs and placed them in the pit.

Lakaloklek is elfin and pretty in appearance, though

she wears a smear of black grease across her face and her hair hangs down across her eyes. She is gay and quick in all her movements, in no way oppressed by her woman's life. Supuk's mother is a big woman with the plaintive jollity of middle years, and the young wife, who can't yet be fifteen, is graceful and big-breasted, complete in the thick torpid way of a fleshy, unopened flower. From the inferno of the smoke, the three women laughed.

Originally this young wife was to have married Supuk's father, but, arriving in the sili for the first time, she fell in love immediately with Weaklekek; when she refused to go to Palek, Weaklekek accepted her philosophically into his household. Palek, having small choice in the matter, was philosophical about it also.

Palek's son Wamatue appeared, a diminutive boy with red hair; the red hair, of a deep rust color, is typical of the children and glows like a halo on their dark heads when the sun is low, toward twilight. Wamatue wore fern bracelets on his wrists, and a miniature horim. The horim was the diameter of an arrow, too small even for Wamatue; it hung in a token way in the area of his navel. Wamatue is a shy sort of creature and stood camouflaged in the brown shadows by the entrance, thinking long thoughts, but finally his presence was remarked upon, and he came forward.

For nearly an hour the pig steamed with fine redolence, and in this time the chortling of the honey eaters in the casuarina trees around the village gave way to the rigid twilight chant of huge cicadas. Weaklekek sat off to one side, holding his baby daughter on his lap; he squeezed her in inarticulate delight, and once he placed his lips against her head in a sort of mute instinctive kiss. Weaklekek is ashamed of nothing, and the great life in him shines outward, with nothing withheld behind the eyes.

Asukwan, lank and indolent, arrived in time to help

take the browned thatch from the fire. When this was done he sat down to one side to await his dinner. Wamatue sat next to him, shoulder to shoulder, and Asukwan punched the little boy playfully on the back. Wamatue cried out, seeking attention from his mother. His mother did not bother with him, and he stopped.

The food was laid on fresh banana fronds: except for the sliver knife of bamboo and a concave length of bark which serves as a sort of tray for discarded scraps, there are no utensils of any kind. Though clays of several colors are common in the valley, the art of pottery has not been learned; the people are content with their string nets, leaf packets, and small water gourds.

Stern Asok-meke, the guest, divided up the meat. The men were given the best pieces, while the women, sitting separately in the darkness, were passed a few poor scraps. The tripes Asok-meke slung disdainfully at the yegerek, who also ate some of the bloodied ferns used in the cooking: all the household consumed hiperi and toa and the spinach-like leaves of mallow, eaten with gray salt from the wells at Iluerainma: the precious salt was sprinkled carefully from a long tube of banana leaf. They ate in silence, without greed or haste.

When the men had retired to the pilai, and the women to the huts across the way, Lakaloklek remained seated by the embers, weaving a new net; the fiber stretched in a long band from her stump fingers to her toes, vibrated by old rhythms of her hands. As she worked she hummed and smiled, at peace in her own world. But soon she too retired, and the fire died.

The sky of night was high with stars shining on other centuries beyond the mountains. This was the time of the night feeding, the nocturnal animals, creeping forth in the last flickers of man's embers. In the shed rats and mice came from the walls with their tight squeakings, and bats on fingered wings flopped to the village—the tiny twilight bat, with its high ascending shriek, and the flying fox, which did not cry but sounded its coming with the quaking flaps of five-foot wings. The bats circled beneath the stars, in the ringing of the tree frogs and the crickets. In the light wind of night weather, the banana fronds stirred with a loud, lonely clacking, and the great dog-faced bats pumped back and forth, thump, thump-thump, thump, to their rude landings on the hanging fruit.

As the night grew, the feeding hour declined, and cold descended from the mountains; the bats vanished, and the rodents withdrew to their dank passages. Even the mosquitoes sought their corners, to shrivel in the dim, dry sleep of insects.

The soft voices in the pilai died, and Weaklekek came out alone, to visit Lakaloklek in her ebeai. The earth turned beneath the stars, and Weaklekek cried out in the night, a pure, sweet cry of pain, and all was quiet.

The nightjar, done with its wide-mouthed hunt for insects, grunted digestively in the black evergreens. Slowly it began its hollow, metronomic tok, tok . . . tok, and the sound wore away the night. Weaklekek came from the ebeai and went into the cooking shed, where he drew a fire from the straw to warm himself and smoke. With his fingers he worked his swollen calf where an arrow tip, broken off, was deep embedded. Of late this old wound had given him much pain.

At first light a dusky green emerged slowly from the gray, and the surrounding woods took shape. Somewhere, on a limb, the nightjar ruffled its loose feathers and blinked its yellow eye; camouflaged like a great moth, it would grow into the wood until night came again. Its place was taken by the honey eater, for this was the morning-of-bird-voices.

Weaklekek, at his small fire, sighed. He squatted there immobile, his silhouette like a statue of black igneous rock against the transient flickering on the walls. A woman came, and they spoke gently to each other, but she moved off to her own shadows and built up her own fire. When it flamed, she took sweet potatoes from a net slumped by the wall and stacked them against the embers.

A mountain pigeon called, and day appeared.

■ Tukum, that morning, found a bird's nest in a pink-flowered myrtle tree. The nest was a miniature cup of soft grass, circled around with bright green sphagnum moss. There were two tiny birds in it, olive and yellow, and, though they had never done so before Tukum found them, they could be made to flutter for short distances.

Tukum carried the nest about all morning, making the little birds fly; they would buzz along on a downward angle, careening inevitably into the ground. The birds delighted Tukum, who talked to them and encouraged them, but he had no recognition of his feeling, any more than Aku and Eken and Werekma had understood why they had picked their flowers. Late in the day he would take them home and eat them.

■ High in the dark cloud forests of the upper Elokera stands a huge beech, and high in this tree hangs a
ponderous nest of the great black hawk. Weaklekek wished
to obtain this hawk, the feathers of which are valuable, and
he set off with his bow and arrow to investigate the nest,
the news of which had spread down to the valley. With him
he took Asukwan, the young warrior of his pilai, who is
credited with a sense of birds and a keen eye. They were
accompanied by Tukum, who is credited with almost nothing.

The three went up the valley along the stream bed of
a tributary, wading the quiet pools under the banks and
leaping from rock to mossy rock; honey eaters and birds of
paradise shrieked at their passing, and mountain pigeons,
veering off, broke the humid airs with the sharp clap of
pigeon wings. Farther on, they took to high ground, crossing abandoned fields; in the hillside woods small flocks of
parakeets, red under wing, criss-crossed the treetops in loud
senseless consternation.

At a place along the trail the grass was crushed and
flattened; Asukwan laughed. He poked the forefinger of one
hand back and forth between the second and third fingers
of the other, and Weaklekek grinned. Tukum, embarrassed,
grinned as well.

In the forest of the upper slopes, with its black mud
and thorned rattan, its hanging shapes and gloom, the pale
clear boles of the canopy trees soared to crests which closed
away the sky; the trail crossed sagging pig fences, and hidden
animals grunted hollowly from the shadows of these dark
pastures. The trail skirted dismal wells where the limestone
had caved in; one well was a hundred feet or more in depth,
and strongly fenced around, though the fence was water-

logged and rotten. Asukwan tossed a stone into the well, and the three exclaimed at the time which passed before the splash resounded. Lagging behind, Tukum tossed another stone, but this time a sound came back immediately, for Tukum's stone, barely clearing the edge, had fallen on a ledge inside the rim. Tukum glared balefully at the well and trotted onward.

Farther still, in a steep clearing, lay a new pig village, perched on a ledge of mud. Here miniature blue butterflies fluttered like gentian petals, alighting as one on the mud's black gleam and all but vanishing, for with closed wings they were nothing more than small scraps of drab gray. Then the blue color would explode again as the butterflies danced in their odd motion. Tukum laughed, pronouncing their apt name—si*gisigit.*

At the village a man joined them, and the four went on to the high forest above. A black hawk soared in the gray cloud which hung upon the forest, and Weaklekek whispered at it, making gestures, in order that it circle lower. But the hawk slid off and disappeared, and its nest, when they came to the base of the tree, had no bird at its edge. Weaklekek crept higher on the slope but could not attain the nest level. After a while he came down again and, on the way home, out of frustration, wasted an old arrow in a shot at one of the green parakeets.

■ **The season turned, and the night was clear and** cold. The akuni kept to their warm huts until the morning was well started, and out in the crisp air built high brush fires. The brush was of dead sticks and dry brown leaves, and around a large fire built under the pines the air sparkled with autumn; light filtered down in long delicate columns onto the fallen needles. But in the undergrowth just at the wood edge the sun was hot, and the bushes flowered in the rich green of the valley's ceaseless spring.

Once or twice a year, depending on its current fortunes, a clan will hold a ceremony which renews the power of the holy stones and invigorates and protects in battle the warriors of the clan that holds the stones: the cleaning of the stones with grease of ceremonial pig, wam wisa, is the most sacred of all rituals practiced by the akuni.

In early June a stone ceremony was held by the clan Wilil, in the small village which adjoins Abulopak. Because this place is more safely located than Wuperainma, which lies close to the frontier, the ancestral stones are still maintained there. They are entrusted to the care of big Woknabin, the only Wilil warrior left in the pilai.

As political kain of the southern Wilil, the man most important in the ceremony is U-mue. He came to the sili in the middle of the morning, bringing three of the pigs that would be slaughtered. He was accompanied by Weaklekek, and on the way past Abulopak he stopped by to invite Wereklowe and Polik. None of these men are Wilil, but the feast is attended by kains, relatives, leading warriors, and boys of all the other clans, depending upon their significance and kinship.

Other Wilil were arriving at the sili, and a period of greeting and singing began, in which a crying takes place very like the windy sound of mourning. The crying lasted ten or fifteen minutes and was followed by excited chatter: this part of the ceremony is designed to bury feuds or ill feeling within the clan itself, and to restore an atmosphere of friendship.

Behind the pilai, Aloro and other men cleared all weeds and refuse from a special yard, using digging sticks to scrape the earth. The yard is a pretty and sequestered place, shaded by banana trees and casuarina and pandanus. All morning large hiperi had been brought in, and wood and cooking stones and leaves. Ekali brought a pig, and Apeore and others brought bundles of split timbers; they marched in procession through the sili and stacked the wood under the trees in the small yard. Old cooking pits were cleared and new ones dug. Loliluk appeared and went into the pilai, followed by old Elomaholan. Elomaholan wore his usual array of fur bits and small bags; only the old men carry such bags, which are slung at the waist from a fiber shoulder strap. Elomaholan's voice is high and squeaky, scarcely audible, and he is prey to the young warriors, who sneak up behind him on the paths and shout Wittaia shouts. Elomaholan is a *wisakun*, or "medicine man": the wisakuns, in addition to their medical duties, supervise the rituals pertaining to the holy stones.

U-mue, freshly greased for the occasion, returned into the pilai from the yard, and the sobbing of greeting was resumed. He would utter a phrase, and Wereklowe and the rest would join it at the end, carrying it onward in a soft dying wail. All held their fingers to the bridges of their noses, snuffling wetly.

The pilai itself is small and old and littered as a witch's den. Dark packets cling to all the walls and rafters, and strange-shaped gourds and long straw bundles, old arrows and feathers; the ceiling shines with black accumulated grease. It is no longer a pilai of warriors, all its strongest men having long since moved away. Some years ago the Wilil were having trouble with the other clans living at Abulopak, and U-mue felt it time, in any case, to start a new sili of his own, as a mark of power. Most of the Wilil went with him to Wuperainma, though a few, like Aloro and Woknabin, remained in the old villages.

Fat hiperi and new banana fronds were brought into the pilai, and the leaves were spread out in the rear, before a kind of cupboard on the wall. Elomaholan took eight flat wrapped packets from the cupboard and laid them on the leaves: these were the holy stones, and he peered into the packets to see which was which. Then he sat back and stroked two very big hiperi, which lay between the stones and the fire. After a moment he left the pilai, taking a bow and arrows into the yard; these U-mue would use to kill the pigs. There were no women anywhere in sight.

The gathering men sat on a mat of straw before the pilai, in the sun. Aloro held the first pig by the head, and Woknabin held it by the haunches, and U-mue shot it through the lungs; the process was repeated with the others. U-mue bit his lower lip as his arms strained at the bow; he smiled briefly upon the release of every arrow, as if in response to some private satisfaction.

A large sow was wheedled toward its doom by Tegearek and Apeore; U-mue awaited them, posed on one knee. But the sow broke free repeatedly and had finally to be seized and overpowered by eight strong warriors. They struggled forward, and the men laughed. A lath was held under the pig's chin to support its head, and the pig bellowed, shuddering all over. U-mue shot it gingerly, and it wrenched free, scattering the people in its path. The grunts and laughter of the men made him look cross. More small pigs were brought and killed; they ran bleeding down the yard, in flight from death, and kept on running even after they had fallen.

The big sow was cornered once again and thrown to earth. Tegearek pumped at its lungs with his foot, but it had been shot badly, and Aloro brought a spear to finish it.

It was carried up the yard at last, big dewlaps quaking, its bloodied bristles stiffening in the sun. There were nine pigs in all. Each pig was earmarked, and each man in the company of more than fifty knew not only who had brought them but exactly which was which; they had a very good idea, as well, as to which piece of which pig each man would receive, for the akuni world is a world of protocol and gesture, and those details not preordained by time are painstakingly determined at the slow small fires.

The sow was a long time at the fire, hoisted and kicked and rolled and scraped by Apeore and Tegearek. The dressing of the eight small pigs was already in progress, with two or three men working on each. U-mue stood regally above his people as they bent over their work, the new clay like yellow gold on his black shoulders.

While the pig-dressing proceeded, the sili became quiet once again. Voices drifted from the shadows, to the fitful chopping of stone adze on bone. Behind the pilai, in the yard, a large fire was constructed, like a pyre: here the cooking stones were piled and heated. From the steep hill above the sili men rolled more rocks down the hill; the rocks rumbled through the woods.

Behind the fire, under a pandanus, a small fencing guards the spirits of the dead. The fencing was replaced now with new laths, and its earth weeded and tamped down, to show the spirits that they are not neglected. In the center of the fencing stands a pole of cane with dried ferns attached; this is a warning sign, to indicate that the place must not be violated.

On a rack by the pilai Aloro and Tegearek hung bloody slabs of meat. The hands of both warriors were crimson, and when they were through they drank water from a gourd and wiped their hands with ferns.

Apeore stood in the cooking pit, covering its earthen

sides with long fresh grass; the strands of grass fanned outward several feet from the edge, until the pit looked like a gigantic blossom. Wet leaves were placed around the rim, like a bright green heart of the grass flower; nearby lay purple hiperi. The rock fire popped loudly as a stone exploded; the stones were seized and borne away in tongs to line the pit, mounting the sides until an igneous center had been formed. The stones were covered with wet grass, and the big hiperi laid in the steam. U-mue appeared and shouted orders, but in the general exhilaration everyone else was shouting orders too. The voices meant nothing; everyone worked hard and willingly, with swift efficiency. The hiperi were brought, and more wet grass; the rock fire rose above the ground. More stones were laid into the core, while Polik and others wove the grass sides tight: Polik does not hesitate to work side by side with the warriors, or even the yegerek, though he is an older and a greater kain than U-mue. The tong men came and went, grunting like penitents; they moved mechanically from pit to fire, fire to pit, their six-foot implements clacking dismally on the rocks. On the pit's edge Apeore sprang about, demonic in the steam.

More stones, more leaves, and a large packet of ceremonial pig, wrapped in banana leaf. And still more stones. The stones exploded and a fragment burned hard-faced Huonke, who cried out. More grass, and now a heap of fern, brought forward in huge bundles and sprinkled with water from a sunlit gourd. Tegearek ran forward with the raw sow hide, heaving it flesh down onto the ferns. More pig meat was arranged around it, in fern packets. More stones, more ferns, more silver water, sparkling in the sunlight—and a cry passed on from a distant kaio. *Kaio, kaio,* a man shouted, and there was a brief stir, but no one left the feast: today the other clans must take care of the enemy.

The grass extending outward from the pit was folded upward, enveloping the whole, and the entire edifice, like a small haystack, was bound around with a long coil of rattan. The finished job was handsome and compact, the product of uncounted years of practice; the voices had been profligate, but scarcely a gesture had been wasted.

Aloro removed the spare meat from the rack and hung it in the pilai; it would be eaten in the ceremonies of the second day. Nilik came, walking quietly up the yard: the name Nilik derives from this man's lifelong knack for finding himself in the vicinity of pig-eating. There is something ominous in Nilik's hungry presence, and his arrival seemed foreshadowed by the clouding-over of the sun. The west wind freshened, and the skeletal fronds rising above the roofs stirred in hollow, ruined apprehension. He greeted, unsmiling, Asikanalek and other men who passed him in the yard; they were taking advantage of the cooking time to go and investigate what had happened at the kaios.

The rock fire was stripped in the late afternoon, and the browned ferns spread out in a great mat before the pilai. More than one hundred men had now assembled, and most of them sat in a circle around the ferns. Many of the ferns were eaten, and on the rest the pig meat was arranged. The fatty skin of the large sow was hoisted up, and U-mue sliced it in thin strips: these were passed to the individuals and groups deserving them, and there was no sign of quarreling, for each knew and received his share. The warriors ate the meat with gusto but without haste or greed, saving some of the hot lard next to the hide to rub on their own skins. The grease of the ceremonial pig is beneficial in every way, providing both strength and good appearance; by the end of the afternoon the dark skins were gleaming.

The sow rump and other special cuts had been taken

into the pilai, where U-mue and the old kains had disappeared; there a bundle of new fiber strings, worn at the throat to protect the men in war, were rubbed in wisa grease. The fibers were dispensed to warriors like Yeke Asuk, whose recent wound, a serious one, indicated his need of new protection; Yeke Asuk handed some spare strings through the door, and the men outside grasped at them eagerly.

In the rear of the pilai the holy stones, still wrapped, lay in a line on the banana leaf. The following morning, the cleansing of the stones was to take place. Noisily, in the near-darkness of the hut, the old men ate, while behind them, slung from the rafters, the raw meat dripped cold blood, turning slowly against the chinks of light.

■ For several days the Wittaia, unable to effect a death in battle or in their field raids from the Tokolik, had attempted a raid near the river, coming across early in the morning from the Turaba. The akuni were aware of this, and Weaklekek's kaio had been strengthened by Aloro, Husuk, and other warriors, who attempted to ambush the raiders; despite several alarms, no real battle had occurred.

This morning the men did not go to the kaio, for the feast of the Wilil was taking place. Aloro was an important Wilil, Weaklekek an important guest, and Husuk went off to war on the north frontier. No women were permitted in Weaklekek's fields, and the kaio was abandoned for the day. The Aike frontier, with the looming Turaba, had always been a dangerous place, and as Weaklekek's absence, like all other important matters, was common knowledge, no trouble was expected.

But the day was hot, and in the afternoon the solitary Woluklek went to the river to drink water. The people tire of the stale, silted waters of the ditches—they have no drink but water—and in dry weather will often go a long way to the river, where they squat on the bank and drink slowly and steadily for minutes. Woluklek took with him three little boys who were playing near Mapiatma.

One of the boys was Weake, whose father had been killed the year before on the Waraba. His mother had since run off to the Wittaia, and Weake was now the ward of his uncle, the warrior Huonke. He was a small yegerek, a friend of Tukum, with the large eyes and thick eyebrows which make many of the children beautiful. His name meant "Bad Path," and recently he had hurt his leg. For this reason, on this day, he was slower than his friends.

Near the Aike, on a little rise just short of the side path to Weaklekek's kaio, Woluklek and the three boys were ambushed by a party of Wittaia; the raiders sprang from the low reeds and bushes. Afterward Woluklek was not sure about their numbers, but a raiding party is usually comprised of about thirty men. There was nothing to be done. He dropped his spear and fled, the boys behind him.

All his life Weake had been taught to hate and fear the enemy, and when he saw the strange men with their spears he turned with the rest and ran. But he was not fast enough and was almost immediately run down. He screamed for help, but the others were running for their lives and did not turn. The face of a man, of several men, loomed above him on the bright blue sky, with harsh, loud breathing. The men rammed their spears through him over and over, pinning him to the ground, and then they were gone, and Weake was carried home.

The cry of *Kaio, kaio* carried swiftly past Homuak and to the pig feast: the hot stone fragment that had burned Huonke must have struck him close to the same instant that his nephew had been pierced by the long spears. While the rock fire was still steaming, word came from Abulopak about the boy. The two villages almost adjoin, and the pilai where Weake lived was scarcely a hundred yards across the fences from the Wilil fire. Huonke and Tamugi, his brother-in-law, ran toward Abulopak, where the women's wailing had already started.

In the long yard of the sili two women were kneeling, facing the mute pilai. The sili lies under the mountain, at the north end of the great grove of araucaria, and the pilai at its southern end is shaded by the tall pines against the hill. Inside the pilai were a few old men, and then Asikanalek arrived, and Tamugi and Huonke, and Siloba.

Weake lay on a banana frond beside the fire. He was

still alive, and his clear childish voice seemed out of place in the brown solemnity of the men's round house: it cut through the decrepit snuffling of the old men as the shaft of daylight in the doorway cut through the motes of dust. Weake spoke of his own etai-eken, his seed-of-singing, the life he clung to with all his strength, as if the mourning he could hear must be some dark mistake. *An etai-eken werek!* But I'm alive! Though he not once screamed or whined, his voice was broken as he spoke by little calls of pain, and the blood flowed steadily onto the frond beneath him.

Huonke tried to quiet him, repeating the same terse phrase over and over, like a chant: *Hat nahalok loguluk! Hat nahalok loguluk!*—But you're not going to die! Huonke's voice was the only firm one in the pilai. Tamugi, a large-muscled man whose ready smile is bolder than his nature, sobbed as loudly as he could, while Asikanalek cried silently. The boy's voice answered Huonke obediently—*Oh, oh,* he repeated gently. Yes, yes. But now and then pain or terror overcame him, and he cried out and fought to escape the death that he felt in their hands. Huonke held his left arm and Siloba his right, while Tamugi and Asikanalek held down his legs. Siloba neither talked nor cried, but breathed earnestly and ceaselessly into the boy's ear, oo-Phuh, oo-Phuh: this ritual breathing, which brought health, would be used in the next hour on the wisa pig meat in the pilai of the Wilil.

Weake twisted in their grasp, his back arching; his legs were released and he drew his knees up to his chin, covering the gleam of the neat spear holes at his navel and lower belly. The old cut on the boy's leg still had its green patch of leaf dressing, but the spear holes, like small mouths in his chest and sides, his arm and leg and stomach, had not been tended. Some fresh leaf was brought at last, and the two stomach wounds were bound up hastily, almost carelessly, as if the true purpose of the leaf was to protect the pilai floor from blood; in their distress the men handled him ineptly, and he cried out. The figures hunched over him in the near-darkness, with the old men's snuffling and the steady oo-Phuh, oo-Phuh, and the harsh tearing of the leaf.

Behind Huonke, in the shadows, a woman sat as rigid as a stone. The custom excluding women from the pilai had been waived while the child lived, but nevertheless she maintained silence: when she spoke, but once, out of the darkness, her voice came clear and tragic, like a song. The woman was Huonke's sister, married to Tamugi; she has a wild sad quality in her face and is one of the handsomest women in the Kurelu. She counseled the men to take the boy down to the stream.

Weake clung to life and would not die. His writhings had covered him with blood, and he lay in a pool of darkness. When the woman finished speaking, the men agreed to take him to the water, which, entering his wounds, would leach out the dark blood of illness. He was picked up and carried outside, Siloba holding his head up by the hair. The women in the yard began an outcry, but the men did not pass through the yard. They took Weake through a hole in the back fencing, across a pig pasture, over a stile, down through a small garden to a ditch. There they laid him in the muddy water, so that it lapped up to his chest.

Tamugi did not come. After leaving the pilai with the other men, he kept on going, for the Wilil fire was now open, and he wished some pig. The others accompanied Huonke to the ditch. Soon they too left, for there was nothing to be done. Only Siloba remained, and his friend Yonokma. Yonokma sat in water up to his waist, holding the legs, while Huonke and Siloba, their own lower legs submerged, held the child's arms: Weake's head rested on Huonke's right thigh.

Fitfully Weake talked and now and then cried out: the voice rang through the silent garden, against the soft background of lament and the low hum of the men's voices at the pig feast. Once he cried, *Tegel Tegel* in terror of the spears, and Huonke shouted him down: *Hat ninom werek! Hat ninom werek!*—over and over and over: You are here with us, you are here with us! He said this dully every time Weake called out. You are here with us. Then Weake would resume his own meek, rhythmic *Oh, oh, oh,* of assent. *Hat ninom werek—oh. Hat ninom werek—oh.* His eyes closed, opened wide, and closed again; he seemed to doze. In the muddy ditch, with its water spiders, round black beetles, and detritus of old leaves, his blood drifted peacefully away. Against the firmament above soared the great arches of the banana trees, and the hill crest in a softening light, and the blue sky. Taro and hiperi grew about him, and the blue-flowered spiderwort lined the steep banks. Swiftlets coursed the garden, hunting insects, and the mosquitoes came; the men slapped one another.

Huonke sighed and leaned his head against the bank. In grief, Huonke's face had lost its hard, furtive quality and become handsome. Yonokma, sitting in the water, yawned with cold. Okal, who had gone with Weake to the river, came and stared down at his friend; he looked restless and unhappy and soon went away again.

In his last sleep Weake cried, a small, pure sound which came with every breath. When pain awakened him, he tried to talk, but his voice was faint and drowsy. Siloba breathed fitfully into his ear, but his efforts were disheartened: he only did it, guiltily, when the little boy called out. The small slim body had more than twenty wounds, and the wonder was that the boy had lived so long. But Weake would live until the twilight, asleep in the healing water, while the men attending him grew tired and cold. They coughed and slapped themselves and stared into the water, and the little boy's chest twitched up and down, up and down. Sometimes Siloba poured water on the wounds above the surface, and more blood was drawn forth, flowing down his side. Huonke said, You will stay with us, You will stay with us, and the child said Yes, yes, yes, and did not speak again.

Siba came and stared at the little boy. He broke off the stem of a taro leaf and with it probed the wound on the left side. The belly leaf was floating, and the small horim: Siba attempted to push back a trace of white intestine which protruded near the navel as if, by concealing the evidence of hurt, he might somehow be of help. Weake was failing rapidly and did not cry out; his mouth was open, and his lips had puffed and dried. In the attack he had received a heavy blow, for the side of his face had grown swollen and distorted.

Yonokma leaned forward and removed a bit of straw from the dry lips.

Siba ran across the garden and sprang onto the roof of the pig shed by the fence. There, with a great cracking sound like anger, he broke off a banana frond and hurled it down into the sili yard: this leaf would be the little boy's last bed. Returning, he picked Weake up out of the water and carried him homeward through the garden. Huonke and the two elege trailed Siba through the dusk, shaking with cold.

The small body was limp, with one foot lying on the other, and arms hanging: the blood dripped very slowly on the weeds. His breathing had silenced, and his eyes, half closed, had glazed, like those of a fresh-killed animal. Nilik, Wereklowe, and Polik had come to look at him in his pilai, but it was evening now and he was dead.

The next morning, in the middle of the yard, Huonke and Tamugi built the chair. Four women emerged from the cooking shed and kneeled before it, and more women were already climbing the stile which separated the small sili from the main yard of Wereklowe. The wailing had commenced, and the Alua clan was coming through the fields from all across the southern Kurelu.

In the pilai crouched Asikanalek, twisted by grief. Against the wall, where sunlight filtered through the chinks, sat Weake's small silhouette, already arranged in the position he would be given in the chair. Asikanalek went to him and carried him outside into the day. Still holding the boy, he kneeled in the bright sun before the pilai and, staring upward at the sky, lamented. The men about him looked disheveled and distraught, and Asikanalek's shoulders were smeared with yellow clay. Weake's appearance in the yard had caused a stir among the women; the long day of fierce wailing had begun.

Weake was draped with two large shell bibs, which covered not only his mutilated chest but his torn stomach; the wife of Tamugi kneeled before him, binding up his legs. A man adjusted a new funeral horim to replace the one which had floated off in the brown ditch. Beside the chair Huonke and Tamugi cried out and rubbed their legs. Now and then Huonke would rub his hands together in a strange, stiff-fingered way, and glance about him, as if uneasy in the light of day.

Weake was carried to his chair. His bound legs were hung over the cross piece, and his head was held up by a strip of leaf passed by Tamugi beneath his chin. At the foot of the chair, wailing, Tamugi's wife crouched upon the ground and mopped at it with torn-up grass; she made a circular motion with her hand, scarring the earth. Other women, with girls and small children, filed steadily into the yard and arranged themselves upon the ground before lending their voices to the waves of sound.

A lizard darted from the fence to seize an insect. It gulped busily, its small head switching back and forth, and moved in quick fits and starts back to the shadows. Above, a honey eater bounded to the limb of an albizzia. It too cocked its head, unsettled by the wailing, but calmed before it fled, and sat there preening. In the blue sky over the hill the kites harassed one another, screeching.

The men draped shell belts on Weake, binding his brow with the bright colors and building the belts into a kind of crown. But his head was small, and most of the belts were lain along his sides and down the chair arms. While his attendants scratched and shuffled and thought thoughts, in the warm doldrums of their existence, the child sat alone in cold serenity. He seemed to grieve, nevertheless, as if oppressed by all his trappings; when the women came and draped their nets, they almost hid him in the shadows. Huonke came and smeared him with fresh pig grease, and his shins, still in the sun, took on a gleam: Tukum, himself gleaming from the pig grease of the day before, perched by the fence on a small stone and watched Weake. Tukum was one of the few children who seemed upset, though, like all his companions, he had seen many funerals and would see many more.

A group led by Polik sang wheezily and long the ancient chants of mourning, working the ground with gnarled old toes and rubbing spavined thighs. One of them, his wrinkled skin reptilian, felt peevishly for the tobacco roll buried in the pouch strung on his back. At the same time he contributed his mourning, a frail *woo, woo, woo,* and his long nose ran tumultuously with all the rest: the hole for boars' tusks in his septum had stretched wide with old age, so that the light shone through it.

Some of the men brought belts, and Huonke called out to them in greeting, a loud *wah-h, wah-h,* somehow impertinent, and at the same time self-ingratiating. He and his brother-in-law stood at the chair and haggled covertly about the placement of the belts. While haggling, Tamugi contrived to sob, rolling his eyes in the frank, open face of cant.

Four pigs came forth, and the pilai's owner destroyed them with a kind of sad authority. All four died speedily, snouting the ground, legs kicking, as if they were trying to bore into the earth. They were dressed swiftly, and the yegerek brought logs. Weake's friend Okal was among them: he wore the yellow clay of mourning and a pad of leaves to protect his shoulder from the wood. Like all the other boys, he played a large part in the funeral of his friend.

Nilik, with his affinity for pig, had come in time to finger the bloody pieces, which were hung on a rack behind the chair. Before the chair an old woman beat her breast with stumpy hands: *Aulk, aulk, aulk, aulk,* she cried—*Loo, loo, loo, loo.* The yellow clay was crusted in the skin folds of old breasts, of fallen hips. On the far side of the yard a giant butterfly, dead white and black, danced out of the shadows of the woods and, passing through the akuni, danced back again.

Huonke and Tamugi cried loud and long, mouths trembling and eyes alert. They watched the entrance of Weaklekek, his people behind him carrying three large flat *ye* stones decorated around the middle with fur and cowries. The ye stones are valuable but not sacred, though they may later become so; they are used, like cowrie belts, as a medium of exchange. *Wah! Wah!* cried Huonke. *Wah! Wah!* cried Tamugi. The party stopped before the chair to grieve, and then the men went onward toward the pilai, while the women and small children remained in the upper yard.

Weaklekek sat down quietly and stared into the earth. He was one of Weake's namis, and plainly he blamed himself for the boy's death, since it was his kaio that had been abandoned. But the raid and death were part of akuni existence, and neither Weaklekek nor Woluklek were blamed by any of the others. Even so, Woluklek, who had been unwise enough to lead the three boys to the river, did not come to the funeral at all.

U-mue's wives had come, and with them the children of his sili. Aku and Holake joined the little girls of the village, who were going about on small self-conscious errands; the girls smiled modestly at everyone, in the pretty illusion that all eyes were upon them. Nylare, who is very young, had a poor grasp of the situation, but she took up the wail of mourning, humming it contentedly to her own rhythms. Natorek, escaping his mother repeatedly, played in the narrow path through the massed women; like most akuni children, he accepted his mother's cuffs and cries in great good spirits and smiled expansively at all and everything even when latecomers stepped upon him. He was finally placed under the care of his brother Uwar, who took him to a corner of the yard and picked his lice.

While the food cooked, more men arrived; they overflowed into the woods behind the fencing. The mourning faltered in the midday pall, and nothing stirred. Only the stinging bees, black and yellow, toiled remorselessly on a small open hive, hanging upside down from a pandanus leaf beyond the fence; they hung in the air below the hive, their hair legs dangling, or clasped one another in dry, delicate embrace.

Near the main entrance of Abulopak the tips of the long grasses had been tied together in three places in the weeds: the tied grass forbids trespassing. The signs were a warning to the women, who were nearly two hundred strong, and whose use of the near weeds to urinate had become an offense to Wereklowe.

The rock fire was dismantled, and pig distributed among the men: a few bits were borne to certain women. Asikanalek's daughter Namilike walked around with her small net stuffed with hiperi, passing it out; Weake's little sister Iki Abusake was also there, as pretty in a baby way as Namilike herself. Iki Abusake's curious name means "Hand That Could Not Help Itself," the expression used by the akuni to account for the phenomenon of pig-stealing.

During the eating, soft waves of mourning rose and fell. The sun, sliding down into the west, burned hotly on Weake, and women tried to shield him with their nets. But now the men came forward and stripped him of his belts: the meal was over, and the day's business must begin. The belts were stretched on a frond before the pilai, with the kains seated in a line along each side. When the belts had been admired for a time, and their destiny decided, Wereklowe stood up to dispense them.

Until this time Wereklowe had remained out of the way, ceding the administration of the funeral to Asikanalek: Asikanalek was not only a sub-kain of the Alua but a fine warrior who had killed two, and a close relative of the dead boy. But the exchange of goods was an end purpose of the funeral, and the greatest leader of the clan usually directs it. With a weighty pause between the names, Wereklowe gave out the belts; he was attended by respectful silence. One belt was awarded to Weaklekek, but Weaklekek was still morose and waved it off; in his despair, and despite all his rich gifts, he felt he did not deserve it. Lakaloklek, more practical, came forth and took it in her husband's name.

Despite the great amount of grieving, there seemed small hint of outrage. Huonke complained that the *pavi* should not have done it, but then, Huonke has killed once himself, a harmless woman found near the frontier who had run away from the Siep-Elortak. Revenge there would be, inevitably, but without moral judgments. Nevertheless, for the funeral of a small boy, well over two hundred people had pushed into the small sili: more presents were brought, and more pigs killed, than for the funeral of Ekitamalek, a kain's son and a warrior. Only a few could have come there in real sorrow, and only a few for the exchange of goods. The rest had come because the killing of a child, despite its ancient sanctions, had made them unhappy and uneasy.

His back to Wereklowe, the child sat naked in the chair. The women came to remove the nets, and Weake stirred; his head dropped slowly to his breast, for his chin strap had been loosened from behind. Then suddenly a man began to shout, and a complete silence fell. The speaker was Polik, and he was warning the people that they might be in danger.

In the fortnight previous Amoli, the violent kain of the Haiman, had killed the young brother of a man with whom he was having a dispute: taking the life of a relative of one's antagonist, or even that of his small child, is not unusual, being not only a more subtle punishment but a less dangerous one. The man had fled to the Siep-Kosi but had sworn revenge, and Polik, on behalf of Amoli, warned any of the latter's friends or kinsmen to be on guard. The fugitive's wife was ordered to come to him the next morning in Abulopak, so that he and Wereklowe might have a full explanation of the affair: it is one of the duties of the great kains to settle feuds within the tribe, not infrequently at the expense of their own pigs. When Polik had finished speaking, the guests fidgeted uneasily, but after a while the voices mounted once again, and the women returned to remove Weake's nets.

People were already departing from the sili. The thongs were loosened, and Weake was carried back to the banana leaves where the shell belts had lain. The yegerek, grim, brought timber for the pyre: Tukum looked frightened and was openly upset. The mourning quickened. Huonke greased the body a last time and, when he was finished, took up the bow and arrow. Another man held up the great thatch bundle. The arrow was shot into it, releasing the spirit from the body, and the man ran with the bundle up the yard; he laid the bundle on the sili fence.

The fire had been assembled quickly, and a loud outcry erupted with the flames: the body was hurried to its pyre. Weake was laid upon his side, in the way that small boys sleep, with a rough timber pillowing his head. The flames came up beside him, and more wood was laid on top of him, and he disappeared.

The mourning died after a time, and the sili emptied quickly. Huonke brought out a red parrot feather and performed the purification ceremony on the men who had handled the boy's body. The men, seated in a circle, held out both their hands, and Huonke passed the parrot feather through the air above the outstretched fingers. Afterward, as much was done for him.

The last of Weake was a sweet choking smell, carried upward by an acrid smoke from the crackling pyre, and diffusing itself at last against the pine trees, the high crest of the mountain wall, the sky.

■ The second part of the stone ceremony had been postponed a day, out of respect for the funeral of Weake, and meanwhile the hanging pig meat had acquired a sweet stink which filled the Wilil pilai, overpowering the old resident smell of grease and sweat and strong tobacco. The ears, tails, jaws, sow rump, and other pieces lay separately on burned fern leaves before the pilai fire: the blood had dried a purple brown, and the meat itself, its juices gone, had shriveled into charred, amorphous lumps. Only the pig mandibles, teeth gleaming in the lean smile of death, stood out from the rest; these were arranged in a neat row beside the fire.

Early in the morning, in the presence of Elomaholan and other wisakun old men, as well as the warriors Aloro, Tegearek, and Yeke Asuk, and a single non-Wilil, Wereklowe, U-mue removed the holy stones from their crisp packets. The stones are rarely exposed to view, and the ritual was performed in awe and silence.

Each holy stone is far older than the reckoning of the clan, and its particular powers are well known. The stones are of the dark green color of the ye stones, a deep, opaque jade, though a few are black; they are shaped beautifully in the same spatulate flat way, narrowed sometimes in the center, but they are smaller and they are undecorated. U-mue took each one up—he was on his knees—and smeared it gently and lovingly with grease of the wam wisa until, in the firelight, the stone seemed to glow. The stones were then put in their packets and replaced upon the mat.

Now U-mue returned to the front of the pilai, where, taking up the pig tails, he sliced off the tufts with a bamboo knife. Some of these tufts he threaded on a sliver; these will be worn by important men as decoration. Another tuft was hung up by Wereklowe among the fetish objects on the frame above the fire, and a last one was inserted by Elomaholen into one of the stone packets to assure the ghosts of dead Wilil that they had not been forgotten. The packets were replaced in the high cupboard behind the hanging bundles in the rear.

Elomaholan now went outside, followed by U-mue and the warriors. Through the wide carpet of ferns and grasses on which the pig had been devoured two days before, Elomaholan cleared a path to facilitate the departure of the ghosts: these would now go forth in concert and set the Wilil community to rights.

Since the eating of the wisa pig, the men had been under a wisa ban and could not smoke or drink or touch their wives. It was now time to remove the ban. A large company of men went from the sili, taking sticks. In the fields and undergrowth they beat the cane brakes and the grass, searched coverts, and dug under stumps, in a search for small wild creatures. All the men and boys took part in this, even Elomaholan, as well as such guests as Wereklowe and Polik—all, that is, except U-mue himself, who, supremely careful of his own dignity, stood to one side, arms folded on his chest.

Wild creatures, when blown upon by the wisakun, then eaten, have the power to remove the wisa ban. The people do not know the basis of this power; they only say it has always been this way. Although anyone can do the blowing, only the true wisakuns are effective, and the power is passed on from father to son. The blood line is not important: Asok-meke is a wisakun and can transfer his power to his stepson Tukum. If Tukum should not wish it when the time comes, Asok-meke's gift will be inherited by Siba.

In a half-morning of search and shouting, twenty-one large mice and field rats were taken, and a beehive with its edible larvae, and a large yellow-faced grasshopper. The first animals, four mice, were given to Elomaholan, and he cupped them in his hand; the tails hung neatly in a row out to one side, and on the other a bouquet of mice heads, their round black eyes beady with terror.

A little girl came running from Abulopak in hysterics; she was one of those supposed to undergo the mourning mutilation. She was caught and thrashed by an old woman, and, as the thrashing of a child is a very rare event, it created a pleasant diversion for the hunters.

Toward midday U-mue returned to the pilai, carrying the creatures with him in a net bag: they were wrapped with women's neatness in leaves and grass. A banana frond was laid on top of the wam wisa, and the dead rats and mice, the grasshopper and the small open hive, were laid in a row along its spine. U-mue smoothed the rodent's fur with the same delicacy and care that he had used to handle the green stones; he then straightened the rat whiskers, a touch which a less fastidious kain might not have thought of. When he was finished he sat back, and the other men shouted violently at the ghosts, Go out, go out! The men rushed out of the pilai, chasing the ghosts before them.

The animals were given to young boys, who opened them with bone needles and removed the entrails. Stones were being heated in a pyre, and the cleaned rats were placed along the edges of the fire to be singed: their backs arched as they shrank, and their teeth protruded. Okal toasted one rat on the end of a pointed stick; like all children, he did not turn his body from the flames but leaned backward from his own hand, squinching his face to alleviate the heat. The charred rats were wrapped up in leaf and returned into the pilai, where the ritual blowing was performed on them, prior to their baking in the fire.

Big Woknabin, the only Wilil warrior still living in the pilai of the holy stones, sat by himself. Woknabin's blind eye saddens his face, though true sadness may stem from the knowledge that his wife is a known slut. The woman is condemned by the community as kepu, in the sense of "worthless," but this knowledge must be small consolation to her husband.

Tukum, sucking his thumb, sat on a rock and watched the older boys. In a little while he joined some smaller children—Natorek and Oluma and U-mue's tiny daughter Nylare, the only female in the company. Together they gnawed on some old pig bones left over from two days before and watched the construction of the cooking pit. Yeke Asuk, who labors rarely, sat by the pit, chewing on a pig ear; he was nearly burned by the boy Weneluke, who dropped a hot stone from his tongs while trying to help the older boys construct the fire. Weneluke always tries very hard. He is high-hipped and gangly and a sissy, with the sissy's unhappy recourse to sneaky giggling and dirty jokes; it is he who has done the finest rock drawings at the fire sites across the mountainside. Yeke Asuk sneered at him, though mildly: he had recovered now from his bad arrow wound, and with his full belly, new fiber string, and fresh coat of grease, was fat with good spirits. He took up a piece of raw ginger and ate it with a happy crunch. Ordinarily ginger is eaten wrapped in its own leaves, which cool it, and Yeke Asuk, gasping for breath, rolled his eyes and moaned and clapped his hands over his ears as if otherwise his poor skull might explode. A moment later he ate another piece, with the same ceremony.

Natorek, with his ferocious energy, toddled from group to group, assaulting people. For his girth he is very quick and strong, and he snapped a piece of savory fern right out of Tukum's mouth. Tukum retrieved it, looking injured and owlish, but a moment later he laughed huskily to himself with a kind of jolly fiendishness, the sort of laugh that might issue from a stump.

Natorek had concealed himself behind the grass stack of the fire and was throwing grass spears at his brother Uwar. The stack was as tall as Natorek, so that only his rust curls could be seen, agitating furiously as he plotted; every few moments a pudgy hand would rise out of the smoke and hurl a spear, then disappear again. His concealment was superior to his accuracy, but nonetheless Uwar got up with his lank grace and drove him disdainfully into the open. The embattled boy leapt and cavorted to avoid Uwar's missiles, but most of his energy was exerted before, between, and long after the moments that the spears were thrown, for his timing was primitive: Natorek is very much an earthbound creature, and despite all his precautions the battle ended as it was doomed to end, and an old man came to comfort him when he cried.

The pit was opened, and the men gathered in the small yard. Pig meat and rats were passed around, and though everyone was supposed to receive at least a small scrap of the latter, U-mue and other men passed it by: the bulk of the rats was consumed by the yegerek and by Woluklek. The boys gnawed fiercely at the rats, which, quite aside from their curative powers, are a delicacy. Okal and his twin—they are the sole identical twins in the southern Kurelu, distinguishable only by the fact that Okal's right ear is cropped in mourning—ate rats most avidly of all. Their sharp ears and quick slanted eyes, their vulpine faces, gave them a predatory air, like wolf-children.

The yard filled with the soft, slippery sound of pig-eating and a faint scent of putrefaction. Everyone ate the cooked ferns and hiperi, sitting cross-legged in the sun, and at the end of the feast, before going home, they greased one another once again, with jovial rubs and slappings. The yegerek did the same, and Natorek stood up for his anointing, which was administered by Uwar. He stretched his arms high above his head, as if on the point of clapping for the world's attention.

■ When the feast was over, Tukum ran straight around to Weake's sili in Abulopak. There, early that morning, a very different ceremony, *iki palin*, had taken place. Out of respect for the dead boy, the two outer joints had been removed from two fingers of Weake's sister, Iki Abusake, and three other little girls. In addition, the upper third of a young boy's left ear had been sliced off with a bamboo knife.

A half-hour before the ceremony the fingers of the little girls had been bound tight, to cut off circulation; just prior to the operation the children were struck forcibly on the upper arm, to render the hand numb. The fingers were placed on a piece of wood and severed with a blow of a stone adze. This latter task had been performed by Tamugi, who is considered skillful in such matters. The fingers are hung in the cooking shed to dry, and the next day burned, then buried in a special place behind the pilai.

The boy is a member of Wereklowe's sili, and his ear served as a token of that sili's grief. One little girl is Wereklowe's niece, another the daughter of a warrior who, having neither pig nor stone to bring to the funeral, offered the fingers of his child. A third is the daughter of Tamugi, and

Iki Abusake is an orphan. One of these girls had taken the place of a fifth child, the one who had gotten hysterical and run off. Though this little girl had been beaten, she had not been forced back to the ceremony; as in the case of kepu men in time of war, her shame is thought to be sufficient punishment.

At three, Iki Abusake is the smallest of the girls, though the other children cannot be more than four. The children sat together in the cooking shed. Their hands had been bandaged heavily in leaves, bound round with grass, and to slow the bleeding each held the green mass upright, beside her face, like a toy or present to be shown to friends. The hands bled badly all that morning, and each little girl held a clump of grass under her elbow to absorb the blood. None of them gave evidence of more than slight discomfort, but all were silent in a way that children rarely are, and the eyes of Iki Abusake, whom the children call Kibusake, were round with shock.

Their relatives talked quietly to the little girls, and after a while the children were taken out into the yard. Many women had come, for this was their occasion, and they sat talking cheerfully by the funeral ashes. The women made a kind, mild fuss over the little girls, but otherwise no notice was taken of them. They were fed hiperi and ate it. Later the little boy with the sliced ear went to the men's feast of the Wilil and gnawed his rat meat with the rest; the side of his head had been smeared carelessly with clay.

Tamugi's wife sat by herself, picking the bones of Weake out of the ashes. She used small wooden tongs, and she laid the white scraps in a little pile on a banana leaf. The motion of her arm, though sure and graceful, was infinitely slow, as if she were entranced. Her eyes were wide and sad, and she looked peacefully at the others without really seeing them. When her task was finished, she folded the leaf over the bones and took it away into the cooking shed.

The few men in the sili kept out of the women's way. Weaklekek was silent still and spent most of the day weaving fiber, hunched in upon himself. But late in the afternoon the men asserted themselves once more. They raised a shout, and the yegerek came flying up the yard through the packed women, hurling stones at the fences and gateway of the sili and crying out: this was the banishment of Weake's ghost, reminding it of its journey to the Wittaia. The yegerek came back laughing, and all the women laughed as well, for the ghost-stoning is a constructive ceremony from which nothing but good can come. More hiperi were taken from the fires, and Tukum, still greasy with his pig, secured two round ones for himself and made off with them to the terrains of the men.

On the third day of the funeral another hiperi feast was given, this time in the sili of Wereklowe. Among matters discussed were steps to be taken in the future to safeguard the Aike frontier, as well as the details of the retaliatory raid which was to come: the death of Weake, who had claimed Weaklekek as his nami and who had not only been a member of Wereklowe's village but related closely to Asikanalek and other important Alua, was not going to pass unavenged. Huwai had died for the death of Ekitamalek, and another enemy, and preferably more than one, would pay for the death of Weake: that Weake had died as a result of the death of Huwai, or of Torobia, or of Owak, Tegaolok, Wie, Haknisek, or Mali, all five of whom had died of wounds received in recent moons on the Tokolik and Waraba, was not the point: revenge was an ancient rhythm of akuni life, a cycle without end.

The feast was scarcely started when an alarm cry came, and this time the sili emptied of its warriors. The Wittaia were said to have struck again, on the mountain path to Lokoparek, killing both women and children.

The warriors ran through the araucarias in a swift, loping stride, past Wuperainma and up across the fields above Homaklep, into the trees. But the alarm was born of the high tensions of days past; if there had been Wittaia on the mountain, no trace of them was found. The men came down the hill, and most returned to Abulopak, where the feasting was resumed. Once again, to shouts and laughter, Weake's ghost was sent upon its way in a hail of stones. The ceremony was enacted a final time on the following afternoon, and on all these days the grass near the place of ambush was burned and burned again. Weake's ghost would linger near even a faint trace of his blood and would not, until all blood was gone, be free to cross into the country of the enemy.

The bones of Weake had already been placed in a fenced shelter behind the pilai. Until his death has been avenged, a kind of altar will be maintained in the cooking shed of his sili, where two of the funeral nets still hang upon the wall. The tails of the slaughtered pigs are fastened to the nets, and with them a stalk of toa, the heavy-bodied cultivated grass which tastes like a fine mixture of artichoke and celery; Weake had been very fond of toa, and its place on the nets is designed to please his ghost. In the rafters above hangs the grass bundle used as a sign to ghosts that all has been taken care of in the sili and that therefore they need not loiter but should get on about their business. When a Wittaia has been killed by Weake's people, the grass will be burned and the altar taken down.

The death of Weake was not called out to the Wittaia, for this was scarcely necessary; nonetheless, the enemy celebrated an etai. The boy's mother, who lives with the Wittaia, was certainly aware of Weake's identity, but what part she played in the celebration the akuni did not know.

■ When the sun had risen from behind the wall, Yeke Asuk and Tekman Bio came up through the fields, bound for the mountains to cut weapons. Yeke Asuk wore a new head net and carried a stone adze slung upon his shoulder; his mouth harp was stuck jauntily through a hole in his earlobe, a hard red berry dangling on the end of its string. Tekman Bio wore a fine hawk-feather pouch slung on his back, and carried a pale laurel spear. The boy Supuk went with them. They traveled slowly up the hillside, observing the mountain morning.

Above their heads loomed the limestone walls, and the men called out, *Yeke Asuk-a-o, Tekman Bio-e,* and the spirits answered them—*asuk-a-o,—bio-e. Mokat, mokat,* they said, and laughed: these were their own spirits and did not frighten them. Farther on, the path was intersected by a small stream where it flowed over a large pale boulder buried in the ground. Here the people sharpen their stone tools, and the boulder's surface is scraped and scarred with ancient labors. Yeke Asuk put down his adze, removed the stone from its fiber binding, and scraped it back and forth under the water: white powder issued from the limestone and flowed away in the clear rivulet, toward the valley.

The men went upward. In a beech tree, in a bower of graybeard lichen, a bird of paradise flapped and spun, cawing more loudly and more harshly than any of its drab crow kin across the world; the sound is a strange grating squeal, the dominant noise of the mountain forests. Protruding sideways from its breast like a brilliant double-pointed shield was its bib of iridescent blue. The bib flashed against the mist which felt its way along the wall above.

They had entered the cloud forest: here the clouds convene in all but a few hours of the day. The mosses flourish, climbing from a dense carpet on the ground to thicken the twigs and tree trunks; in the constant damp, the mosses have made their kingdom. The mossy forest drips with moisture; the naked men moved carefully, avoiding the cold branches.

They went on higher, to one of the numerous congregations of squared boulders on the hillside; the boulders form natural amphitheaters of great majesty, and the people choose these places for their fires. The men had now climbed very high, and the whole course of the Aike, which descends from the mountains through a narrow gorge, twisted out onto the plain before them.

Supuk built a fire, using dead pandanus leaf and graybeard lichen for his tinder. A stick split at the end—a stone holds the split open—is placed on the ground, the tinder within the split, and a strip of rattan is run around beneath: the rattan, one end taken in each hand, is pulled up and down until a spark ignites the tinder, which is protected from the wind by the split wood. On the fire Supuk laid the sapling, to dry it and sear its bark.

Tekman Bio, meanwhile, had found a fine straight laurel pole, fourteen feet long when dressed; with Yeke Asuk, he split it down its length, using log wedges. One piece was split again in two, and the best of the three lengths was stood against a boulder and its bark chipped away.

Yeke Asuk, perched on a rock, carved some new arrow points from a split piece of myrtle, using a boar's-tusk scraper which he carries hooked in his fur armlet. Yeke Asuk avoided the heavy work, attributing his reticence to his recent wounds. Now and again he described excitedly to Tekman Bio the activities of the enemy, which he imagined he could see: the distance was great, but the men have kept their hunters' eyes, and Yeke Asuk is an imaginative man.

When the bulk of the spear pole had been chipped away, with only the finer work remaining, Tekman Bio laid it on his shoulder; Yeke Asuk took up the adze and Tekman Bio's spear, and the boy followed them down the mountain. The rains of afternoon were gathering on the rim, and they moved swiftly. On the way Tekman Bio gathered a bundle of coarse grass, which will be used in the last stages as a kind of sandpaper.

Early in the morning Tekman Bio brought his new spear to Homuak, where he laid it in the waters of the spring. He broke rocks to make new edges and, after removing the spear from the spring, took it up to the council ledge above, where he built a fire. He scraped the long pole with the stones, and finally he rubbed it with the gritty grass to make it smooth.

The spear-rubbing with *leno* or *hugi* grass is a suggestive motion to the akuni, and the words appear in a kind of chorus to a sportive song which Tekman Bio sang softly as he worked. The song concerns two promiscuous women named Kiluge and Yai-ige who give themselves—*lelokano*—to the young men along the paths "all the way from Homuak to Abulopak":

> *Kiluge Yai-ige*
> *Homuak lelokano*
> *Araken arahalok*
> *Abulopak lelokano*

(Vigorously): *Hugi are ara*
Leno are ara.

The shape of the spear was still unsatisfactory, and with the stone adze Tekman Bio did some more light chipping. Again he scraped the whole spear with a boar's tusk, and especially the long white blade, on each face of which he carved two facets, so that the cross section of the blade was like a flattened diamond. All this work, performed steadily but without haste, took a long time, and it was not until afternoon that he took a substance from a leaf and rubbed it on the spear: this is a kind of wax made from the cocoon of the black and yellow caterpillar, a creature esteemed highly as a food. The wax is thought to cure the wood, and he rubbed it painstakingly all over. Warm pig fat was then applied, for the grease is said to give the spear resilience and to facilitate its final straightening. Finally he rubbed on another coat of wax, turning the spear carefully against the flames.

On the day following, Tekman Bio helped Werene and Tegearek with the heavy work in their new gardens, but the day after, he completed his new spear. He pared it finer with the boar's tusk, bent it continually at the fire, and rubbed it all over again with the magic grease of pig. At last it was ready for its simple decoration. Just at the base of the long blade he wound a sleeve of fern pith, copper-colored. He held its point up to the sky, pleased with the feel of it, with the knowledge in his own hands.

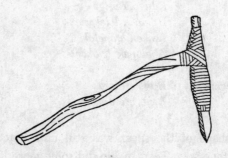

■ Tekman Bio had left his new spear for a day to help Werene and Tegearek in their new gardens. He did this out of friendly obligation, as they must do another day for him. The men had worked in these gardens for a month or more, between wars and feasts, etais and funerals, and only now were they beginning to emerge out of the broken litter of dead bushes. The roots and trash had been removed, and the hiperi beds, laid out, were climbing slowly with the excavation of the ditches.

Aloro was there, with Woluklek and Siloba, toiling and grunting. Aloro worked savagely, driving his hiperi stick like a plunged spear. In the heavy postures of field labor his shriveled leg swung clumsily, recalcitrant. He seemed to sense this and stumped angrily about his work. Unlike Aloro, Woluklek worked slothfully, picking and poking and gazing philosophically across the land, while Siloba, laughing, worked in furious fits and starts.

The men dug and levered, scraped and pried, and the sticks thunked stupidly into the ground. Tegearek worked hard, but often he straightened to offer an opinion he had come to, usually on the subject of war; unlike the rest, he found it hard to think and work at the same time.

The rain came swiftly through the sun, but it was transient and the men worked on—not against time, for time is not of meaning in the valley, or against seasons, for seasons are weak and fitful, untouched by laws of distant springs, temperate autumns. The men worked against the field itself, the weak soil of it and the wild growth which would not relinquish it without a struggle, nor for very long.

The rain passed. The sun reflected from the copper

wings of a black hornet, from the thatch of a small shelter which, in this light, was gold, from the white fiber sleeves at the bases of the long spear blades. The spears were planted at the corners of the fields, the only sharpness in the swollen landscapes of hot middle day.

■ Like most of the young unmarried men, Walimo visits a good deal among the other villages and sleeps casually in the pilai where night finds him. Last night he slept in a sili of the Haiman, beyond the Elokera, but this time his visit was not casual. The village belongs to Maitmo, who fiercely believes that Walimo should be killed for having crossed enemy lands to visit clansmen on the far side of the Baliem. It was Walimo's idea to sound out the people there in order to keep closely in touch with Maitmo's state of mind.

It appeared that Maitmo still held the same opinion, and Walimo returned to the southern Kurelu as downcast as before. He wandered about in his airy way, playful and equable as ever: Walimo is liked by everybody, perhaps even Maitmo and Wereklowe, who are anxious that he die. On the savanna he took up some strands of sedge and wove grass toys; he fashioned a tiny decorative basket, a replica of the men's back pouch, some miniature coil skirts, and a cat's-cradle.

When his toys were completed, he abandoned them to the mice and insects, trailing homeward toward Hulibara.

■ In eight months or ten, or in a year, a *mauwe* feast will be called by Kurelu. The most elaborate festival of the akuni, the mauwe is held once every few years, its timing determined by the tribe's need of the ceremonies which comprise it as well as by the supply of pigs. Though the mauwe is called formally by Kurelu, it is celebrated in all the villages, under the direction of the local kains; the ceremonies require more than a week, and the period surrounding the mauwe is a time of peace, of restoration and renewal—from the sili fence and buildings and whatever else may need repair, to friendships and clan relationships—and a cleaning of the holy stones.

The ceremonies of the mauwe surround the initiation of young boys and girls into the tribe, followed by marriage of the eligible girls; there are no spinsters, for no girl is so poor or ugly that she will not be taken, if only as an extra wife, by some old or poor or ugly man. There is a song that the young men sing:

> Where are all the young girls gone?
> We danced with them at the Liberek
> And now they are all married.
> Well, what can be done,
> When the kains take all the women?

The initiation of the girls is little more than a first step in their marriage: the rush skirt is removed and thrown away, and a woman's coil skirt given in replacement. At the next mauwe Loliluk's Werekma may reach womanhood in this way, and, if she wishes it, and is wished in turn, she may be married. The marriage is arranged between the families, since it involves a complex set of obligations and exchange. The arrangements concluded, Loliluk will cry ceremonially at his loss, and matters will proceed.

On the day before the marriage Werekma, with her mother and other women of her family, will be presented by her male relatives with a large amount of pig meat; this is perhaps the one time in her life when Werekma will eat more than a few scraps of meat. The pigs are given ordinarily by the girl's brothers, but since Natorek and Uwar are not yet pig-owners, the animals must be supplied by Loliluk himself. Should Loliluk be poor at the time of mauwe, the pigs would probably be given by U-mue, as the kain closest to the household, though U-mue will expect to be repaid.

The following day Werekma will remain at home in Wuperainma. The man—it may be Walimo, who is thinking these days of marriage and who, as an Alua and therefore waia, is eligible to marry a Wilil girl—comes to Wuperainma, where he is feted with fine pig meat; he is accompanied by sisters or other female members of his family. Werekma remains inside the cooking shed, protesting modesty and indifference, but after a while she wanders out. The sisters then ask if they may take her back with them to their village, and, when permission is granted, a request is made for all her property—not only the nets, ye stones, shell goods that she may have been given by her family, but the leftover pig meat of the late feast. Werekma then goes off with the women, while the man remains behind; he is now forbidden his own village and must skulk about in other pilais. His family, meanwhile, holds a feast—part of the mauwe— in honor of Werekma. In two or three days the husband is sent for and returns.

With Werekma and a small number of his people, he enters a new ebeai built for the marriage. The couple sit together on her net, where they receive marriage instruction, including the advice not to be shy with each other. Pig and hiperi are eaten in a kind of marriage supper, and, after a few hours of pleasant conversation, Werekma will be left alone with her new husband. At this time Werekma may or may not be a virgin, but, as she is a self-righteous child of prudent character, she probably will be, and the first night of her marriage gives every promise of being a forlorn one.

Should Werekma's brother Uwar be among those boys initiated at the mauwe, his ordeal, a gentle one, will be approximately as follows.

For a period of four days or so he will be largely confined to the lower floor of U-mue's pilai; he is not allowed to go up into the loft, for he is meant to abstain from sleep as best he can. This is a test of his ability to undergo privation. To sustain himself, he is given a piglet and four sweet potatoes. He may go out to relieve himself, and for a period each day he is taken to a field with other boys, where they are taught the niceties of war and ambush, and where they join for the first time in a kind of etai and fierce dancing.

At the end of this period he will be required to shoot arrows through a circlet of grass, to establish his skill in this most important regard: from now on he may go to war if he likes, though he is not forced to do so. His nami, a Siep-Kosi, will be present and will present him with his own bow and arrows and a ye stone. For perhaps half an hour he must stand still, with the bow and arrows in his left hand and the ye stone in his right. The nami also gives him a small net bag for his belongings, and a cowrie belt, which is wrapped around his head; this is the second of three occasions in his life on which he wears the shell belt, the others being birth and death. At this point the initiation is concluded, and pigs are killed and eaten in celebration.

Throughout this period of initiations and marriage, purification rituals are held in all villages holding sacred stones, with a continual round of feasting and exchange of goods in the guise of gifts: the presentations and rewards, the settlement and creation of obligations, are one of the main reasons for the mauwe. Guests and relatives are entertained, for visitors come to mauwes from as far off as the Yalimo: except in time of mauwe, the Yali men, in their extraordinary corsets of hard hoops, appear very infrequently, on trading missions. Every effort is made by the great kains to strengthen ties and promote good feeling and to bury the more dangerous feuds, which weaken the whole tribe. Pigs are awarded by the kains to the slayer of each enemy, as well as to children who had ears or fingers cut in sign of mourning. Hundreds of pigs are slaughtered during mauwe, and it will be another year or two or three before the tribe can afford another.

■ A woman in Hulibara, village of Walimo's father, Yoli, was visited last night by a man. She was half asleep when he crawled up into her sleeping-loft, and in her drowsiness she did not pay full attention to him; he was in haste and was already inside her when it came to her that he was not her husband. She shouted for help, and another woman in the ebeai came flying to her assistance. Between them they grasped the man, but with their cropped fingers they were not able to hold him. The husbands came finally from the pilai, but by this time the intruder had departed, leaving his horim behind.

Though there is really not much hope, horims being difficult to trace, the villagers are most anxious that the man be identified, for they are short of grease and in dire need of the pig that he must forfeit.

■ Not far from Lokoparek, just to the north, the upper Tabara flows through the forest, under the mountain wall. Here a man named Pumeka came to cut wood. He had been working for some days, and rough laths roughly pointed at both ends were stacked beneath an overhanging rock. The woodcutters knew of the techniques of ringing trees or building fire at their bases, and the latter method was employed infrequently on the old dead giants among the beech and oak. But for the most part they confined themselves to smaller laths, to which their building had long since been adapted.

On the face of the rock where Pumeka stacked his wood, above a shallow fire site protected from the rain, was a rich pattern of charcoal drawings. Most of the drawings on this rock had been done in the past year by the boy Weneluke. Of all the rock drawings in the region, these were the most complex and original, though so many had been made, overlapping one another, that some were difficult to pick out from the rest. Nevertheless, rude human figures were discernible, and several big puna lizards, and some pigs, including a pig splayed open with its ribs showing, in a strong pattern quite unlike any other drawing on the fire rocks. There was a sad-faced woman in a few simple lines—head, eyes, nose, and genitalia—and a remarkable man, nearly four feet tall, whose head and arms had been blacked in—this technique, too, was unusual—over a blank ovoid body, like a great spider perched atop an egg. This drawing was so unlike anything else on all the rock faces that Pumeka at first imagined the black thing to be not a human head but an awesome sort of insect. His son then pointed out the inevitable penis, situated in this case just beneath the chin; the lower body appeared to have been an afterthought, contributed perhaps by another artist.

Pumeka, whose name means "Water Snake," is a toothless, kindly man with foolish wrinkles on his face and a high, delighted laugh. He is a village kain of Sinisiek, in the Kosi-Alua. Though he has a withered arm and cannot fight, he has become an expert woodcutter, using his strong left side. The Kosi-Alua, living far out on the valley floor where the forest has disappeared, are in constant need of wood, and Pumeka spends much of his time in the cloud forest near the Tabara. Sometimes he is assisted in his work by his son and by one or more old men. They lop the branches where the tree falls in the forest, then haul the poles to the clearing where Weneluke's rock drawings are located. Here the bark is beaten with a heavy chunk of wood, to soften it, after which it is stripped and the pole leaned against one of the open rocks, out in the sun, to cure.

Pumeka started off down the mountain, bearing on one shoulder a long tapered pole of kai and on the other his stone adze; he moved in the long, swift stride of the akuni and within a short time was below the cloud forest, on the hillside tundra. The trail followed a small stream bed, and the wet white sand between the rocks was cool beneath his feet. Down he went, skirting the giant boulders, some of them fifty feet in height, and on through the cool myrtle woods of the lower hill, emerging at last in the old fields above Homaklep. Women came up through the fields, bound homeward to the mountain villages with their vegetables, and he greeted all of them in his cheerful toothless way.

Pumeka is dismissed by other men, as all cripples but Aloro are dismissed, with a wrinkling of the nose in a face jerked sideways, the shrug and simultaneous motion of the hand back past the face—Why talk about him? the gesture seems to say. But he is liked and, in his way, respected.

He strode along the path below Wuperainma. He had not eaten since early morning, and, as it was now midafternoon, he was quite hungry. In the grove grew wild raspberries and the small puffball mushrooms, but he did not stop to eat them, nor did it occur to him to visit in Wuperainma. The Wilil and the Kosi-Alua were in a state of tension, as they often were, due most recently to the abduction by Kosi-Alua of U-mue's wife Yuli and to the spearing of a Kosi by Tegearek and Yeke Asuk: the Kosi had recovered, but the grudge had not been settled. Furthermore, now that U-mue had established his new pig village at Lokoparek, he was trying to claim that the forest near there was his domain; he had expressed great anger that the Kosi-Alua should use it without asking his permission. Husuk, for one, was open in the opinion that U-mue was kepu; at the very mention of U-mue, Husuk's nose wrinkled, and his hand rose past his face as if waving off a fly, but Husuk, like U-mue, was an intriguer, maneuvering for future power, and he suppressed his sardonic smile in U-mue's presence. Nevertheless, the Kosi-Alua went right on cutting wood. For all these reasons, Pumeka would not have felt welcome in U-mue's village.

Tukum and Supuk were coming through the wood. At the edge of the grove they stopped and shook the small willowy trunks, then picked up the large stinkbugs of brilliant green which rained in the grass. Passing Pumeka, the boys offered him a bug, and he accepted it. *Kain-a-laok*, Pumeka said, sucking in his breath: the phrase, with the sucking-in of breath denoting awe, is used customarily in accepting a gift, whether or not the giver is a kain, for generosity is the ultimate sign of kainship. The stinkbug had a violent smell and taste, from musk secreted from its glands, and while this musk had evolved across millenniums to repel the lean stomachs of birds, Pumeka bit into the bright bug with his rear teeth, screwing up his face with pleasure. *Kain-motok*. Pumeka grinned. Great kain—the exaggerated phrase was used affectionately, half joking.

■ The knoll of Anelarok lies at a crossing of the paths, a way station where the warriors pause to search the landscape, to build a fire, to smoke at midday in the shade of the small trees. Here women dance on days of etai, and the yegerek come to play a game of war.

The symplocos tree bears quantities of seeds like small hard olives. Each seed represents a warrior, and the yegerek, beneath the trees where the grass of decades has been rubbed away, move companies of warriors about in sudden charges, much as the companies move up and down the Waraba or Tokolik. Sometimes small kaios are erected and seeds are posted on the high straw platforms.

One sunny morning Uwar played war with Weneluke, and Kabilek with Supuk; Natorek, Uwar's round brother, large-eyed as a cuscus, sat in a small hole between the war grounds. Uwar had a sharpened stick, a dart, and this he threw into the ranks of Weneluke's warriors; Weneluke picked it up and drove it into the army led by Uwar. Now and then a seed would be run through and was carried to the side; the army claiming the most punctured seeds would win the game.

During the battle the boys kept up a ceaseless whistling and sighing, to simulate the howls and chanting of real war. Natorek sighed and whistled too, and now and then reared up to hurl an impartial pudgy spear into one side or the other, only to be banished back into his hole.

Off to one side thin Aloka, blind in one eye, played by himself. A root emerged from the bare soil between his armies, and this he called the Waraba. Aloka is jeered at for his deformity, as Aloro must have been, but, unlike Aloro, he is timid and will not escape from his condition.

Perched on a rock beneath the tree, in black, enigmatic silence, the war kain Husuk watched the yegerek. He wore a pair of long sedge tassels in his hair, like horns. Natorek, hissing furiously, rose suddenly from his hole, his spear of bent grass cocked back to throw; he jockeyed and feinted on his tuberous legs, then threw himself flat to escape the arrow that his recklessness might invite. Husuk's face twitched briefly in a smile; he turned his head, as he had done each little while, and gazed across the fields toward the frontier.

Weneluke is the sensitive boy who did the fine rock drawings near Lokoparek; he stays at times in the third sili of Wuperainma, which belongs to the Wilil wisakun, old Elomaholan.

Supuk, son of Palek of Homaklep, is one of the leaders of the yegerek, a boy of great spirit and humor whose merry face is the very face of childhood. Like many of the akuni, he was given his name in remembrance of an event in the life of a parent or nami—in Supuk's case, his mother.

Supuk's mother was originally a Wittaia woman who, unlike U-mue's wife Ekapuwe, came to the Kurelu of her own will. A woman who crosses an enemy frontier usually does so with an eye to suicide, but if she cries out that she wishes to live, and takes the fancy of the warriors, she may be accepted into the tribe. Supuk's mother was escorted as far as a village, where, her charms proving inadequate, it was agreed by the inhabitants that she should be executed after all.

The unlucky woman fled into an ebeai and barred the door. The villagers besieged the door and, getting nowhere, decided at last to get at her from above. Without further ado, they fell upon the thatching and proceeded to dismantle that part of the roof known as the *supuk*. At this point Wereklowe happened along and decried what they were doing: the destruction of the woman, however laudable, did not justify the destruction of a fine ebeai. The people deferred to Wereklowe, and, cooler heads having prevailed, the poor woman was given a pardon. Later she married Palek, a hapless man without a wife, and their first child was named for the supuk of the ebeai which had saved her life.

■ Heavy rains of the dark of the moon had delayed the raid which was to avenge Weake. But one morning the sun glinted in an iron sky, and warriors came to the southern Kurelu from as far away as the Loro-Mabell. The raid was planned for Wittaia fields near the Aike, and parties of warriors which would support the war to follow assembled inobtrusively at Anelarok, at Puakaloba, and at other vantage points; at some places there were thirty or forty warriors. The men moved covertly, in small bands, so as not to alert the Wittaia sentries on the hills across the swamps. One group concealed itself in the stand of wild sugar cane, close to the Aike, where the Wittaia had lain who killed Weake. This is a pretty place just above the winding river, but today it had a blasted look from the grass fires which had burned away all trace of Weake's blood.

The raid was a failure, and withdrew almost before it started. Asikanalek had led a band to the top of the Turaba, where they lay in ambush for any passing enemy, but the ambush too was frustrated, and in the late afternoon they returned, picking their way nimbly and swiftly down among the tumbled badlands. From Puakaloba the men watched them, and in a little while they took up their own spears and started home.

The next day, despite the rain, a war was called. Tekman Bio was delighted, as the war would give him his first chance to carry his new spear.

Because of Weake, the Kurelu had its heart set on a kill, and though the war was a formal one, to be fought according to the ancient pattern, a preliminary ambush had been prepared. Led by Weaklekek, a party crept up the east flank of the Waraba, under cover of an advance goup which, in plain view, had taken possession of the north end in the usual manner: the men went up the grass slope on their bellies. Weaklekek wore his shell bib on his back, and Asukwan, finding himself encumbered, took off his horim and carried it in his spear hand. The plan was to assault in sudden numbers the few Wittaia who would dance out in the first forays.

Meanwhile a second ambush party was stalking the Waraba from the north. An hour earlier Nilik had come to the Kosi-Alua kaio nearest the Waraba, where he was met by Maitmo and Wereklowe with nearly a hundred men. Wereklowe was very excited and talked ceaselessly, walking in and out among the warriors; at one point he scrambled up the kaio like a boy, to look over the situation for himself. The Wittaia warriors were visible from the kaio, a dark crest of black bodies and long spears on the far southern knoll of the Waraba. Wereklowe jumped down again, and, after a brief discussion with the other kains, he told the ambush party to move forward. They crept out in small bands, keeping low, dragging their spears behind them by the tips. Farther on these warriors were joined by Husuk and his men, and the entire party slid silently into the low wood which adjoins the flats on the inside corner of the Waraba. In theory, Wittaia warriors advancing toward the crest above would be cut off in pincers.

But the first party had been discovered by the Wittaia, who were now on the alert; when the skirmishing started, they avoided the lower woods. Wereklowe went forward from the northern knoll, speaking under his breath with a soft fierce intensity. *Eme*, he said, *eme*. Come. Nilik followed, spectral and bony against a hellish rain smoke on the northern rim; the rain came and went all afternoon, but neither side withdrew. In the downpours the men retired, but they did not retire very far; they wrenched tall grasses from the ground and held these on their heads to guard their feathers.

Asikanalek and Huonke led the fighting on the heights. This is not a usual position for Huonke, but today, as the uncle of Weake, he was obliged to choose the forefront. Aloro, as usual, was down on the lower flats, where the fighting is closer and where the terrain is better suited to his bad leg. He had brought a spear, but on the battle line itself another warrior lent to him a bow and arrows. Aloro moved forward with his curious oblique gait, the bow, with its arrow poised and set, held in one strong hand where bow and arrow met; with the other hand, which held spare arrows, he could snap the bowstring in a second.

A few yards to his right the ambush party hid; a suspense hung upon the ridge, in the gray pall. Aloro tried to lure the Wittaia men who faced him to a point at which they might successfully be cut off and overwhelmed, but the Wittaia remained wary and skirted wide. What they did not imagine was the large numbers of the ambush party, and when suddenly the bushes burst and fifty or sixty men charged at their flank, they howled in alarm and bolted. The main body of the Kurelu howled also, rushing forward in support; they streamed in waves along the hillsides and across the rocks, pouring down the rain horizon. Polik ran after them, bawling orders like a man possessed.

The Wittaia, outnumbered, fled in panic, and the Kurelu swept them back almost a mile; though the enemy tried briefly to hold the final knoll, they were soon driven off, pursued by the screeching Kurelu onto the flats. They made sporadic efforts to recoup and return, but they were badly demoralized. The Kurelu, far stronger, held the heights, and the day was won.

Despite the victory, no warrior of the enemy had been run down and killed, and the returning warriors were disgruntled. A number of the enemy had been wounded, however, and on the Kurelu side several men had been hurt. Feckless Siloba had an arrow in his shin, and Werene, carried away to an unusual degree by the exhilaration of the rout, returned with a wound in his shoulder. The stunned man, in the thick of things for the first time that the akuni could remember, drew as much attention to the wound as possible, under cover of outrage and anger; he was plainly delighted by the prestige that had come his way through his own miscalculation, and was determined to make the most of it.

One warrior was all but pierced through by an arrow entering below the collarbone; he was carried back on another's shoulders, supported on both sides. Aloro tried to remove the arrow, using sharp bamboo splinters. He picked and pried, and the blood came, but, though he probed deeply, the shaft remained. Another man, feeling in the back, located the arrow point beside the shoulder blade, and the onlookers remarked on this excitedly. Bending forward, Aloro tried to grasp the broken splinter with his teeth; he came away with bloody lips. Yeke Asuk squatted nearby, giving advice, while Tuesike, who in the previous moon had sat with an arrow in his stomach only a few feet from this spot, looked on in silence. Tekman Bio came, and Aloro ceded his place: Tekman Bio picked and worried at the arrow and was able, after a quarter of an hour, to grasp and withdraw it with his teeth. The blood started, and leaves were brought to stanch the wound.

Uwar stood watching on the slope above, arms wrapped around his neck, hands clasped on his nape; his elbows were pressed together before his chin. All akuni assume this posture when they are cold, in evening and early morning and in rain, but the children adopt it also when they are thoughtful.

A man brought sphagnum from the swamp, and the wounded man was sponged with its cold water. He was then stood upon his feet. Two men grasped folds of his stomach skin and pinched them hard, and these Tekman Bio sawed through with a bamboo sliver, in three places, to bleed out the black blood. The splinter was then inserted into one wound and jabbed upward into the abdomen, to bring more blood; the warrior went weak in the knees and sank down to the ground. He coughed harshly, vomiting white fluid. More moss was brought to wash away the blood, and a stretcher was prepared behind him; the men chewed strands of cane to soften them, and these were strung loosely between two parallel poles braced at each end with three short sticks.

In the first part of the operation the man had remained entirely stoic, frowning without outcry, and talking now and then in a quiet, controlled voice. When Tekman Bio bled him, he did not cry out either, but his face was shrunk with agony. He ground his teeth loudly, and his toes clawed at the ground. His resistance was failing fast, as if at any moment he must scream. They had bled him on the field of war because his wound was thought a serious one; another man came forward and blew into his ear, oo-Phuh, oo-Phuh.

Pumeka the Woodcutter squatted beside the wounded man, clutching his own crippled wrist, his merry toothless face clownish with pity, while Limo, passing, scarcely glanced aside, erect and expressionless as a god.

They bandaged the man with leaves and laid him in the stretcher, which had been lined with grass; more grass was laid on top of him, covering his face, and the whole parcel lashed around with thongs. Toward dusk the faceless shape was borne off through the swamps. He was one of Kurelu's men, from the north, but the warriors who had treated him did not know his name.

■ Siba's boar was sick and finally died. Siba kept the fact as quiet as possible, so as not to have to share the meat with the half-hundred people who, getting wind of it, might happen to pass by, and who, according to the codes of hospitality, might be refused only with rudeness. The men of Siba's sili were welcome to a share of it, and a few others were invited also. The men of U-mue's sili he did not invite, and most of the latter went out to work in the field of Yeke Asuk. U-mue himself heard the news of the dead boar from Aloro when their paths chanced to cross at Homuak, and though he was annoyed at not having known about the feast —U-mue likes very much to know of everything—he did not loiter in the vicinity in order to get invited.

■ One night not long ago in Wuperainma, Ekali left the pilai to visit his young wife. Ekali is neither young nor brave, nor is he as potent as he has been, and this fine evening his wife decided that she would not receive him. She barred the door of his ebeai and listened to him shout.
Barring the door is a common recourse of disgruntled

wives and is usually the occasion for a loud commotion; all up and down the sili yard the heads pop in and out and voices fly, and marital disputes on all sides get an airing. The men take the part of the husband and bellow about their rights, while the women take advantage of this opportunity to laugh at them. In spite of the fierceness of the din, almost everyone is amused except the husband, thwarted at his own portal under the naked moon; since the door is small and there is no practicable way to force it, he has the poor choice of retreat or setting fire to his own property. Unless he is in a position to lend force to his fulminations, he must retreat, and this is what befell poor Ekali. He did not even have the satisfaction, in the morning, of thrashing his young wife soundly with a stick, for he knows very well that the first time he should try it would be the last. She is a pretty woman and would not hesitate to run away, for she can easily find another husband. It is the opinion of her neighbors that she may leave Ekali soon in any case.

■ Tamugi has had a small pig stolen and wanders about seeking sympathy or staring vacantly at one and all, as if unable to comprehend his loss, much less the idea that anyone could play him such a trick. His suspicion is that the pig was taken by the elege, big wayward youths like Siloba and Yonokma, and devoured in some dark feast in the woods, but he cannot account sensibly for this intuition, and no one takes his anguish very seriously.

The case is reversed with Walimo, whose plight has worried the whole region. Eight pigs, the entire herd of Walimo and his father Yoli, were taken from the fallow fields near Hulibara, and this is the least serious aspect of the matter: the pigs were not stolen but seized, in the light of noon, by men of Amoli, as if the small boy tending them had not been there at all. Amoli, kain of the Haiman under Maitmo, lives just across the river in Hulainmo.

The seizure seems to be a provocation on the part of Maitmo. Walimo can disregard the act, but if he does so he will be much poorer and he will be thought kepu: even should this high price be acceptable, his chances of forgiveness would not be improved but lessened.

His alternative is to muster such assistance as he can and either attempt to retrieve his pigs or seize eight others. But this is not an ordinary theft, and, since Amoli is very much more powerful than Walimo, reprisal might well end in the latter's death. Walimo's father, Yoli, is the village kain of Hulibara, but he is not a steadfast man, nor is he likely to stand up strongly for his son: Yoli's first act, when he heard of his son's peril, was to retire to his new village in the mountains, out of harm's way. And while the men of the southern

Kurelu are fond of Walimo and give him sympathy, they are afraid of Maitmo, and they know too that their own war kain, Wereklowe, shares Maitmo's conviction that Walimo should be killed. For these reasons, in addition to the fact that Walimo's guilt is recognized, the chances are that he will find no friends to help him.

Walimo has lost his careless air, and looks like the frightened boy he is. His whimsical smile is fleeting and unhappy, and his hand strays continuously about his body, rubbing his knee as he squats, or running a finger along the side of his nose.

■ Aku, small net on her back, trudged up into the mountains to fetch beech fagots and lisanika leaves to wrap tobacco; she was accompanied by her uncle, Yeke Asuk, whose work on his fields is temporarily at an end. At Sulaki they met Huonke starting downhill with a herd of pigs. Yeke Asuk talked with Huonke while Aku chattered at an old woman of the village: the woman was preparing banana stalks for a journey to the salt wells the next day. Strips of stalk are used to absorb the brine, but before the stalk is peeled it is scraped down with a rough stick to break its hard glossy surface. This the old woman was doing. The long stalk leaned against a rock, while Aku stood on top of the rock itself, belly and behind gracefully protruded, hands folded on the top of her quick head. Yeke Asuk hissed at her to come, and they started off again. Aku kept her hands on top of her head, and Yeke Asuk marched along with his arms folded behind his back.

The slope was grassy, and its limestone soil was reddish with a tint of iron; on the path the soil was greasy from the rains, but Aku skipped upward lightly, a new gold skirt of rushes at her hips. On the spine of the ridge they met two men bound for the high forest with their adzes. The four moved eastward, up the slow incline of the rim, to a small village nestled in a cleft: this was the pig village of Patosaki. Here, just outside the village, they came upon two crotched poles, in the clefts of which were rat bodies turning to skeletons in brown, dry nests.

These mountain villages, of which Lokoparek is the largest, are largely inhabited by pigs and women, who are put there for their own safekeeping. At Patosaki, which is owned by Tegearek and Asok-meke, the piglets had been growing very slowly, and Tegearek at last decided, with the assistance of Asok-meke, that the failure of the piglets was a consequence of eating rats. Rats were not bad for pigs, which hunt out and eat with relish almost anything, but the ghosts of their rodent victims had banded together in revenge against the pigs and conspired against the piglets' growth. To warn the rat ghosts that he is on to them, and to banish their influence from Patosaki, Tegearek had erected these two poles. If this precaution does not work, Yeke Asuk informed his niece, then Tegearek will be driven to sterner measures.

A short distance above Patosaki the clouds awaited them like mountain fogs, and the forest changed. The forest was ruled by oaks and beeches: in a weak sunlight glinting through the mist shone yellow young leaves of the oak and the new red leaves of the beech, cresting great trees which arose from a subsidiary gorge beyond the rim.

Aku walked on a narrow spine between two worlds, the cloud forest below her on her left and the sunlit floor of the wide valley far below her on her right.

The woodcutters followed a trail far back into the beech forest, and Yeke Asuk and Aku pursued them a short way; they paused among the buttressed roots of tall pale beeches, awed by the silence of the mossy floors. Strange bird calls, of a liquid note heard rarely in the valley, rang here and there, but the only birds visible were parakeets, hurtling through the canopy in nervous bands, like green leaves taken wing. In the air, dense as cold smoke, hung the rich dark fungus smell of mossy earth and wood decay; Aku wrapped her thin arms about her neck. Around them, sinking beneath beds of moss, lay fallen trunks of beech; the fine red wood of all these trees, girdled and killed long, long before, would be split and hauled to Patosaki and the villages below.

Yeke Asuk and Aku wandered toward the rim. Already Aku had gathered her lisanika, back on the grassy ridges, and the woolly leaves were tucked into her net; a few steps earlier she had come on a fresh-fallen limb of beech, and from this she had snapped and wrestled a large bundle of good fagots. Aku placed some ferns upon her head, and Yeke Asuk placed her heavy bundle on the ferns. He preceded his niece along the rim, bandy-legged and self-assured, his arms still folded behind his back. Once he paused to powder his shell bib with the white spores of a lycopod; then on he went, the burdened child tottering behind him like a bundle of sticks with legs.

They perched on a rock lookout. Behind them, the stone tools of the woodcutters resounded from the forest, like the hollow tok . . . tok of the nightjar calling at night from Homuak. They were now above seven thousand feet, and Lokoparek lay eight hundred feet below them. They called out to Aku's father, who was working there—*U-mue-a-oo*. U-mue did not answer, but a woman responded with a long, impassioned outcry; high on their pinnacle, Yeke Asuk and

Aku nudged each other, laughing. Against the deep mountain silences the words of the woman wandered, and the voice thinned to a wail of mortal bitterness.

■ Tekman Bio's tribal father, who lives in the village of Abulopak, is getting old, and as the holy stones belonging to him will go to Tekman Bio as well as to his own son, Yonokma, and as it is more suitable that a man move to the village of the stones rather than vice versa, Tekman Bio is preparing now to move away from Wuperainma. In the past few weeks he has constructed a new sili leading off the great yard of Wereklowe, directly opposite the one in which Weake died. The cooking shed was completed a little while ago, and today, with the completion of the pilai, a consecration ceremony was held.

In the middle of the morning Tekman Bio, accompanied by Tuesike, came from Wuperainma with a pig. Polik, who is Tekman Bio's uncle—they are both of the clan Halluk—was already at the new sili, and Wereklowe, who has strong ties with the Halluk, came shortly after, from his own pilai across the fence.

The kains gathered in the new pilai built sturdily of chestnut laths and beams of oak, with a cane ceiling and a cone roof of saplings and thick thatch. Already the pig jaws of past feasts had been brought from the old pilai of Yonokma's father, and with them his collection of ye stones; the stones and jaws lined the rear of an otherwise bare wall. As yet, the new pilai has not acquired the fine dense smell of tobacco and men and woodsmoke.

The Halluk's wisakun old men arrived and were greeted warmly, with handshakes and embraces and the gentle, soft *wah-h, wah-h.* Wereklowe, who cannot sit still, fell to splitting bamboo sections to make knives; he used a pig-bone scraper, pounding it down the length of the upright bamboo with his gnarled hand. Some of the large sacramental hiperi for the feast were brought into the hut, and at the sight of them Polik started a new chant of approval, a short fast *wah-wah-wah, noro-a, noro-a,* less because he looked forward to the eating—in the course of a feast Polik is apt to stand quietly, hands behind his back, observing the seated men—than because he rarely avoids an opportunity to chant or sing.

Outside, Tekman Bio and Tuesike, with Yonokma and his friends, were hacking down banana trees to make room for the new cooking pit; this part of the yard had not been cleared as yet and will eventually be occupied by ebeais. More men arrived, most of them old; there were few warriors other than Tekman Bio's own close friends. The men passed ceremonially around the group seated before the pilai, taking hands and murmuring low greetings. This courtesy is no less pure for being protocol: the affection is there, and the will to show it, for these men have counted on one another in the past and will do so again before too long. A day earlier a Kosi-Alua had died of an arrow wound suffered four days before at the Waraba, and in his village, a few miles across the fields, was seated at this moment in his final sun. Including Weake, there were now two who would have to be revenged.

Wereklowe emerged from the pilai with a bow and arrows, but he did not kill the seven pigs; at the last moment he presented the bow to one of his men. To kill the pigs is a small honor which may be transferred, and the man was surprised and very nervous. His face trembled as he drew his bow, but nevertheless he worked efficiently, and the pigs died quickly. The rock fire was ready, and, while it cooked, the holy stones, wrapped in their packets, were brought to the new pilai. The rock fire was opened in midafternoon, and the elege served the hiperi and pig and fern, depositing the food quietly in the center of grass circles around which the men sat. As usual, there was no haste or greed; only Si-loba's old father, he of the extruded rectum, seemed more intent on his share of the food than on the talk. He squatted by himself, small eyes flicking back and forth and old loose muzzle sliding over and around the shank of bone.

A mild rain came, despite Polik, who called out to the sky that it should stop: his craggy face was silhouetted on the storm clouds, the big face of a leader. *Hah! Miso lan! Hah! Legasin!* Rain, go away! At the end of the feast Polik took grease from the wam wisa and cleaned the holy stones. The holy stones were now restored, and good fortune would befall the Halluk warriors.

■ Asikanalek's old father, in recent moons, has been too weak to move from his son's pilai; a woman, taking advantage of this situation, stole hiperi from the old man's garden. The other women caught her at it and were very angry, and when Asikanalek got wind of it he went out to the gardens and beat her with a stick. The women cheered him on, and when he gave it up at last and went away, the quiet air of early afternoon was rent by the squalling of the culprit. Ekapuwe, the wife of U-mue, was among the spectators and expressed for some time afterward a loud and cheerful satisfaction over the outcome of the matter. A few weeks later the guilty woman ran away to the Siep-Kosi.

■ Kabilek, son of Ekali, who may be twelve, wishes now to be known to his people as Lokopma. The latter name will commemorate the death of Kabilek's nami, who was killed in a Wittaia raid near a stand of *lokop* cane, or "place of cane"—*lokop-ma*. Kabilek sees no reason to retain his present name, Kabi-lek, which means "Sharp Not," or Dull. While the people try as best they can to adapt to the frequent name changes, the chances are that Kabilek will henceforth go by two names rather than one. This is common enough: Asikanalek is also known as Walilo, U-mue as Wali, Polik as Mokat.

Yeke Asuk too is in the process of a name change,

though his reasons are quite different. Having been wounded twice in recent months, he has decided that Yeke Asuk is an unlucky person and that he will fare better under the name of Iki, which means "Finger."

A few days after Kabilek and Yeke Asuk decided to change their names, Tukum announced that he was henceforth to be dealt with under the name of Pua. *Tukum* lek, he growled at everyone. *An etara Pua.* I am called Pua. When asked the reason for the change, he said, *Mel . . . mel . . . mel . . . Welegat.* Unlike all other name words among the akuni, the word Pua means absolutely nothing, though Tukum himself insists that it means "Mud."

Some time afterward, Tukum admitted that he had named himself in memory of his friend Weake; Pua was short for Puakaloba, the kaio near which Weake had died.

■ A Wittaia man died in the first days of July, but he had been wounded in the northern wars, and the southern Kurelu did not consider themselves avenged for the death of Weake. Revenge had been delayed by weather, cold and wet, which had continued all through the full moon. Now two days of sun had dried the land, and a raid was set in motion. In the early morning of the second day the men streamed toward the Aike, but only a few of them were in full view, out in the fields; the rest moved by way of Homuak, down through the wood and up across the knoll of Anelarok. From there they descended into the gorge of the lower Tabara. Across the path was placed a branch which pointed at the gorge, to remind those who came after that they must not take the open path toward the river.

The raiders, led by Wereklowe himself, convened at the place on the Aike where the natural bridge occurs, above Puakaloba; they climbed quickly to the top of the Turaba and disappeared on the far side. Others gathered at Puakaloba itself, and these sang a chant, with ritual weeping, which might protect the raiders.

We will fight at the Alogalik [between Turaba and Waraba].
Wereklowe! Weaklekek! Hide carefully!
Husuk; take care they do not see your neck, your back,
And you, Tegearek, with that big wife of yours, keep hidden!
Beware, beware of the cutting grass,
Wereklowe! Weaklekek! Keep hidden!
They will hurl their weapons, but be brave,
Keep on!

There would be a wait of several hours while Wereklowe and his men crept down the length of the Turaba, recrossed the river, and stalked the people working in the Wittaia gardens; if everything worked out, one or more of these men, women, or children would raise their heads, like Weake, and see too late the fierce men rushing down on them with spears.

The sun of the morning disappeared behind low grays; the clouds drifted at all levels, from the rain smoke in the gorges to a dirty cumulus high in the east. A falcon came across the plain and stooped to the crest of a river casuarina; it perched a moment, turning its dark head. Then it flew on across the river and alighted on the highest rock of the Turaba. From there, shifting its wings, it glared back across its shoulder, feathers pressed flat by the southeast wind.

Toward noon men from the northern Kurelu appeared, slipping down the Tabara or angling out through garden ditches to crouch near the southern kaios. A few came to

Puakaloba, strong, heavy warriors with heavy faces, heavy names. Politely they passed from hand to hand of the waiting men, and, though the precaution was unnecessary, no voice rose above a whisper, as if the burden of suspense which must be frightening the creeping raiders should be shared.

Limo came, striding alone across the gardens; his arrival caused a stir, and some of the warriors, at his command, moved off into the woods. Limo feared that too many men had concentrated at Puakaloba and might give the raid away. Soon he himself went back into the Aike woods, followed by U-mue. Almost all the best warriors of the southern Kurelu not with the raiders were already in hiding, until the moment when they should slip downriver in support of Wereklowe and his men. Only Yeke Asuk, still complaining of his wounds, held back, remaining in the shelter with the old men. Yeke Asuk is brave enough so that he can malinger from time to time without being called kepu. The old men spoke rapidly of a kain of the Siep-Elortak; word has drifted across the hills that the Siep-Elortak were responsible for Weake's death.

A low whooping rode the wind from a point on the Turaba; the raid was starting. The warriors gathered in the woods streamed down along the Aike, between Puakaloba and the water. They moved low and swiftly in two lines, one skirting the river bank, the other through the tall grass near the shelter: Asikanalek, passing, flipped his tobacco roll under the thatch and disappeared again into the grass. In a few minutes more than a hundred men had come and gone, trailing the long spears by the blades.

Rain came, and with it heavy gusts of wind. The Turaba forms a barrier toward the southeast and keeps this corner of the valley almost windless, but today the wind was far stronger than usual, howling audibly through the pocked eroded rocks of the badland's summit. From the Aike, farther down, a scattering of ducks rose as the warriors passed; the birds swept outward across the gardens, veering wildly in the tumult of the air.

Maitmo appeared in his roosterish red crest—like Limo, he had come alone—and paused briefly in the shelter to smoke. He too spoke excitedly of the Siep-Elortak, and the other men, most of them old, regarded him with deference and vague disquiet: they seemed relieved when he got up and went away downriver.

Soon all but the oldest men moved after him. Below Puakaloba they crossed a deep inlet of the Aike, up to their chests, and moved on down along the bank. Already word had filtered back that Tekman Bio had been wounded. Siba ran by, followed by young Siloba; Siloba panted loudly in excitement.

At a sudden rise of rock the old men and yegerek climbed to the crest; the warriors ran on, across the fields of Likinapma. Likinapma is a village near the river, abandoned a few seasons past. Its thatch roofs are sagging, and its banana trees sink away in the surging shrubbery. The ditches of the gardens have filled in, and the coarse grass has usurped the plots, bedding them over with gold tussock, for the village is now in no man's land. It belongs to the men of U-mue's pilai, but its proximity to the enemy makes it unsafe. Beyond it and below is a wide, low swale of bright marshy green, ending at a neck of woods; on the far side of the neck is the Wittaia end of the Tokolik, with a large kaio.

From the wood itself there came shrill howling, and now a large number of Wittaia burst out upon the swale, driving back the Kurelu; more Kurelu were strung out along the trail from the dead village. There was a brief vicious skirmish and exchange of arrows before both sides suddenly drew back. The Kurelu on the rock crest, like those at the gate of the old village and on the swale itself, stood in silence in a cold, driving rain. They watched the Wittaia, who had formed a large leaping circle and were chanting in etai.

The raid had not avenged Weake, and a Kurelu had been killed. Four or five other men were wounded. Already the injured hobbled or were carried back, one after the other. One was Tekman Bio with a spear through his front thigh, another Siba with an arrow in his leg, a third Wereklowe's wild-smiling son; Wereklowe's son had been speared twice, in the back and side.

The dead man was Yonokma, who, with Tekman Bio, was to inherit the pilai and holy stones of his old father in Abulopak. Yonokma was a stocky, cheerful boy, close friend of Siloba, and he had been in the advance raid. The raiders had attacked a garden, chasing the Wittaia into a wood; the Wittaia had rallied in the wood and waited in ambush for pursuers. The frustrated Kurelu had rushed ahead, Yonokma in the lead, and in a furious fight Yonokma had been cut off; he was set upon and speared, over and over.

Already word had flown back to the villages, and a few Wilil women crept out across the fields. Wailing softly, arms around their necks, they sat on the high rocks in the rain, like owls. Far below the men stood in groups, staring at the woods into which the Wittaia had disappeared. Not only was Yonokma dead, but the Wittaia had his body: the warriors waited in the cold to see what the enemy meant to do.

The Wittaia could very well have thrown Yonokma's body into a field to rot, but they did not do so, less out of courtesy than because, should they do so, Yonokma's ghost would never leave their territory: they called out that they wished to return the body. Meanwhile, in the shelter of the woods, they went on with their etai, in full view of the waiting Kurelu.

Kurelu himself came back alone across the marsh and

climbed into the rocks. With the rest he gazed back for a time toward the woods, then went on down the far side of the rock and began his long walk home.

A band of Wittaia left the wood, bearing the body of Yonokma. The group hurried toward the battle line, escorted by dancing warriors. The Kurelu came forward, and both sides feinted with spears, but no arrows were exchanged. The Wittaia dropped the body in the grass and fled, for the Kurelu immediately attacked. In the fighting the Wittaia were driven back toward the woods, and under cover of the melee the body was retrieved, and a man ran forward with a brand and some dry thatching and set a fire where it had lain: thick smoke billowed up against the high Wittaia hills.

The body was carried back a little way and laid to earth while the warriors conferred; in a few minutes it was picked up again and hurried toward the old village, and its second resting place burned behind it. The rain had stopped, but the air was very cold; it was nearly dark. The line of men accompanying the body paused at the village, where a stretcher was constructed; the body was wrapped in grass between two poles and carried on. One of the bearers was Siloba, Yonokma's friend. The procession went northward across the fields to the central kaio, the people falling into line behind it.

A young pig had been brought out from the villages; it was killed as the stretcher came near. The body was put down and warm blood from the pig rubbed on it. Then U-mue, outlined against the silver sky of rainy twilight, shot four arrows over the body toward Wittaia land, one to the northwest, one due west, and two over Yonokma's head, toward the southwest, where he had died: the arrows would drive back all unfriendly ghosts which might have trailed the body. The stretcher was taken up again and carried back toward the villages under the mountain wall.

■ Like most of the elege, Yonokma had lived in many pilais but, since U-mue's wife Koalaro was his elder sister, he stayed most commonly in Wuperainma. For this reason his loss was as upsetting to the Wilil as it was to his own Halluk. The fact of Yonokma's death and Tekman Bio's wounding but five days after the consecration of their holy stones would decrease the power and prestige of the stones, which would now go to Tekman Bio.

The death was thought of as a most important one, not only because Yonokma had been brave and a good warrior but because his death compounded the grief and bitterness caused by the killing of Weake, because he was one of "Werek's" men, and because he had been widely known and liked; the mourning was entirely serious. Even Maitmo came from the northern Kurelu, though he stood off by himself and was not a part of the gathering of southern kains before the pilai.

All day the mourning rose and fell, counterpointed by the split of wood and the clacking of wood tongs on the rock fires. The women's requiem was soft and steady, while inside the pilai the old kains sighed and quavered in a harmony resonant and old. From time to time the younger men took up the chant, in a strong, pure refrain, as if all breathed together.

The moaning persisted until late afternoon, though it was weary now, and stray voices of the women rose brokenly from the rest. One sang out of harmony with her sisters, *Yay-y, yay, egh-egh-egh.* Often the women's wail began with a single uttered word hurled out as a point of departure: *nyerakenare-e-e, ay, ay, hitu nan a-ay-ay, egh-egh-*

egh. The *nyerakenare* is the long shell belt; *hitu nan*—fire-eaten—described the burning which would come.

The nets were removed, the chair dismantled. Yonokma was carried back to the banana fronds before the pilai. There Tuesike supported him while others greased him, while the laths were brought and stacked, while the pyre rose. Pigs squealed hungrily in the stalls, and the restless infants caterwauled. At the pyre the adzes rang, and a clamor rose over the mourning.

Yonokma was hurried to the fire, and a howl like fear vibrated on the windless air. The men worked in the smoke, adjusting him on his side, and finally they fell back, staring, for there was no more to be done. The fire burned slowly and badly, and it was near twilight before the flames took hold and rose into the sky.

The one-eyed Aloka had retreated to the hill above before the funeral had ended. There, on a grassy knoll, singing to himself, the boy built a toy sili out of twigs and grass, complete with entrance way and fence. He hunched over it, content, staring and picking at what he had accomplished. The sinking sun fell through the western clouds and gleamed on the savanna pools with promise of fair weather. Below the hill where Aloka was playing, the flames turned cold and thin, and dark figures hurried back and forth through a thick smoke.

■ Nylare, U-mue's daughter by Koalaro, was one little girl certain to lose her fingers, for not only was Koalaro the sister of the dead boy, but Nylare had never undergone iki palin and was of age to do so. At dawn she accompanied her mother from Wuperainma to Abulopak, under a fresh pink and blue dawn sky.

The sun had not yet fired the mountain rim, and in Abulopak the sili yard lay in a dense blue shadow. Two old women squatted at the funeral embers, picking out the bones with tongs, while other women and small children filled the entrances of the cooking shed, their backs to the warm smoke. Hugunaro and Yuli came with hiperi, and as the sun touched the bushes outside the village, then the village door itself, other women clambered through this entrance, all sticks and string and knees. Aku had come with Nylare and strolled about with her arm around her little sister's shoulder.

In the pilai the kain men sat, nursing their cold bones around the fire. One of them, in slow, measured strokes, raked bits of wood and ash onto fat hiperi placed side by side among the embers. No agreement had been reached as to which children were to undergo iki palin, for this was an important matter involving pigs and shells and obligations.

In the yard a tall man smeared with yellow clay arrived alone. Standing near the funeral ashes where the two women were picking bones, he burst into loud mourning. Strangely, he had carried his spear with him into the yard and held it upright while he cried, a breach of custom probably caused by confusion and distress. This was Yonokma's nami, from the Siep-Kosi, who had come across the hills for the second day of the funeral. The women near the stranger's feet and those collected in the yard—there were fifty or sixty—took up the man's mourning in a low chorus of their own, and big Woknabin came forward to join him. Woknabin is a friendly man, and his gesture seemed intended, at least in part, to spare the man from far away from having to sing alone among the women.

The women, even as they mourned, investigated the pile of ceremonial nets heaped up before them, and soon their wails turned into chatter. Hugunaro sat at one end of the nets, leading negotiations. Koalaro was on the inner circle, her blunt hand on Nylare's small shoulder. Nylare stared about her out of round dark eyes, a miniature figure in the humped avid circle of brown flesh. After a while she spoke to Oluma, who stood nearby, next to his mother; their heads were on a level with the women's. Across the circle, Loliluk's wife listened intently to Hugunaro, in no way distracted by her small son Natorek, who was drumming on her head with a piece of bark. Hugunaro was sifting through the nets, discussing each with everyone; the discussion was quiet until joined by Ekapuwe who, arriving late, made a place for herself quickly. The young wife Yuli stayed aside, straying idly where the men might see her and keeping her own dim counsel.

Ekapuwe confined herself, at first, to an ill-tempered and contemptuous dismissal of Hugunaro's authority; for a while she kept her back half turned, tossing remarks over her shoulder. Hugunaro took notice of this, and her own voice grew hard; Hugunaro's large eyes are in no way gentle, and clearly she has little taste for avoiding trouble. Within a few minutes the voices of U-mue's wives dominated all the rest, and at one point both women had risen to their knees, each clutching one end of the same net. Yeke Asuk, observing the rivals from the far end of the yard, squealed in hoarse hushed laughter, clenching two fingers in his teeth in a pantomime of terror. From time to time akuni women go at one another with their sticks, almost always over a man, but this prospect was avoided by the appearance of a crone. It was she who was to distribute the nets, and Hugunaro and Ekapuwe subsided.

The old woman stood among her seated sisters, leaning

on a stick, a ragtag of nets twice her own bulk collected like blown trash on her bent back. In a weak voice, as each net was passed up to her, she uttered the name of a woman; she was tottery and confused, and the real business was transacted around her legs by younger women. Another old woman, cold as a dawn lizard, crept into the sun's warmth: the sun gleamed on the ranks of naked shoulders and fired the rusty heads of the small children.

The iki palin was now postponed a day, until its principals could be determined, but the real reason for the delay was a reluctance on the part of the kains to take on further obligations: the giving of one's daughter's fingers is worth a small pig or shell belt, but, unlike other gifts, a small child's finger is not currency. The waiving of the iki palin is quite unusual in a funeral of such importance, and U-mue is already hinting darkly that Wereklowe, in discouraging the women from the ceremony, is *we-ak*—bad. But as it has been put off a day, and thus lost its order in the ritual, the chances are that the iki palin will not occur at all. The women's feast will proceed as usual, and the banishment of the ghost will occur for several days to come, but U-mue's Nylare and the other children will keep their fingers for a little longer.

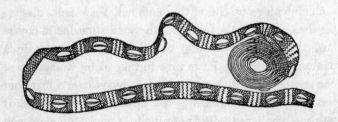

■ Just after dark, Yonokma's ghost paid a visit to Wuperainma. The men of U-mue's pilai were at the fire, and the shadow of the ghost passed along the wall, then up into the loft. There was a stir of exclamation and uneasiness. Yonokma's ghost should have been in the land of the Wittaia, causing trouble, and while the men did not feel it wished them harm—indeed, they laughed about it when light came again—its restlessness seemed a bad omen.

The next morning an armed party went out to the floating marsh beyond the abandoned village, to the point where the Wittaia had brought the body. While the enemy jeered at them from the hill beyond, they gathered and burned the grass near every place where the body had lain, to make sure no drop of blood had been overlooked. U-mue himself was there, looking worried and morose. The people are stunned by the bad circumstances of Yonokma's death, and the inevitable revenge has yet to be attempted, as if first they must determine why their sacred powers have forsaken them.

■ Uwar and Tukum, Okal and his friend Weneluke, and Supuk went on a crayfish hunt in a grassy little stream which trickles down past the salt-burning rocks and around the fences of Wuperainma, through the grove and down into the gardens. They arrived at the brook on the run and leapt into it with a great shout, though the stream, even in time of flood, is rarely more than two feet wide and one foot deep. Coming down off the steep bank, Tukum misjudged the opening and hurt his leg; he sat dolefully in the grass, feet in the water, consoling himself, uncertain about crying.

The boys moved quickly up the stream, extravagant and inefficient in their power; they felt in the mud with their swift feet, darted their hands under the grassy banks, and flew ahead. Soon Kabilek came and joined them, leaving his pigs to fend for themselves. *Kok-meke! Kok-meke!* they cried out—Big one! Big one!—and in a file, Tukum zigzagging in the rear, they would crowd and pummel into one small lead, leaving untouched long stretches of stream behind them. In the shadows of the grass, facing each other as they probed, the tops of two heads would press together in concentration.

Weneluke found a first small crayfish, and because Weneluke is a sissy his feat irritated Uwar; he hurled grass spears at Weneluke in false playfulness, while Weneluke, backing off, smiled miserably. *Kok-meke! Kok-meke!* Tukum cried, for no reason at all, and the boys rushed ahead, darting upstream through grass and sedge and the wild sugar cane.

Namilike came flitting past, correcting the vagaries of her pigs by smiting the burly creatures with a fern. For some piggish reason they minded her, and she danced away behind them, calling out to the other children over her shoulder.

At Wuperainma, Oluma and Natorek came out to watch, as did Eken, who strayed down along the path from Homaklep. Eken's left ear is smeared with clay, and she kept touching it with her short fingers, for in the last day or two it has been cropped, in a belated gesture toward Yonokma. Eken joined briefly in the hunt herself. But, drunk with the fellowship of their male associates, her swineherd companions paid no attention to her. Eken soon fell behind, then stopped entirely, plucking a grass stem and working it in her fingers in the lonely sun of childhood's afternoon.

More crayfish were captured, to fierce cries, the largest of them two inches in length. Some large dragonfly nymphs were caught as well, and these were eaten on the spot; the crayfish would be broiled upon the fire.

Now and then the hunt was interrupted by a cry of *Puna!* or *Pelal!*—at which the children would explode out of the ditch: the puna is the large frilled lizard, and the pelal any sort of snake, and the yegerek affect great fear of them, to render life more perilous. In their glee in the face of danger, they are like the men in war. But the cries had been raised by Uwar and were probably baseless, for Uwar is bored readily; he likes to tease and disconcert the other children, who have retained their innocence.

Uwar has intelligence and charm, courage and great prowess with grass spears, and he is beautiful, but he is a child no longer, and a mean streak gleams in him which may only be the first sense of his own power. Again he fired grass spears at Weneluke, who again wilted in the face of it, and now, still smiling in his wild, bright-eyed way, he hurled missiles at the rest. The little boys raised their heads out of the grass and stared at him. Tukum growled fiercely, breaking off in his pride a fat bundle of spears which his instinct told him not to throw; like the great frogmouth in the woods of night, he huffed and squawked in a hideous voice, depending on the terrible nature of his appearance to dissuade attackers. Kabilek and Supuk, though in no way timid, are gentle children, without Uwar's itch, and fought back mildly until the storm should pass.

Okal, on the other hand, is a contender: he popped up out of the grass, thin shoulders smeared with the yellow clay of war and death, and fired spears until Uwar himself affected boredom. But the spell of the hunt had been broken, and the boys regarded one another in discomfort. They dispersed.

■ Eak, the old father of Asikanalek and the grandfather of Namilike, died during the night. He had shrunk away to nothing, and when his body was seated against the wall he looked no bigger than a child. In the morning he was draped with shell belts, like an old packet badly wrapped. Sitting there in the brown darkness where his life had ended, he was reduced by the dim light to a strange pattern of white luminescent cowrie shells, as if, after all, he had gone away long ago.

Eak had been decorated in the pilai because he was an old man and had died naturally; the mourning would be no more than a formality, like the funerals of women. No chair was to be built, no fingers cut, and two small pigs would honor him. A few people came to grieve, but most of these were neighbors from Homaklep and Wuperainma, come out of respect for Asikanalek. Werene wore a head-net of fresh spider webs, acquired by rolling his hair through the vast gossamers of a large spider harbored in banana groves for just this purpose.

Since there was no chair to mourn before—the old man

was kept all day in the pilai—the men mourned at the fire of rocks. Tamugi, who loves to grieve, came and ululated like a dog, but no one else mourned for very long, and many came who did not mourn at all. U-mue sat glumly in the pilai with Weaklekek and Wereklowe. Since the cooking pit was not ready and the men were hungry, they roasted sweet potatoes on the pilai fire, oblivious of the choking smoke. In the dense pall, Eak's body floated eerily.

The children moved cheerfully about the yard. Nami-like herself fled happily from group to group, self-conscious and a little spoiled; at one point she nearly choked herself over the embers, attempting to light tobacco for a woman guest. Wamatue leaned against the entrance, sad-faced and solitary, his miniature horim in its usual offset position.

Altogether about fifty people had arrived in time for the opening of the pit.

The eating finished, the belts were stripped from Eak and brought outside, where they were distributed by Weaklekek; though Wereklowe was present, he was an honorary guest, and it is Weaklekek who is head of the Alua in the three villages near the Aike frontier. One of the belts was awarded to Tuesike, who sat down with it, smiling modestly, near other men and yet somehow not with them; when the belt ceremony was at an end, Tuesike seized the chance to help Eak's kinsmen build the pyre. Because Tuesike is quiet and not articulate, yet wishes to take part in things, he often does much of the heavy work at other people's ceremonies.

Eak was brought out of the pilai, carried like an injured child. His face was composed and pure. In the light of day it was discovered that two cowries were still fastened to his collar; a delay occurred while these were tugged at, and finally the neckband had to be cut free. Because the fire was already burning, the tugging had been hasty; it shattered the serenity of the funeral, not only in its own implications but because, during the process, the old man's mouth fell open wide and his eyes bulged, as if suddenly he had come to life and glimpsed the pyre. An uneasy murmur swept the women, who were seated in a line under the eaves.

As a final courtesy, and to placate Eak's spirit, his body had been smeared for the last time with grease. Shiny and hairless, he was hurried to the pyre. The men tucked Eak down among the logs with something like affection, and at this late moment a real grieving began. As if to compensate the dead old man for their long day of apathy, the men and women sobbed and wailed in earnest. In this desiccated thing they seemed to glimpse themselves, just for a moment; this was the way that all of them would go, under a blue sky, in a late twilight.

■ The children of Wuperainma engaged in the morning tussle with the village pigs, shouting and banging and hissing and squealing through the pig stalls and the yard and in the weeds outside. Loliluk's pretty Werekma, running through the bushes to cut off a sow, ran afoul of excrement; she squeaked with distaste and chagrin and fled to clean her foot, while the younger children laughed; Werekma, who may marry at the next mauwe, has been giving herself airs.

The children were watched dourly by Ekapuwe, her baby creaking in her net—Ekapuwe is restless and is looking at the men—and by Loliluk, who is crippled these days by the long infection of a spear wound in his hip; the hip has collapsed rather than swollen, as if his body were slowly being eaten out from the inside. Suddenly the man is old and squats, staring at nothing, or creeps about his yard among the women. Perhaps this is age, which comes on early in the valley, as if the eternal spring burned lives out swiftly. Loliluk may be thirty-five. At forty-five he will be a village elder, and at fifty-five, if he is still alive, he will be a decrepit and spindly old man.

The elder wife of Loliluk is a woman of the Wukahupi, a people down the valley, on the far side of the Baliem. Through their success in killing and pig-stealing, the Wukahupi had incurred the violent anger of the Huwikiak; the latter joined forces with the Wittaia and other tribes and, in a rare maneuver, attacked the Wukahupi villages at night, killing and burning. The Wukahupi fought back, but their allies failed to come to their assistance. They shall be scattered like the mokoko heron, the kain of the Huwikiak had said, and indeed they were scattered all across the valley: they had even lost their tribal name and were now known as the Mokoko. The wife of Loliluk was one of several Mokoko women among the Kurelu.

In recent moons this woman had grown weak and sick, with bad internal pains, and lately she has been called Wako Aik, which means "Worm Biting in the Stomach." Her people are very worried, and early this morning a hunt took place in the savannas below the village. The hunters were not content with rats but caught small songbirds, for the ritual to come was very serious.

Loliluk, with Hanumoak and Yeke Asuk, went out in the morning-of-bird-voices, followed by Uwar and Kabilek; Uwar is the son of Wako Aik, but the mother-son relationship is not emphasized, and Uwar was as lighthearted as ever. The men were joined by Walimo and Asukwan, and the boys were joined by other yegerek. All these people came along for the fun of throwing sticks.

Songbirds are hunted in a kind of bush-beating or drive. Each hunter breaks off several lengths of madder or other branching shrub and strips the leaves. The party forms a driving line through the tall grass, or encircles a brushy copse; when the birds fly out they are met with a hail of missiles. The boys and men, trained from infancy to hurl spears of grass, then cane, then wood, throw with great force and skill, and though few birds are retrieved—the small bodies are easily lost in the dense undergrowth and grass—a surprising number are brought down.

The sun pierced dull black clouds over the cliff and caught the red leaves of vaccinium; the leaves and grasses were wet with the night rain, and the sun, still low, brought the whole world sparkling to life. The men were haloed by the sun's gleam on their shoulders; they stalked the bushes, arms cocked, saying *Hoo-sha, Hoo-sha.* A gray rail fluttered up, wavering slowly before Yeke Asuk; it was the first easy shot, and the others laughed and hooted when he missed it.

Three birds were soon recovered. Wrapped in neat leaf packets, they were borne back in triumph to Wuperainma.

It was agreed that the spirit of Wako Aik had deserted her, and that ceremonies must be held to lure the spirit back. Yoli's wife, a well-known woman wisakun, was called in to assist, and Yoli, his expansive self once more now that the danger brought on him by his son Walimo seemed less imminent, came along to help eat up the pig.

The pig was slaughtered in the early afternoon and was butchered by Tuesike, who came in to help. Behind the fence, in the banana grove, a small rock fire was built and the small pig placed in it, with sweet potato. Werekma helped build the fire, after she and Uwar had cleaned pig guts. Aku watched them from a doorway, but she and the other children took no part.

During the cooking, the men gathered in U-mue's pilai. They talked, and Yoli wove at a long shell belt. Loliluk asked Hanumoak for a feather of egret, and this he sent with Uwar to his ebeai. Yeke Asuk went down into the wood; he returned with three saplings and with these constructed a kind of sturdy tripod, in which the largest pole, almost erect, was braced by the two others. Loliluk called out to the women, who were in the ebeai of Ekapuwe. The sick woman appeared with the egret feather in her hair. She was draped with nets, and the men withdrew to the end of the yard: this was a woman's ceremony, and they had no part in it.

The pig had been killed because spirits, like people, cannot resist the smell of cooking pig. The tripod, which Wako Aik now mounted with the help of others, was to render her as nearly airborne as possible; the spirit is a flying thing and might be more prone to re-enter a body found in its own element. Natorek was handed up to his mother, and she held him, not because he would be of much assistance in the cure, but because he was underfoot and threatened to jostle the tripod; Natorek clung for dear life to the longest pole, enjoying himself hugely. Finally Wako Aik was handed a bow and arrow by Yoli's wife; she clutched them for half a minute while this woman muttered healing imprecations. She was then relieved of both bow and Natorek and helped back down to earth. She went into the ebeai with the bow and arrow, followed by Yoli's wife and Loliluk. The other women went into the cooking shed, and Yeke Asuk returned into the pilai.

The egret feather worn by Wako Aik had been a sign, a first warning to the bad spirits which infested her that they were unwelcome. The bow and arrow was a second warning: perceiving by this weapon that she was armed against them, they would certainly by frightened off. The next morning the rout of the bad spirits, represented by the hunted birds, was made complete: the birds were laid upon the ground, and Wako Aik attacked them with her hiperi stick, dancing around and jabbing the air over the bodies.

The ceremony over, the birds lost their significance and were eaten by the men.

The next day the women held a hiperi feast to bring to a close the banishment of Wako Aik's illness. The women themselves built the fire, assisted by Ekali. Ekali's wife worked opposite him, hauling with more strength than his own on the rattan binding. The rain began before the fire was completed, but they finished it hastily and retired to the cooking shed, leaving it smoking in the yard. Although the women had worked merrily together—a merriment from which Ekali had been excluded—they sat around their separate fires, once inside.

There are five fires in the cooking shed. The two at the west end, nearest the sili entrance, belong to old Aneake and whichever of U-mue's wives are present: Aneake sat at the far-thest fire, weaving a net dyed purple and bright yellow. Aneake is having trouble these days with her etai-eken, which is giving her stomach ache, but she is impatient rather than complaining, as if she had only to speak to it in her spirited way for it to cease its nonsense. She is a hot-tempered little person, and her name, derived from *ane-weak*, or "Voice Bad," suits her at certain moments very well: she maintained a rapid peevish chattering. Two of Aneake's neighbors, younger than herself, were far sicker than she was: Asok-meke, the stepfather of Tukum, had not even been able to attend the pilai consecration of Tekman Bio, and a special wisakun man had been sent for from the Siep-Kosi. As for one old woman of Abulopak, she was not far from death. Within a few days she would be bundled up in her own nets and given to the flames.

With Aneake sat Hugunaro and Aku, and Hugunaro's smoky laughter and her wild, hard eye tightened the whole atmosphere. At the next fire Ekali's wife and the second wife of Loliluk sat in dull silence. With them was the boy Wene-luke, and Werekma, and Natorek: Natorek, though prostrate on his stomach, and despite the fact that Werekma was be-hind him, contrived to strike her with a stick. The movement was a strange, rubbery, convulsive one, peculiar to this boy, and possibly it was unintentional, but Natorek has a bad character and was not given the benefit of the doubt: We-rekma spanked him smartly where he lay. Werekma promises to be a scold; she is just coming into puberty and young breasts, and the put-upon air that so often accompanies fe-male adolescence; hence the talk that she will be married at the next mauwe. However, she is still young, perhaps twelve, and the talk for the moment is mostly for its own sake.

Wako Aik, looking disconsolate and weak, came and

squatted by the fire of the younger wife: though there appears to be no animosity between them, the latter chose this occasion to move down to the next fire. The young wife, a thin-faced, withdrawn girl who looks discontented without quite knowing why, is presently nursing a small baby. Wearing taro leaves upon her head in a kind of bonnet, she watched the other women without interest. She had removed her nets, and on her small shoulders and round back shone the silk skin of girlhood, for she is no more than a child.

The boy Weneluke wove hand patterns with a string, working it skillfully into abstract designs on all eight fingers: one of these represented a man and woman facing each other, and, by manipulating each sex, he arrived at a nice parody of copulation. Self-consciously Werekma tossed her head, and the uneasy boy grinned furtively at his own talent.

Awaiting the baking of the food, the women ate toa stalks and rolled fiber thread. They laughed and chatted peacefully in the fine warmth, out of the rain.

■ Asukwan of Homaklep is a strong, indolent warrior with a huge head of hair and a heroic nose made fierce by its black band of charcoal; his handsome demeanor, coupled with a rare talent for grinding his teeth, have made him much admired by the women. But these days Asukwan is plagued by an old arrow wound in his ankle which does not heal, as well as a fresh arrow wound in the back of the same leg, suffered in the raid in which Yonokma lost his life;

he is reduced to hobbling about with a heavy walking stick, a kind of club, used commonly by men recuperating.

Finally he went to old Elomaholan, the wisakun. Like almost all medical treatments of the akuni, his cure would be external and spiritual in nature, though there is an internal medicine imported from the Yali which is taken sometimes for arrow wounds. Asukwan sat on the council ledge above Homuak, while Elomaholan, hunched on his knees over the wounds, fingered each in order. As he massaged, he blew on the wounds, oo-Phuh, oo-Phuh, and between puffs chattered a litany of healing words: the simultaneous nature of his treatments soon had him short of breath. Now and again he would raise his head and inquire of Asukwan in a soothing manner about other factors that might influence the treatment, and Asukwan answered him seriously, brow furrowed in concentration, with the modest self-importance of the ill.

Asukwan was still hobbling on his cane when, on the afternoon of the women's feast, he caught and raped the wife of Palek, mother of the boy Supuk; this is the same woman who was almost killed by the akuni after fleeing the Wittaia. Palek did not wish to remain with Asukwan in the same sili, and that same day he moved his family away to Wuperainma. Palek is a kepu man with neither wealth nor power, while Asukwan is a warrior of Weaklekek's pilai: to demand a pig of Asukwan in compensation could only lead to further ignominy. It is not a question of Weaklekek's lending support to a man who is in the wrong, for Asukwan is not really in the wrong. Asukwan took Palek's wife because his strength gave him that right; the only wrong involved is Palek's weakness.

Though Asukwan is young, he has a history of disorder in his love life. Only last year a wife of Amoli, the fierce kain of the Haiman, was so overcome by Asukwan's imposing appearance that she ran away to join him in Homaklep. Amoli demanded her return and at last came to fetch her, bringing with him an armed party. A skirmish took place in which several men were wounded, but in the end the love-drunk woman was still with Asukwan. This episode, unresolved in the eyes of Amoli, is one of a number at the seat of trouble between north and south.

■ The only salt available to the Kurelu occurs in a briny spring on the mountainside two hours north of Homuak. Weaklekek's wives set out early in the morning, taking with them banana fiber to absorb the brine. Lakaloklek's daughter Eken accompanied the women, and with her came two other girls from the sili of Werene. Supuk also went along, accompanied by Tukum. Weaklekek went too, for to reach the salt wells the party would have to traverse the territories of Amoli and Maitmo; the enmities between north and south had been building again in recent days over the episode of Walimo and his pigs, and Weaklekek wished to protect his women. The party was joined before it had got very far by Woluklek and Siloba, who, as usual, were on the lookout for some distraction to occupy their minds.

Despite the time of the full moon, the rains had been very heavy, and the paths across the fields and around the villages were waterlogged and greasy. At the sloughs and ditches the pole bridges were slick with mud, but nevertheless the burdened women and the men moved quickly, as they always did, in a fast walk which was almost a short trot; with centuries of instinct in their feet, they could run the thin poles with scarcely a break in pace. Very shortly they came to the Elokera River, just south of the place where it bends outward from the mountain wall toward the Baliem. Here, in a grove of fig and myrtle trees, a large myrtle had been felled across the river, which flows about five feet below the log. The grove is on the farther side, with shady grass beneath the trees and a bank where the people go to drink.

The Elokera is the tacit boundary between the Kurelu of north and south. The two groups, regardless of close ties of clan and family, are dominated by separate kains; in the old days, despite their ties, they feuded regularly, and even now they rarely overlook a chance to quarrel. The northern villages threaten constantly to deny the southerners access to the salt wells, and this too is a source of trouble and the subject of a southern song:

We wish to go to Iluerainma
But the men of the north forbid us.
Forget them, then, we will not help them in their wars. . . .

Near the west bank of the Elokera, not far from the grove, is the village of Hulainmo, run by Amoli. The party skirted Amoli's village and kept going.

The trail went west under the mountains, across old fields and shrubby grasslands, down across a quiet stream and up again through a small wood of araucaria and chestnut. The travelers were passing now through the lands of Kurelu, and one of his villages, where four or five of his eleven wives are kept, lay in sight on the savanna. The trail approached the mountains at the mouth of a steep gorge; here Weaklekek and the young warriors sat down under a tree to wait, while the women and children went on upward to the well.

The mountain trail to the salt well and onward to the Yalimo is worn down to bare rock, and the rock itself is polished smooth by the generations of bare feet; in many places it is stained with purple, for juices dripping from the burdens of soaked fiber have this color. Among the stones wind exposed roots, these also polished smooth; the roots change, as the path ascends, to the beech and oak of the mossy forest. Here the strange stiltroot pandanus fills the clearings. The trail itself is bordered with deep greens—ferns and lilies, orchids and begonias, glistening with that ageless damp and splendor peculiar to the silver air of mountain gorges—the whole infused with the warm, secret smell of wood decay and fungus. Below the trail flows the bouldered stream, its white rush smothering the calls of birds in a huge silence. The water voice is a forest voice, part of the rocks and greens and filtered light; near where Weaklekek waited, the water voice would die. The stream would wander in slow sun and silent grass, seeking the river, the broad lowlands, and the sea.

The bent women crept upward on the rocks, dark bodies muted by the shades. Light fell in shafts and splinters, in warm pools of green gold. Here and there the trail traversed the stream on boulders slick with algae, and on one of these the child Eken's foot went out from under her, so that she landed on her head. Her woolly red-black hair protected her, though she was shaken; she cried quietly and briefly. Lakaloklek tied a bow of grass and laid it on the rock in warning. Another bow, half rotten now, lay there beside it.

Not far below the crest of the pass lies the salt spring, Iluerainma. This is one of two salt springs in the valley; the other is far off to the southward, in another country. The spring occurs in the stream itself, in a clearing formed by a broad outcropping of boulders. A pool has been dammed, and here the women descend into the water. There are always women at the salt wells, sometimes forty or fifty at a time, and from the bank comes a steady whack and chop—the breaking up of the small banana stalks with flat wood knives. The dark pool is small, scarcely ten feet across, and so the women must stand and bend and press together, the pale fibers floating at their knees. The gloom of the cloud forest and the packed, straining flesh, the primal browns and the salt waters from the inner earth, are somehow infernal—and a butterfly passes, a magenta scrap of light, like the tip of a wand.

When the cargo is well soaked it is carried back down to the villages: dried in the sun, it is then burned on a special salt rock behind Wuperainma. The gray residue of salt and ash will be packed away in neat leaf bottles and stored for use at feasts.

Lakaloklek, finished with her work, sat on a rock and smoked. Then she rose slowly with her wet heavy load and started homeward. At the mouth of the pass Weaklekek joined them silently, and they moved southward swiftly through the fields.

■ This morning the pigs of Walimo were returned to him, at the end of a dangerous sequence of events.

Three men of Amoli appeared yesterday at Homuak, where Walimo and Husuk and several others of the southern Kurelu were at the fire. The three declared to anyone who would listen that the reason Walimo's pigs had been taken was that Walimo had stolen one of theirs, and not only that, but Walimo had made improper advances to one of the wives of Amoli, who had already lost a wife to Walimo's friend, the young warrior Asukwan.

Walimo listened in silence for a time. Then, without a word, he grabbed two spears which leaned on a near araucaria and drove one of the men out of the grove; in the course of the chase he succeeded in spearing this man in the thigh. The other two left promptly.

When the wounded man was brought back to Hulainmo, Amoli became enraged; Amoli is known as hunuk palin, a man of violence. He knew already that Weaklekek's party had passed by early that morning on the way to the salt wells, and he also knew exactly who was in the party: Siloba and Woluklek were both friends of Walimo, and it was immediately decided to waylay the party on its return and kill whichever one might tarry or wander aside. If this was not possible, one of the small children would do as well, especially Tukum, whose father is dead, and from whose clan a less serious reprisal might be expected.

Near Kurelu's village Weaklekek was stopped on his return by an old woman. The woman knew only that a man had been speared in the southern country and that there might be trouble.

Weaklekek went on. He stopped every man he met, in order to make inquiries. Many avoided him, and the others gazed at him and at his people in an uneasy and embarrassed way. He learned at last that he was walking straight into an ambush. The party halted for a little while and talked, but for want of a better choice—they were deep in unfriendly territory, with no way to slip off or hide—it was decided to proceed.

People were now openly avoiding them, stepping off the

path a long way ahead. The villages they passed, in the oily haze of the hot afternoon, were silent. They went onward, single file, across the wide savanna, the women and children herded close, and the men before them and behind. All but Weaklekek and Woluklek were frightened: Woluklek walked jauntily, lifting his feet high off the ground in an unconscious parody of himself, a coy, self-deprecating smile on his strange face.

Weaklekek guessed that the ambush would occur at the Elokera, near Amoli's village, for this crossing could not be avoided, and there was a cover of heavy cane a short distance from both banks. Nearing Hulainmo, they came upon a place where the grass had been stamped flat; here the men danced before a war or ambush, to work up a fierce spirit, and there had been dancing in the past few hours. Ahead of them a group of women, surprised in the path, took fright and fled into the bushes. In the village itself the banana fronds were still.

Hulainmo lies a few hundred yards to the north of the Elokera. Upon reaching it, Weaklekek went alone into the village, leaving his party on the path. He did not know that, a few minutes before, Amoli had withdrawn the ambush party: Amoli had learned that the party was moving in close array and cautiously, and, since it appeared impossible to cut out and kill any single member, he had decided against attacking the whole group—not out of fear of failure, for it would have been simple to kill them all, but out of respect for the consequences. To kill Weaklekek would be a very serious step and one which, Amoli knew, would probably not be approved by Maitmo, for it would insure open warfare within the tribe which might not be settled for years to come.

Weaklekek sought out Amoli and talked to him. Amoli was candid about the purpose of the ambush, and Weaklekek warned him that he was very angry about it and that Amoli and Maitmo were risking serious trouble. Wereklowe himself was already disturbed: apparently he no longer feels so violently that Walimo should be killed, or not, at least, at the cost of intertribal war.

Maitmo may also be of this opinion, for the next morning word was sent to Walimo, in the disdainful way that these things are done, that he might come and fetch his pigs. Walimo did not go himself, for tempers were still high, but sent some boys who would not be molested. For the moment Walimo's emergency has passed, but this does not mean that the whole business is concluded.

■ Strong winds careened from the southeast, clearing the cloud shreds from the last corners of the valley; the mountain Arolik was naked in a crystal air, with scars of snow tracing the crevasses of its upper flanks. The wind and sun of several days had dried the banana fronds soaked by Lakaloklek at the salt wells, and early this morning she went with her daughter Eken to the special rock west of her village where, in a hollow like an oven, the salted fronds were burned. Weaklekek went with them. He sat in the grass, finishing a new shell belt and glancing every little while, as the men do, toward the frontier.

Eken plucked dry leaves of cane as tinder—she had brought a firebrand from the village—and the long strands were heaped onto the flame. The strands were soon reduced to a gray ash. Lakaloklek picked out the roughage, then transferred the fine residue to a piece of banana leaf, taking it in pinches with her fingers. She had filled her mouth with water from a gourd, and as she worked she let the water fall onto the ash so that the salt would cake. The final pinch, constantly moistened so that more ash would adhere to it, was rolled around the fire base to retrieve any salt that she was unable to pick up with her stub hands. Even so, there was some left, and Uwar came by and salvaged it, employing a wet fingertip.

Asukwan also came along, seeking diversion; he limps less than he did before his cure and seems much happier in his mind. Asukwan sat upon a rock, weaving pretty bracelets out of fern. While Lakaloklek packed the salt in round thick cakes and bound them neatly in fresh leaves, he and Weaklekek talked of the day's events. Asok-meke had made a good recovery and was once more up and about, but in Abulopak an old woman had died over the night; that afternoon she would be taken by the fire. Maitmo was giving a large feast in which twenty-three pigs would be killed: this ceremony would finally close the mourning period held in honor of his three wives, killed four moons before by the Wittaia. Apparently U-mue had been invited but was nervous and upset, for he was supposed to bring a pig; he was short of pigs these days, as a consequence of the funeral of Yonokma.

■ When Palek moved away from Homaklep, unable to suffer or revenge the disgrace put upon him by Asukwan, he took his family to the sili of Elomaholan in Wuperainma. Though Elomaholan himself is one of the important wisakun men of the Wilil, the other inhabitants of the sili, like Palek himself, are kepu men of middle age. The sili is a small and undistinguished one, with a pilai almost innocent of weapons, and because most of its inhabitants spend their time in the mountain villages, the sili yard is patched with stubborn weeds.

Palek stayed but a week or two in Wuperainma. He came originally from the lands of Kurelu—the name Palek, which means "No Family," was given to describe his status in the southern villages—and he decided to return at last to his native territories. With him he took his luckless wife and his sons Supuk and Wamatue.

Supuk was one of the best boys in the villages, and the society of yegerek will miss him, though he himself is probably glad to leave behind the land of his father's disgrace. Wamatue is too young to care, and doubtless stands this very moment just inside the door of a cooking shed very like the one in Homaklep, his toy horim still dangling free from the region of his navel.

■ In a lull in the rains an ambush was attempted in the same gardens where the enemy Huwai had been killed. The men lay in hiding all day long, but the Wittaia were alert, knowing that raids would be inevitable. No chance was offered for a surprise attack, though the raiders waited until late afternoon. They then returned to the Waraba, where they were joined on the crest by the supporting party. The men stood there in the Place of Fear until dusk settled in the valley, as if at a loss to know how to change their fortunes.

Another moon had come and gone since the death of Weake, and he was still unavenged. Of four attempts at ambush, three had ended in frustration and the fourth in the loss of Yonokma. The days turned past in half-light and gray rains, a prevailing gloom and dankness which muted the voices of the children, of the cloud-drenched birds: the people made no secret of their conviction that their fortunes had taken a bad turn for the worse and that any further attempt at raids must end disastrously. Their faith in their holy stones had been shaken by Yonokma's death but five days after the stone-cleaning of his father, and as they had no gods to invoke, they sank into despondency. *Nit nai-uk,* they said. We are afraid.

But the full moon's coming brought three fresh clear nights, and the Southern Cross glittered with promise in the sky. Day by day the people's spirits rose. Gold-green mornings danced with the bird voices, sparkling in the sun and gleaming leaves, and the clouds, white and without weight, drifted off into the blue, and one day Weaklekek and Asikanalek went off with other warriors to join a war on the north frontier.

That morning a party of Wittaia had staged a raid on the Kurelu gardens. They had swum a stream which winds through the heavy cane brake of the region, then crept through the dense swamps to the garden edge. No people were in the garden, nor were there sentries in the nearby kaio. Disgusted, the Wittaia rose to their feet, and a warrior went forward to the kaio and climbed up to look around.

But the raid had been detected by the Kurelu, who had guessed where it was headed. They prepared an ambush and were lying in wait by the time the enemy had crept up through the cane. The warrior, nearing the platform of the kaio, spied the ambushers; he uttered a howl of fear and warning, and his own party fled, leaving some weapons behind them. The warrior himself jumped to the ground, still howling, but he was cut off and killed.

In the war that followed, no man on either side was seriously hurt, and at the end of the afternoon a Kurelu victory dance was held at the northern etai field. The singing spread across the Elokera to the paths and gardens of the southern Kurelu.

Weaklekek and the other men returned in the wake of the noise, triumphant, and by twilight a formal chanting had started in Abulopak. Though the victory was not theirs, and would not remove the need to avenge Weake, the southern Kurelu felt that their luck had changed. For the first time in many weeks the whooping rang from all the fields and villages, taken up and carried onward, to die for a little while and resume again.

The following day a formal etai was held in the north and a smaller one at the Liberek. The dancing at the Liberek was led by the warriors who had gone to war the day before, all but Weaklekek, who rarely dances. Woluklek rarely dances either, but today he ran fiercely with the rest, as if his life depended on it.

Walimo, whose blitheness has returned, attended both celebrations, going early to the north, then hurrying back four or five miles to dance with his own people.

■ In the fields above Homaklep, with Kabilek and Uwar, Tukum played a game of whirligig: the point of the game was to whirl, arms outstretched like wings, over and down a steep bank of grass, and to land gracefully on one's feet at the bottom. Since Tukum landed regularly on his back, in a stunned, crucified position, the point of the game was lost on him, and after a while he trudged away.

Down in the little stream which flows past Wuperainma, some children much smaller than himself, mostly small girls like Namilike and U-mue's daughter Nylare, were throwing twigs at dragonflies; they threw delicately, from ambush, as the dragonflies zipped past. Tukum took charge of this game, barking orders in his commanding voice, but as he was no more successful than themselves at downing dragonflies, and as his frontal assault drove all the dragonflies away, the game soon ended.

Left to himself, he dug a long, deep burrow in a bank. Into this he placed an ear-shaped fungus he had found nearby. He packed it in with earth, then hiperi leaves and grass, then more earth, then more leaves, and so on, until the burrow was full. The fungus he called *mokat-asuk,* or ghost-ear, and his idea was that the mokat-asuk would listen for the return of his father, who is dead. Since Tukum is beset by his mother and stepfather over the matter of his pigs, he misses his father very much and would like to have him back. But, so far as is known, the ceremony of mokat-asuk is not an effective one, and is in fact unknown to any of the akuni except for Tukum.

■ One afternoon in this period four strangers came on a visit to Abulopak. Though the men were of the Asuk-Palek people, a group allied ordinarily with the Wittaia, they considered themselves safe because two of them had close relatives in the sili of Wereklowe.

But, despite the new turn in their fortunes, the Kurelu considered the revenge of Weake and Yonokma incomplete; in addition, a man arrowed in the inner thigh on the afternoon that the Kurelu were routed from the Waraba had since died of this wound in the mountain villages. It was therefore decided to attack the two strangers who had no clansmen, with the excuse that the two had doubtless come to kill somebody.

A fierce howling burst the twilight air. One man fled the sili and, as dark was near, escaped entirely in the heavy brush which lies just opposite Abulopak. The second took refuge in the loft of the pilai; he was dragged out to the yard and speared to death. As most of the men involved were Wilil, U-mue took loud credit for his clan, a credit which, in high excitement, he shortly transferred to himself.

The body was taken by the heels and dragged out along the muddy paths, all the way from Abulopak to the Liberek.

Tegearek led in the hauling, beside himself with the joy of violence.

Some boys had been playing in the fields as twilight came, and these now danced along beside the body, Okal and Tukum among them, and jabbed at it with their cane spears. Though Tukum took part, he seemed frightened by what he was doing, and the next day broke the toy spear he had used over his own head.

The Asuk-Palek was of middle age and strongly made, with a large forehead. He had been breathing when the spearing stopped, a short, ragged sound, but he was dead long before he reached the Liberek. He lay on his back beneath a high, hard moon, his eyes wide open, an eager smile upon his face. The face looked oddly trusting and untroubled.

The people were gathering; they danced beneath the stars.

Husuk came from the Kosi-Alua, an ax gripped in his hand. Taking the body by the hair, he wrenched it into a seated position and inspected the spear holes in the back. The man's mouth fell slack and the eyes stared; for a moment it seemed that Husuk would sever the head.

He let the body fall.

Tegearek, excited still, dragged the body to the field edge. Behind a low fence there lay a slough from which yellow clay is taken in time of war or funeral or etai. The body was dumped over the fence, then thrown face down into the ditch. The men prodded it with spears until it slid beneath the surface, and black bubbles rose. Grass was thrown on top of it.

Later in the evening the body was taken from the ditch, and the two Asuk-Paleks who had not been attacked carried it off beyond the Elokera. The following day a large etai was held, for the score had been settled at long last, and the faltering etai-eken of the people had been restored.

■ For three months Werene had worked on his new garden, and finally it was ready to be planted. The roots and old grass had been burned, the ditches weeded out and excavated, and a series of new trenches dug: these led away from the main cross ditch like fat teeth in a jaw, a kind of harmonious deep scalloping. The ditches were fed by a small stream draining the brushy wetlands below Anelarok, and because the garden lay on a slight slope, toward the Baliem, the large ditch which encircled the whole garden, including the plots worked by Tegearek, was finished in a series of steps, perhaps twelve feet apart, so that in dry weather the water would not pour away. This ditch would also deter pigs from undoing the work of man.

Between the ditches the new plots, perhaps twenty feet across and eighty long, had been built high with the excavated earth, and the clods, dried to a gray clay in the sun, had been broken and leveled. In Werene's half of the new garden the men's work was finished, and in a day or two the women would come and plant the shoots of hiperi. Tegearek, who busies himself with war and other matters, had fallen several weeks behind and still labored fitfully in the old trenches.

For the most part, Werene had worked all by himself, his solitary spear and the thin plume of his small fire isolated on the valley sky. But others had come to help him with the deepening of the ditches, and in the last weeks he was assisted almost every day by Hanumoak.

The quarrel which had separated the two brothers years ago had come about when Werene had ordered Hanumoak, then still a boy, to go to work out in the gardens. Hanumoak had rebelled and, after a dispute which became serious, had left the sili of Werene and gone to live in Wuperainma. Now, long after, he had come to work for Werene at last, and, while the two were not affectionate, they laughed mildly together while they heaved and dug, as if embarrassed and relieved that their quarrel was at an end.

Hanumoak's own garden plot, part of a large new garden worked by the men of his pilai, lay down the stream a little way, across a neck of brushland. This garden, a few days ahead of Werene's, had already been turned over to the women, but since Hanumoak had no wife his plot was planted by the wives of U-mue. For the labor of these women, Hanumoak will be in U-mue's debt, just as Werene will be in debt to Hanumoak. Between the women as they worked lay a net filled with hiperi tendrils. They hollowed each hill and buried in the pit the graceful length of morning-glory vine, so that only the tip, with its cluster of pretty, heart-shaped leaves, was exposed to the air and sun. In the grass along the garden edge the bees hummed sleepily in the midday heat, and a robin chat sang fitfully its rolling song. From across the fields a woman's voice rose monotonously, a keening *o*-ay-*wa*-ay, *o*-*wa*-ay; *o*-ay-*wa*-ay, *o*-*wa*-ay, over and over and over.

■ A pig of the Wittaia, bent on some hoggish errand in the frontier woods, blundered and snuffled within view of one of the Kurelu kaios. The men at the kaio waylaid this pig and escorted it with pomp and ceremony to Abulopak, where they ate it. The pig was only further evidence of their new luck, and the next morning the Kurelu, riding the storms of fortune, went to war. This war was led by Nilik and Yoli: Yoli in recent days had held a holy stone consecration in Hulibara and, feeling more important than usual, had enlisted Nilik's support in the initiation of the stones.

In midmorning a party of warriors slipped down through the woods north of the Waraba, for the war was to start with a raid; another party crept to the base of the Waraba from the Tokolik. The first group crouched and ran along the cover of the high cane brake which fringes the stream between the Waraba and Siobara. Some of the warriors wore mikaks and white feathers which flashed across the fields; whether for this reason or another, they were seen by Wittaia sentries on the crest of the Siobara. The sentries scrambled down among the rocks, silent as ghosts, and by the time the raiders tried to cross the open place between the hills, the Wittaia were prepared. They attacked the raiders at this place, driving them up onto the Waraba, where the first band rushed to support them. The Kurelu's luck had continued, for none of their men was seriously hurt, while a Wittaia was struck in the stomach with an arrow and may die.

Both sides now held back, awaiting reinforcements. In the slow morning hours before the war commenced, Aloro, sitting cross-legged at the fireplace at Homuak, scraped down a new white bow. He was absorbed in it, paring its ends long and sharp, using his boar's tusk; the fine white shavings fell and curled on his cordy shrunken thigh. Later he braced and bent it into shape between two saplings, his face fixed in his intense grimace which is not quite a grin.

At the Kosi-Alua kaio near the Tokolik, men gathered beneath the shelter. It was a damp morning of intermittent rains, and the sparks of the fire, flying high, caught on the thatching of the roof. A heap of blazing ferns was knocked from the crest of the fire, and Wereklowe's son stamped them to ash with his bare foot. He is still limping from two spear wounds suffered in the raid in which Yonokma died, and walks about with a heavy walking stick.

Wereklowe himself came along, striding outward from the mountains with the rain. His white spear swayed against the rim, sharp on gray clouds flowing out of the high forest, down into the valley. He leaned his spear among the rest on the side of the shelter and crouched down to slip beneath the thatch; bent, he picked his way around the fire, taking the men's hands in both his own and smiling his furious wild smile. *Wah*, he sighed in his gentle voice, *wah, wah*. Though he had no special greeting for his son, who lives apart from him in his own small village at the edge of the Kosi-Alua, he came and sat beside him when the round of his greetings was at an end.

The rain diminished for a time, and the men at the outer kaios moved on across the swamp to the Waraba. Already warriors of the Kurelu were bunched on the high rocks toward the Siobara, and on the Siobara itself small parties of Wittaia were convening. But the rain drifted in again, and some of the men returned to the reedy knoll at the corner of the L. Asikanalek and Pumeka came together, and Pumeka was carrying with his good arm Asikanalek's long dark spear. Pumeka looked glad and foolish, carrying this weapon he had never used, and pointed at it in self-deprecation before the other men could tease him. Asikanalek laughed, a shrill, high laugh peculiar to him—*An nai-UK*, he cried, springing away from Pumeka. I am afraid! And they laughed together.

When the rain diminished once again, the Wittaia whooped in challenge, though in fact they were badly outnumbered, not nearly strong enough to take their own end of the Waraba from the Kurelu. The latter were ranked on the farthest knoll, overlooking the small meadow and the stream which separates the Waraba from the Siobara. The Wittaia had come across the stream, and more approached along the extension of the meadow from their villages to the southward. The Kurelu danced down the hill to meet them. But Nilik, asserting his own power, decided that this war should be fought in the corner of the Waraba; he stalked down the slope, screeching at his warriors to pull back, and finally sent a messenger onto the field. This man, an older wisakun, was excited and nervous, and the warriors did not take him very seriously: they shouted, *Mare! Mare!*—Arrow! Arrow!—and howled fearfully, and when the old man skittered in alarm, the hillside laughed. But soon the warriors withdrew until more Wittaia should appear, for the contest was unequal; one old kain from the northern Kurelu drove his men back with a flat blade of his spear.

The warriors climbed up onto the hill, but before they had returned along the ridge the Wittaia danced forward on the meadow, jeering and prancing; they wished to fight on the present ground, suspecting, perhaps, that the Kurelu had hidden men in the low wood at the corner of the L. The jeering goaded the Kurelu, and some Wilihiman-Walalua rushed down the hill again with an awesome drum of feet. They drove the Wittaia back across the stream and far down the meadow to the southward. More Wittaia ran up from the rear, while a few of their best warriors, wheeling and crouching down and switching their arrowheads back and forth on bows drawn taut, dispersed the charge.

The battle line quickly stabilized on the meadow to the southward, where the narrow terrain, bordered on one side by a dense brake and on the other by the tangled growth of the old gardens, offset the advantage in numbers held by the Kurelu. A hundred or more men on each side were now actually fighting, and the line spread out into the brush. The battle was led, for the first time in several moons, by the Wilihiman-Walalua, and particularly by Weaklekek and Asikanalek, who are leaders in a way that a warrior like Aloro, with his own cause to fight, is not. Asikanalek, in the early afternoon, led the dangerous skirmishing in the gardens, ducking and feinting and shooting forward to invite attack from hidden Wittaia who might thereby show themselves. Supported as he was by warriors like Huonke—Huonke looked grim and set but did not venture forward—Asikanalek fought his battle almost single-handed. In war Asikanalek is quite different from the gentle, shyly smiling man who built his pilai all alone, who grieved so passionately for Weake: he is reckless to the point of madness when possessed by battle.

Weaklekek quartered the meadow, moving swiftly and powerfully along the line, directing the other men; Weaklekek has found himself again, after a long period when the old arrow point still in his leg, with the responsibility he took upon himself for the death of Weake, had crippled his huge spirit. His leadership inspired his men, and his strong commands appeared to keep their injuries at a minimum. In an hour of fighting, but two warriors, with arrows through the forearm and the foot, were led back to the hill, while a third arrow, scarcely penetrating, was removed on the battlefield from the shoulder of big Woknabin. Woknabin wandered back unaided, an expression of confusion and hurt feelings on his rough, foolish face.

When Aloro received his inevitable wound, he retired behind the hill. Unlike Woknabin, he did not go home but helped remove the arrow points from the wounded who came later. He still carried his old bow, for the new one is not completed, and after he had drawn the arrow point from the calf of a young elege his bow and arrows were returned to him respectfully by the boy who held them.

Tegearek, Tuesike, Hanumoak, and Siba shot steadily and carefully, and Walimo ran wild in his odd skittish way. Siloba too fought bravely for Weaklekek. Like his friend Yonokma, he has left the ranks of elege to join the adult warriors. Feckless as ever, he dodged arrows all afternoon, running back and forth in his loose, loping stride, shouting and laughing. When Siloba runs, all the bones in his arms and legs seem thrown to the toes and fingers, yanking him in all direction, yet this disjointedness is pure high spirits, a crazy joy in his own being, and despite it he maintains a frantic grace. His courage has not made him a good warrior, but on this afternoon he contrived to escape the wound inflicted on him almost every time he decides to fight, confining himself to a sprained foot acquired in a leap of pure abandon.

Woluklek also spent his afternoon in the forward line, preoccupied and solitary, dallying with spent arrows. Now and again he would pause to gaze around him, as if not quite certain where he was, and smile shyly at his friends. Even Ekali of Wuperainma joined the warriors briefly, but soon he retired to the hill: his long hands shook badly as he lit his tobacco. Ekali is made miserable with dread, with the necessity to save face, in time of war.

Of all the important southern warriors, only Yeke Asuk and Tekman Bio took no part in the fighting. Yeke Asuk has lately acquired a taste for the rear echelons, while Tekman Bio is still chastened by his spear wound. They sat in the ranks on the hill above, three or four hundred strong beneath their spears, and behind them the sun emerged through a turbulence of black clouds, catching the greased shoulders, the long spear tips, the white feathers. With a Wittaia death so recently behind them, they were all in great good spirits, and laughter rang out frequently among the howls of war. In the height of battle a dove hurtled up across the hill, and the men leapt to their feet, straining after it with their spear points, so that the hilltop swayed as with a wind, but the dove escaped, and the men groaned good-naturedly. At other times they cheered and hooted the efforts of their own elege, who were conducting a side war with the older boys of the Wittaia. The elege faced one another across the stream where it broke from the tall stands of cane to cross the soft meadow between the hills. They fired their poor arrows back and forth, shouting insults without rancor in the terrible cracked cries of adolescence.

A Wittaia warrior came and sat among his elege, on the bank directly opposite the elege of the Kurelu. Putting his hands behind his head, he leaned back into the grass, calling out comments on the boys' poor aim and inviting them to shoot at him. Both sides laughed at this, and for a little while it seemed that the war was little more than a harmless game, a sport, for only a few warriors had been hurt all afternoon, none of them badly. The rain had gone and the day was bright, with lovely shadows in the soft harmony of mountains. The men of both sides ran up and down, fine-feathered and with fanfare, tossing their long hair from side to side, stopping suddenly to cock their spears in comic menace at an enemy too far away to threaten them, and leaping up and down for the sheer splendor of it, the sun burnishing their skin.

Yoli remained high on the hill, conferring with Nilik at every opportunity in an effort to identify himself with leadership. Nilik, annoyed that his will had been disobeyed in regard to the choice of battleground, paid no heed to Yoli. High on the hill, he glared out at the battlefield, clutching his beautiful carved arrows. Nilik's head was low and forward, like the head of a falcon, and his hands were clenched.

The men ranged up and down below them, yipping lustily—*Kip, kip, kip, kip—hoo-r-ra, hoo-r-ra*—and now and then there rose the deep abysmal groan vented by both sides when a man is struck. Wereklowe came to the crest, gazing down excitedly on the battle ground, and with him Polik, his hair down across his shoulders, brandishing his great spear and shouting: Polik wished revenge for a woman of his sili killed by Wittaia raiders three days before, and his face with its deep lines and stony eyes wore the wild, haunted expression that it must have had in the violent days when his name was Mokat.

Wari-gi-jee! he bellowed. *Wari-gi-jee!*

Listen, you people . . .

Po-kan Kul-ma! Po-kan Kul-ma!

Now watch the ones along the Kulma stream. . . .

E-lop-i-nima! E-lop-i-nima!

Move back! Move back!

Tugi! Tugi!

Strike them! Strike them!

But Polik's voice is a part of every war, and though the men are in awe of him, and think him a great kain, they paid small heed to his fierce ranting, for Polik is growing old and goes no longer to the battle line.

The battle waned, renewed again, the egret wands whirling on the Wittaia side, the twirling black whisks of cassowary. A bird of paradise sang from the wood behind the Waraba, and some of the warriors took up its strident call.

In a lull some Wittaia fled up and down, running and

feinting with their spears, spinning their white wands, stopping short to snap their bow cords, leaping, menacing, loping back—an elaborate dance, performed and observed in utter silence. The nearest Kurelu was five hundred yards away, yet the dance was part of war and taken seriously. Then these warriors screeched suddenly, as if under attack, and the screech was answered: the Kurelu on the hill talked faster, laughing and pointing but intent, and then as one they leapt away down the hill, spears high, in a din of whooping and running feet struck down forcefully upon the earth, an avalanche of black muscle and white feathers. The battle raged between the silent hills and then, as transient as a thunder squall, it ended, and the men streamed back, singing in etai. The wild battle had been indecisive, and both sides claimed victory.

The Wittaia gathered at the base of the Siobara, and the enemies sat in the warm, waning sun, shouting out insults and shrill laughter. The insults included coarse remarks about the women of their foes—Go home to your sluts before your hiperi grows cold!—and each sally was carried forth on a wave of loud delight, a cheering and whistling. Then the Wittaia would respond, while the Kurelu kept silent; the Kurelu not only wished to hear what the enemy had to say but laughed aloud when it was humorous.

Then, toward twilight, Asikanalek led a wild, sudden charge across the meadow, screeching furiously, legs flying through the grass as he shot forward, long spear tilted on the sky. He spun gracefully to avoid an arrow and rushed onward, infusing his own recklessness in the men behind him, and for a moment the fighting was fierce and silent. Then the Wittaia broke ranks and gave ground. Asikanalek and his men did not pursue them, for the glorious charge had been the point; they raced back to the hill, leaping and smiling.

Dark was coming from the mountains, and the Kurelu

climbed back up onto the hill, against the sky. Woluklek kept off to one side, still smiling sheepishly, as if he had no right to be there. They filed homeward down the Waraba, through the white flowers of rhododendron. Content with Asikanalek's last charge, which had brought their mild victory to an end, they paid no heed to the few Wittaia who pranced back to the battle line as they departed.

Spears on their shoulders, the men splashed across the swamp. They trailed along the Tokolik past the black ponds, then crossed the frontier woods into another world, where gardens breathed the heat of the last sun. A gold light washed the beds of dozing hiperi, in the slow folding of the lavender-hearted flowers. From the day's trash fires a thin smoke strayed and vanished; ducks gabbled in the water lilies of the long ditches ahead, and evening herons flew. Children's voices drifted from the villages, and the gold light rose to the mountain rim, the clouds.

Now the wild duck shot up out of the lilies in neat sprinkles of silver drops; they fled like black shreds of night across the softening sky. Ahead of the men, on the shoulders of their friends, swayed two warriors hurt badly in the last charge.

■ The mother of Tukum has been having trouble with Asok-meke, her husband, and has gone away to her own people at Lukigin, on the far side of the Elokera. Tukum remained behind in Wuperainma, but yesterday he was reprimanded by Asok-meke for permitting one of their pigs to wander away toward the frontier at the Aike. Tukum is at times forgetful about his pigs, being readily distracted by other children, dragonflies, puddles of water, and wild foods, and the chances are that Asok-meke was in the right.

Nevertheless, Tukum is a very proud little boy, and since his nami lives in Lukigin, where his mother has already gone, he has decided to go away for good. This morning he put on his thin neck the cowrie collar with its brief string of shells which is his sole belonging; he smeared his body with pig grease until it shone, in order to make a fine impression at Lukigin. There, perhaps, he will be known as Pua. Then he set off alone on the long journey in the sun across the woods and fields, a small brown figure with a flat head and pot belly. His back was turned on Wuperainma, his pigs and his friends, his childhood, and he clutched a frail stick in his hand.

■ A pig has been stolen from Kurelu, and it may be a sign of his weakening power that he is abroad among the villages, conscripting help. In former days to steal from Kurelu would have invited death, but now someone has dared it. As late as a few moons ago Kurelu appeared quite commonly in the southern villages, and his claim to control all the southern lands was taken seriously. But now he rarely comes, and his appearance on this errand will be noted, for it may signal the beginning of the end of his long leadership and the ascendancy of the hungry Nilik.

Four new moons had come and gone, and the great cicadas, *anikili*, no longer filled the twilight woods with their shrill ringing. In the morning-of-bird-voices, the whistlers sang fitfully, in a kind of wistful torpor, leaving the midday silences to the shrill discords of kites, the searching cries of birds of passage paused a moment in the high limbs of the araucaria. For this—midwinter August—was the season between nestings. At night, the frogmouths and nightjars, the stealthy owls, moved without sound, and the tree frogs clung like wet leaves to their perches.

The red flowers of the ginger plant had vanished from the fields, replaced by scarlet of the myrtle *karoli;* the karoli, drab since early May, had burst forth in new flowering. On other plants, the petals fallen were restored on the next bush, so that the land maintained its dappling of lavenders, of reds and whites and yellows, renewing its cycles without cease under the high sun of the equator.

In the gardens abandoned above Wuperainma, the grass choked off the last weak leaves of hiperi, but new gardens had been hacked and wrenched from the savanna and even now were being planted. Akuni had died and gone up in the fire—Weake, Yonokma, old Eak, a few others, and just recently, despite all her precautions, Wako Aik. The infant daughter of Weaklekek had also died quite suddenly, and Weaklekek, who had delighted in this child, smeared himself with mud and cried, but the grief of his young wife was still more terrible. U-mue's baby, now three months old, had at last been named Woraisige, after the fact that her mother had been picking *worai* orchids at the time of her abduction by the dynamic kain of the Wilil.

Yeke Asuk and Tekman Bio had new spears, Aloro a new bow, and the new bow had already taken life; in recent days the enemy had killed Tikiliak of Mapiatma, but two of the raiders had been cut down, one of them by Aloro's swift arrows.

Tukum had moved away from Wuperainma, but another boy had come. Elomaholan's sili had grown weedy with disuse, but a new one was under construction just behind that of Asok-meke. Natorek in recent days had tied on his first horim, though for the nonce he wore it in much the same casual fashion as had Supuk's little brother. Some of Walimo's pigs, it was now agreed, would be seized and eaten, and if he pretended not to notice it, the whole episode would be forgotten.

In the days after his daughter's funeral, Weaklekek climbed slowly to the top of his kaio tower. He was much saddened by the death and stared heavily at the silent Aike. Two white egrets in a near ditch craned their long necks at a stiff forward angle, rigid as stalks, and a blue-gray mokoko flapped off toward the Tokolik, rasping its cry. The mokoko was a more common heron than the white egret, and Weaklekek saw one every day, flying sometimes with its long neck outstretched or soaring high over the valley, two things which the egret never did. The mokoko was a strange bird, always solitary.

A strange smoke drifted on the wind from down the valley. There the remnants of Wako Aik's Mokoko tribe clustered for protection around the village of the Waro; this people had come out of the sky to live on the Mokokos' abandoned lands.

In the way that *tue* meant "bird," *waro* meant "snake" or "insect." The first Waro had come to the Kurelu just after the last mauwe, through the land of the Wittaia. He had white skin, and he was accompanied by black men dressed like himself. The strangers had been stopped at the frontier, and a warrior named Awulapa, brother of Tamugi, had been shot down and killed by a Waro weapon with a noise that echoed from the mountains. Though these men had fled, the Waro had not left the valley; already they were building huts among the river tribes throughout the valley.

While he kept watch, Weaklekek's hands moved rhythmically in the sun, for once again he had started a long shell belt. He was proud of the old ways, proud that his own people went on as they always had since the time of Nopu. But from the Waro changes in the land had come, brought by the wind: a strange blue flower had rooted in the fields, and in an old oak by Homuak there was a yellow stinging bee. This bee gathered in large swarms, howling in the hollow wood like a bad wind in the rocks of the Turaba; in the past moons it had come across the swamps and gardens from the Waro village on the Baliem. The blue flower and the yellow bee did not belong in the akuni world and had no name.

28 KURELU

29 NILIK

30 NILIK

31 POLIK

33 POLIK

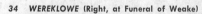

34 WEREKLOWE (Right, at Funeral of Weake)

32 WEREKLOWE

THE GREAT KAINS (Continued)

35 MAITMO

36 LIMO

37 HUSUK

38 U-MUE

U-MUE:
HIS FAMILY
AND
SOME
CHILDREN
OF HIS
VILLAGE

39 WITH EKAPUWE'S BABY

40 OLD ANEAKE

42 AKU AND NYLARE

41 HUGUNARO

43 EKAPUWE

44 UWAR

45 OLUMA (Rear) AND HOLAKE

46 NATOREK

47 KABILEK

48 WEREKMA

49   YONOKMA

51   YOROICK

50   WERENE

SOME TRIBESMEN

52   HANUMOAK

53 YEKE ASUK

54 LOLILUK

55 WALIMO

56

57

58

59   EKEN

56-63. WEAKLEKEK

(58 and 63

60   WITH YEKE ASUK (Left)

61

NOARIGE, Who Died

AND HIS FAMILY

(LAKALOKLEK)

62

63

64 ALORO

65 TEGEAREK

66 APEORE

67 SILOBA AND ASUKWAN

68 TEKMAN BIO

69 SIBA

70 TUESIKE, WITH BODY OF YONOKMA

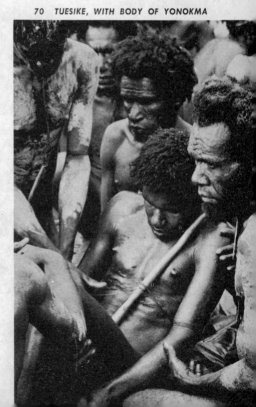

THE WARRIORS

72

73

74

75 ASIKANALEK

76 NAMILIKE, HIS DAUGHTER

ASIKANALEK
AND HIS FAMILY

77 HIS FATHER, EAK

THE DEATH OF WEAKE

78 THE TWINS (Okal standing)

79 WOLUKLEK

80 WEAKE, IN ARMS OF ASIKANALEK

81 HUONKE

82 TAMUGI

84 THE DEAD ASUK-PALEK

3 IKI ABUSAKE

Photographic Section II:

THE PEOPLE OF THE BOOK

■ 257

Acknowledgments

I should like to express my gratitude to the expedition members, not only for the assistance acknowledged in the Preface, but for permission to use the excellent photographs included in this book.

I am also indebted to Mr. Hobart Van Deusen and Dr. Thomas Gilliard of the American Museum of Natural History, who prepared me for the fauna of New Guinea's Central Highlands, and to Miss Lily Perry of the Arnold Arboretum of Harvard, who instructed me in the fundamentals of its flora; Mr. Chris Versteegh, the botanist of the Dutch Government who joined the expedition for a brief period, made an invaluable contribution in the field.

In Hollandia, in addition to Dr. J. V. de Bruyn, Miss Lou Von Zanden of the Office of Native Affairs was very courteous and helpful, and Mr. J. R. Schroo of Hollandia's Bureau of Soils was kind enough to furnish information on the geology and soils of the Baliem Valley.

For many forms of hospitality and kindness received in my journeys to and from New Guinea, I remain indebted to the following: Luisa and Domenico Gnoli (Rome); El Amin Sulfab (Juba, Sudan); Hamdan Mohamed (Nimule, Sudan); Miss Ulla Mai Ekblad (Nairobi, Kenya); Patrick and Hennie Hemingway (Arusha, Tanganyika); Ruth Jhabvala (Delhi); Mr. and Mrs. Clair Weeks (Kathmandu, Nepal); Mme. Françoise Teynac (Angkor Wat, Cambodia–Hong Kong); George Chi (Hong Kong); Jorge Borges (Macao); Mrs. Jean Austin (Heron Island, Australia); Misses Carol and Gay Plowman (Sydney); Joy and Kenneth Plowman (Sydney); Mr. and Mrs. Bryan Warne (Sydney); Betty and George Edwards (Newcastle, Australia); John Haereraaroa (Moorea, French Oceania); Patsy and Mike Goldberg (Belvedere, California); Evan Connell and Max Steele (San Francisco).

For expert advice, and for unstinting interest and patience, I should like to thank my friend and editor, Marshall Best, and the excellent staff at the Viking Press, in the hope that this book will justify their effort.

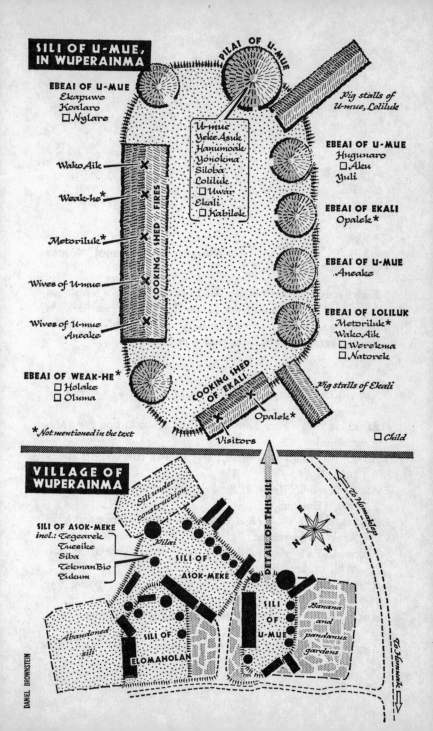

SILI OF U-MUE, IN WUPERAINMA

PILAI OF U-MUE

EBEAI OF U-MUE
Ekapuwe
Koalaro
□ *Nylare*

Pig stalls of
U-mue, Loliluk

U-mue
Yeke Asuk
Hanumoak
Yoniokina
Siloba
Loliluk
□ Uwar
Ekali
□ Kabilek

Wako Aik

EBEAI OF U-MUE
Hugunaro
□ Aku
Yuli

Weak-he *

Metoriluk *

COOKING SHED FIRES

EBEAI OF EKALI
Opalek *

Wives of U-mue

EBEAI OF U-MUE
Aneake

Wives of U-mue
Aneake

EBEAI OF LOLILUK
Metoriluk *
Wako Aik
□ Werekma
□ Natorek

EBEAI OF WEAK-HE *
□ Holake
□ Oluma

COOKING SHED
OF EKALI

Pig stalls of Ekali

Opalek *

* Not mentioned in the text

Visitors

□ Child

VILLAGE OF
WUPERAINMA

Sili under
construction

To Homaklep

SILI OF ASOK-MEKE
incl.: Tegearek
Tuesike
Siba
Tekman Bio
Tukum

Pilai

N
E · S
W

SILI OF
ASOK-MEKE

DETAIL OF THIS SILI

Abandoned
sili

SILI OF
ELOMAHOLAN

SILI
OF
U-MUE

Banana
and
pandanus
gardens

To Homuak

DANIEL BROWNSTEIN

Glossary of Personal Names

Each name is followed by a guide to pronunciation, a translation in italics, identification of the person bearing the name, and, in parentheses, the village in which he lives. The number identifies the photograph in which the person appears.

AKU. a-KOO (*after piece of land toward Siep-Kosi*), daughter of U-mue (Wuperainma), 42

ALOKA. A-lo-ka (*Very Late Born*), boy blind in one eye (Mapiatma)

ALORO. A-lo-ro (*The Cripple*), war kain of clan Wilil (Abulopak), 64

AMOLI. A-mo-li (*He Who Replaces*), violent kain of clan Haiman (Hulainmo)

ANEAKE. a-NAY-a-kay (*Bad Voice*), mother of U-mue and Yeke Asuk (Wuperainma), 40

APEORE. a-PAY-or-ay (*Killed by Strangling*), warrior of clan Wilil (Lokoparek), 66

ASIKANALEK. A-si-KAN-a-lek (*No Sound of Bow*), young war kain of clan Alua (Abukumo), 75, 80

ASISAL. A-si-SAL (*Extruded Rectum*), old father of Siloba (Mapiatma)

ASOK-MEKE. ah-SAWK-mek-KAY (*Outsider*), stepfather of Tukum (Wuperainma)

ASUKWAN. ah-SOOK-wan (*Long Ear*), young warrior of clan Walilo (Homaklep), 67

EAK. AY-ak (*The Little One*), old father of Asikanalek (Abukumo), 77

EKALI. AY-kah-lee (*Shame*), kepu man, father of boy Kabilek (Wuperainma), 12

EKAPUWE. ay-KAP-oo-way (?), wife of U-mue, formerly Wittaia woman (Wuperainma), 43

EKEN. AY-ken (*Seed, or Flower*), daughter of Weaklekek (Homaklep), 59

EKITAMALEK. ay-kee-TAM-a-lek (*Empty Fist*), slain son of Yoroick (Kibitsilimo), 11

ELOMAHOLAN. el-LO-ma-ho-LAHN (*Wife Taken Away*), old "medicine man" of clan Wilil (Wuperainma)

HANUMOAK. HA-num-o-AK (*Tobacco Pipe*), young warrior, brother of Yoroick and Werene (Wuperainma), 52

HOLAKE. HO-la-kay (*Path of Women*), young daughter of Wereklowe (Wuperainma), 45

HUGUNARO. Hoo-GOO-na-ro (*Sitting Opposite*), jealous wife of U-mue, mother of Aku (Wuperainma), 41

HUONKE. HOO-wonk-ay (*Little Stone Ax*), uncle of slain boy Weake (Sulaki), 81

HUSUK. HOO-suk (*Dives under Water*), war kain of clan Kosi (Kibitsilimo), 37

IKI ABUSAKE. EE-kee a-BOO-sa-kay (*Hand That Cannot Help Itself*), little sister of slain boy Weake (Abulopak), 83

KABILEK. KA-bee-lek (*Sharp Not*), son of Ekali (Wuperainma), 47

KOALARO. ko-AH-la-ro (*She Who Left Her Man*), wife of U-mue, sister of slain youth Yonokma (Wuperainma)

KURELU. KOO-rel-OO (*Wise Egret*), great kain of tribe (villages in north Kurelu), 28

LAKALOKLEK. LAK-a-lawk-lek (*She Who Would Not Wait*), wife of Weaklekek (Homaklep), 58, 63

LIMO. LEE-mo (*Treeless Place*), tall war kain of clan Alua (Sinisiek), 36

LOLILUK. LO-lee-LOOK (*Bones Ungathered*), father of Uwar, Werekma, Natorek (Wuperainma), 54

Maitmo. MITE-mo (*Near Village Ditch*), fierce war kain of clan Haiman (north Kurelu), 35

Namilike. na-MEE-lee-kay (*Hope She Won't Die*), small daughter of Asikanalek (Abukumo), 76

Natorek. na-to-REK (*Mauwe Ceremony*—when he was born), small brother of Uwar (Wuperainma), 46

Nilik. NEE-leek (*Present at Pig Eating*), kain of clan Walilo (Kulmo), 29, 30

Nylare. NY-la-ray (*My Village*), small daughter of U-mue (Wuperainma), 42

Okal. OH-kal (*The Roamer*), one of twins: friend of slain boy Weake (Mapiatma), 78

Oluma. OH-loo-ma (*species of tree*—at the foot of which he was born), friend of small boy Natorek (Wuperainma), 45

Palek. PA-lek (*No Family*), father of Supuk, husband of woman raped by Asukwan (Homaklep; later, Wuperainma)

Polik. PO-leek (*He Who Came Up from Behind*), kain of clan Halluk (Abulopak), 31, 33

Pumeka. POO-may-ka (*Water Snake*), crippled woodcutter (Sinisiek)

Siba. SEE-ba (*a kind of insect,* with connotation of beauty as a child), young warrior of clan Wilil (Wuperainma), 69

Siloba. SEE-lo-ba (*He Who Goes Out Even in Rain*), young warrior; friend of slain youth Yonokma (Wuperainma), 67

Supuk. SOO-pook (*roof section of women's hut*), son of Palek (Homaklep)

Tamugi. TA-moo-gee (*a tree marsupial*), brother-in-law of Hu-onke (Abulopak), 82

Tegearek. TAY-GAY-a-REK (*Spear Death*), young war kain of clan Wilil (Wuperainma), 65

Tekman Bio. TEK-man BEE-o (*Remains Away*), warrior of clan Halluk (Wuperainma; Abulopak), 68

Tuesike. too-AY-see-KAY (*Bird Bow*), warrior of clan Wilil (Wuperainma), 70

Tukum. TOO-kum (*area of men's hut in front of hearth*), small swineherd stepson of Asok-meke (Wuperainma), 71–74

U-mue. OO-moo-ay (*The Anxious One*), political kain of clan Wilil (Wuperainma), 38, 39

UWAR. YOU-wahr (*after Uwar River in land of Siep-Kosi*), son of Loliluk (Wuperainma), 44

WAKO AIK. WAH-ko a-EEK (*Worm Biting in Stomach*), dying mother of Uwar (Wuperainma)

WALIMO. WAH-lee-mo (*Shell Bib*), condemned young warrior of clan Alua (Hulibara), 55

WAMATUE. wah-MAH-too-ay (*Bird in Pig Stall*), small brother of Supuk (Homaklep)

WEAKE. WAY-a-kay (*Bad Path*), slain boy, friend of Okal, Tukum (Abulopak), 34, 80

WEAKLEKEK. way-AK-le-kek (*The Bad Man*), young war kain of clan Alua (Homaklep), 56–58, 60–62

WENELUKE. wen-EL-oo-kay (*Pig Thieves*), boy painter of cave drawings (Lokoparek)

WEREKLOWE. way-REK-lo-way (*He Who Never Works in Fields*), great kain of clan Alua (Abulopak), 32, 34

WEREKMA. way-REK-ma (*There Are Daughters*), daughter of Loliluk (Wuperainma), 48

WERENE. Way-re-nay (*Parrot*), brother of Yoroick and Hanu-moak (Homaklep), 50

WOKNABIN. WOK-na-been (*Take Me with You*), half-blind warrior of clan Wilil (Abulopak)

WOLUKLEK. wo-LOO-klek (*Was Not Rewarded*), the solitary man who led Weake to river (Mapiatma), 79

YEKE ASUK. YAY-kay a-SOOK (*Dog Ear*), brother of U-mue (Wuperainma), 53, 60

YOLI. YO-lee (*species of myrtle,* used for spears), father of Wa-limo (Hulibara)

YONOKMA. yo-NAWK-ma (*The Wanderer*), slain young brother of Koalaro (Wuperainma), 49, 70

YOROICK. yo-ROYK (*Pigeon*), father of slain warrior Ekitamalek (Kibitsilino), 51

YULI. YOU-lee (*Piece*), young wife of U-mue (Wuperainma)

Dani Words Used Commonly in Text

AKUNI. a-KOO-nee, the People, i.e., the Kurelu

EBEAI. AY-bay-ai, women's round house

ELEGE. ay-lay-gay, youths

ETAI. AY-tai, "singing," i.e., victory dance

ETAI-EKEN. AY-tai AY-ken, "seed of singing," i.e., soul

HIPERI. HIP-eree, sweet potato (also, food)

HORIM. ho-REEM, gourd penis sheath

HUNUK PALIN. HOO-nuk pa-LEEN, given to fits of violence and manic bravery.

IKI PALIN. ee-kee pa-LEEN, finger-cutting ceremony

KAIN. (as in "swine"), leader

KAIO. KAI-o, lookout tower

KEPU. kay-POO, cowardly: without worth

MAUWE. MOW-way, feasting period of marriage and initiation

MIKAK. MEE-kak, section of large baler shell, worn under chin

PAVI. PA-vee, species of tree (slang: enemy or excrement)

PILAI. PEE-lai, men's round house

SILI. SEE-lee, compound, one or more of which comprises village

TOA. TOE-a, large edible grass

WAM WISA. wom WEE-sa, sacramental pig

WISA. WEE-sa, infused with supernatural power

WISAKUN. WEE-sa-kun, "medicine man"

YEGEREK. YEG-air-ek, children between infancy and puberty

Shell bibs, 12, 24, 27, 89, 121–22, 136, 190, 199
Shell goods, 180; trading in, 127–28
Shells, 12, 91, 137; as currency, 12, 127–28
Silis (family enclosures), 20, 38, 96, 236, 255; consecration of, 200–201
Singing, 81, 104, 123, 144, 238, 251; see also Chanting; Songs
Sinkholes, 34
Skin color, 6, 32, 41, 77, 100, 256
Skinks, 70, 78
Skirts, 21, 53, 89, 99, 179, 198
Smoking, 140, 207; by women, 124, 137, 219, 231; see also Tobacco
Snail shells, 12, 91, 137
Snakes, 78, 126, 217
Soil, 8, 107
Songbirds, 107, 224; hunting of, 222
Songs, 104, 175, 229; see also Singing
Soul, the, 134, 153, 225
Southern Cross, 237
Spear-rubbing, 175–76
Spears, 6, 9–10, 14, 16–17, 26, 32, 39, 63, 82, 103, 173, 189, 191, 232, 245, 246, 249, 255; grass, 81, 168, 217; hiperi, 22; making of, 175–76; value of, 113; wood for, 128, 174
Spirits, 147, 223; see also Ghosts
Spoils, 110, 114, 120
Sport, war as, 11; see also Games
Status, 25
Stealing: pig, 32, 42, 44, 79–80, 196–97, 221, 228, 231–32, 253–254; punishment for, 203; of sweet potatoes, 203; wife, 39, 87, 91, 185
Stick throwing, 222
Stinkbugs, 186
Stoicism, 193
Stomach hoops, 88
Stone ceremony, 144–50, 164–69
Stone culture, 5–6
Stretchers, 30, 86, 193, 209
Sugar cane, 189
Suicide, 126, 188
Sweet potatoes, 5, 7, 46, 146, 169, 212, 219, 223; advent of, 106–107; as basic food, 19, 136; cultivation of, 21–22, 28, 243, see also Gardens; sacramental, 201; stealing of, 203

Swineherds, see Pigs, tending of
Symplocos trees, 30, 187

Table utensils, 139
Taro leaves, 121, 135, 225
Teeth, grinding of, 74, 226
Territorial conquest, 11
Thatch bundles, 162–63, 185
Tinder, 174, 234
Toa, 135, 172, 226
Tobacco, 27, 126, 197
Tobacco pipes, 74; see also Smoking
Topsoil, 107
Toys, 129, 178, 211
Trading, 127–28
Treachery, punishment for, 120
Tripes, 52, 137
Trophy bundles, 123

Victory celebration, 59, 70, 84–85, 111–12, 117, 122–25, 208, 238–239, 241
Villages, 6–7, 19–20, 69, 111, 198, 233; abandoned, 96–97; pig, 18, 143, 185, 198; restoration of, 97
Virginity, 181
Volcanoes, 105

Wallabies, 5
Wands, egret feather, 10–11, 58, 250
War, 6, 9–17, 30, 52, 73–77, 81–86, 99, 113–20, 125, 132–34, 189–92, 244–52; spoils of, 110, 114, 120; see also Raids
War parties, 15; see also Raiding parties
Warriors, 9–10, 13–16, 30, 59–60, 111–13, 115–17, 151, 188, 205–206, 238, 244–52; young, 12–13, 59, 74, 117, 132, 133
Wasps, 51
Water calabashes, 57
Weapons, 9; wood for, 128, 174; see also Arrows; Bows; Spears
Weaver finches, 108
Weaving, 225, 235
Whisks, feather, 11
Whistlers, 9, 100, 254
White men, 256
Wigs, 92, 123
Wio wood, 128
Wisa ban, 166
Wisa things, 29, 66, 101, 150, 165
Wisakun, see Men, wisakun